WORLD TRADE ORGANISATION

(TEXT)

Volume–I

Edited by
K.R. Gupta

ATLANTIC®
PUBLISHERS & DISTRIBUTORS

Published by
ATLANTIC®
PUBLISHERS & DISTRIBUTORS
B-2, Vishal Enclave, Opp. Rajouri Garden,
New Delhi-110027
Phones : 25413460, 25429987, 25466842

Sales Office
7/22, Ansari Road, Darya Ganj,
New Delhi-110002
Phones : 23273880, 23275880, 23280451
Fax : 91-11-23285873
web : www.atlanticbooks.com
e-mail : info@atlanticbooks.com

ISBN 81-7156-888-2 (Vol. 1)
ISBN 81-7156-886-6 (Set)

Printed in India
at Nice Printing Press, Delhi

PREFACE

The book contains full text of the World Trade Organisation. In recent years there has been a lot of discussion on the provisions and policies of this Organisation. The Organisation has great impact on the world trade and economic policies of member countries. In spite of great importance of WTO, the full text of the Organisation has not been easily available. The present book fulfills this gap.

It is hoped that the book would be found useful by the researchers and students of International Economics and International Law, business executives, Government officers concerned with formulation and execution of economic policies, parliamentarians and the common man interested in world economic affairs.

K.R. GUPTA

LIST OF ABBREVIATIONS

AMS	Aggregate Measurement of Support (in Agreement on Agriculture)
BISD	Basic Instruments and Selected Documents (published by GATT)
CCC	Customs Co-operation Council
CCC Secretariat	Secretariat of the Customs Co-operation Council
Dispute Settlement Understanding/DSU	Understanding on Rules and Procedures Governing the Settlement of Disputes
DSB	Dispute Settlement Body
FAO	Food and Agriculture Organization of the United Nations
GATS	General Agreement on Trade in Services
GATT 1994	General Agreement on Tariffs and Trade 1994
HS	Harmonized Commodity Description and Coding System
IMF	International Monetary Fund
ISO	International Organization for Standardization
ISO/IEC	ISO/International Electrotechnical Commission
MFA	Arrangement Regarding International Trade in Textiles
PGE	Permanent Group of Experts (in Agreement on Subsidies and Countervailing Measures)
SCM	Subsidies and Countervailing Measures

Secretariat	Secretariat of the World Trade Organization
SSG	Special Safeguard (in Agreement on Agriculture)
ST	Special Treatment (in Annex 5, Agreement on Agriculture)
TMB	Textiles Monitoring Body
TPRB	Trade Policy Review Body
TPRM	Trade Policy Review Mechanism
TRIMs	Trade-Related Investment Measures
TRIPS	Trade-Related Aspects of Intellectual Property Rights
TSB	Textiles Surveillance Body
World Bank	International Bank for Reconstruction and Development
WTO	World Trade Organization
WTO Agreement	Agreement Establishing the World Trade Organization

CONTENTS

FINAL ACT EMBODYING THE RESULTS OF THE URUGUAY ROUND OF MULTILATERAL TRADE NEGOTIATIONS

1. Having met in order to conclude the Uruguay Round of Multilateral Trade Negotiations, representatives of the governments and of the European Communities, members of the Trade Negotiations Committee, *agree* that the Agreement Establishing the World Trade Organization (referred to in this Final Act as the "WTO Agreement"), the Ministerial Declarations and Decisions, and the Understanding on Commitments in Financial Services, as annexed hereto, embody the results of their negotiations and form an integral part of this Final Act.

2. By signing the present Final Act, the representatives *agree*

(a) to submit, as appropriate, the WTO Agreement for the consideration of their respective competent authorities with a view to seeking approval of the Agreement in accordance with their procedures; and

(b) to adopt the Ministerial Declarations and Decisions.

3. The representatives *agree* on the desirability of acceptance of the WTO Agreement by all participants in the Uruguay Round of Multilateral Trade Negotiations (hereinafter referred to as "participants") with a view to its entry into force by 1 January 1995, or as early as possible thereafter. Not later than late 1994, Ministers will meet, in accordance with the final paragraph of the Punta del Este Ministerial Declaration, to decide on the international implementation of the results, including the timing of their entry into force.

4. The representatives *agree* that the WTO Agreement shall be open for acceptance as a whole, by signature or otherwise, by all participants pursuant to Article XIV thereof. The acceptance and entry into force of a Plurilateral Trade Agreement included in Annex 4 of the WTO Agreement shall be governed by the provisions of that Plurilateral Trade Agreement.

5. Before accepting the WTO Agreement, participants which are not contracting parties to the General Agreement on Tariffs and Trade must first have concluded negotiations for their accession to the General Agreement and become contracting parties thereto. For participants which are not contracting parties to the General Agreement as of the date of the Final Act, the Schedules are not definitive and shall be subsequently completed for the purpose of their accession to the General Agreement and acceptance of the WTO Agreement.

6. This Final Act and the texts annexed hereto shall be deposited with the Director-General to the CONTRACTING PARTIES to the General Agreement on Tariffs and Trade who shall promptly furnish to each participant a certified copy thereof.

DONE at Marrakesh this fifteenth day of April one thousand nine hundred and ninety-four, in a single copy, in the English, French and Spanish languages, each text being authentic.

[List of signatures to be included in the treaty copy of the Final Act for signature]

AGREEMENT ESTABLISHING THE WORLD TRADE ORGANIZATION

The Parties to this Agreement

Recognizing that their relations in the field of trade and economic endeavour should be conducted with a view to raising standards of living, ensuring full employment and a large and steadily growing volume of real income and effective demand, and expanding the production of and trade in goods and services, while allowing for the optimal use of the world's resources in accordance with the objective of sustainable development, seeking both to protect and preserve the environment and to enhance the means for doing so in a manner consistent with their respective needs and concerns at different levels of economic development,

Recognizing further that there is need for positive efforts designed to ensure that developing countries, and especially the least developed among them, secure a share in the growth in international trade commensurate with the needs of their economic development,

Being desirous of contributing to these objectives by entering into reciprocal and mutually advantageous arrangements directed to the substantial reduction of tariffs and other barriers to trade and to the elimination of discriminatory treatment in international trade relations,

Resolved, therefore, to develop an integrated, more viable and durable multilateral trading system encompassing the General Agreement on Tariffs and Trade, the results of past trade liberalization efforts, and all of the results of the Uruguay Round of Multilateral Trade Negotiations,

Determined to preserve the basic principles and to further the objectives underlying this multilateral trading system;

Agree as follows:

ARTICLE I

Establishment of the Organization

The World Trade Organization (hereinafter referred to as "the WTO") is hereby established.

ARTICLE II

Scope of the WTO

1. The WTO shall provide the common institutional framework for the conduct of trade relations among its Members in matters related to the agreements and associated legal instruments included in the Annexes to this Agreement.

2. The agreements and associated legal instruments included in Annexes 1, 2 and 3 (hereinafter referred to as "Multilateral Trade Agreements") are integral parts of this Agreement, binding on all Members.

3. The agreements and associated legal instruments included in Annex 4 (hereinafter referred to as "Plurilateral Trade Agreements") are also part of this Agreement for those Members that have accepted them, and are binding on those Members. The Plurilateral Trade Agreements do not create either obligations or rights for Members that have not accepted them.

4. The General Agreement on Tariffs and Trade 1994 as specified in Annex 1A (hereinafter referred to as "GATT 1994") is legally distinct from the General Agreement on Tariffs and Trade, dated 30 October 1947, annexed to the Final Act Adopted at the Conclusion of the Second Session of the Preparatory Committee of the United Nations Conference on Trade and Employment, as subsequently rectified, amended or modified (hereinafter referred to as "GATT 1947").

ARTICLE III

Functions of the WTO

1. The WTO shall facilitate the implementation, administration and operation, and further the objectives, of this Agreement and of the Multilateral Trade Agreements, and shall also provide the framework for the implementation, administration and operation of the Plurilateral Trade Agreements.

2. The WTO shall provide the forum for negotiations among its Members concerning their multilateral trade relations in matters dealt with under the agreements in the Annexes to this Agreement. The WTO may also provide a forum for further negotiations among its Members concerning their multilateral trade relations, and a framework for the implementation of the results of such negotiations, as may be decided by the Ministerial Conference.

3. The WTO shall administer the Understanding on Rules and Procedures Governing the Settlement of Disputes (hereinafter referred to as the "Dispute Settlement Understanding" or "DSU") in Annex 2 to this Agreement.

4. The WTO shall administer the Trade Policy Review Mechanism (hereinafter referred to as the "TPRM") provided for in Annex 3 to this Agreement.

5. With a view to achieving greater coherence in global economic policy-making, the WTO shall cooperate, as appropriate, with the International Monetary Fund and with the International Bank for Reconstruction and Development and its affiliated agencies.

ARTICLE IV

Structure of the WTO

1. There shall be a Ministerial Conference composed of representatives of all the Members, which shall meet at least once every two years. The Ministerial Conference shall carry out the functions of the WTO and take actions necessary to this effect. The Ministerial Conference shall have the authority to take decisions on all matters under any of the Multilateral Trade Agreements, if so requested by a Member, in accordance with the specific requirements for decision-making in this Agreement and in the relevant Multilateral Trade Agreement.

2. There shall be a General Council composed of representatives

of all the Members, which shall meet as appropriate. In the intervals between meetings of the Ministerial Conference, its functions shall be conducted by the General Council. The General Council shall also carry out the functions assigned to it by this Agreement. The General Council shall establish its rules of procedure and approve the rules of procedure for the Committees provided for in paragraph 7.

3. The General Council shall convene as appropriate to discharge the responsibilities of the Dispute Settlement Body provided for in the Dispute Settlement Understanding. The Dispute Settlement Body may have its own chairman and shall establish such rules of procedure as it deems necessary for the fulfilment of those responsibilities.

4. The General Council shall convene as appropriate to discharge the responsibilities of the Trade Policy Review Body provided for in the TPRM. The Trade Policy Review Body may have its own chairman and shall establish such rules of procedure as it deems necessary for the fulfilment of those responsibilities.

5. There shall be a Council for Trade in Goods, a Council for Trade in Services and a Council for Trade-Related Aspects of Intellectual Property Rights (hereinafter referred to as the "Council for TRIPS"), which shall operate under the general guidance of the General Council. The Council for Trade in Goods shall oversee the functioning of the Multilateral Trade Agreements in Annex 1A. The Council for Trade in Services shall oversee the functioning of the General Agreement on Trade in Services (hereinafter referred to as "GATS"). The Council for TRIPS shall oversee the functioning of the Agreement on Trade-Related Aspects of Intellectual Property Rights (hereinafter referred to as the "Agreement on TRIPS"). These Councils shall carry out the functions assigned to them by their respective agreements and by the General Council. They shall establish their respective rules of procedure subject to the approval of the General Council. Membership in these Councils shall be open to representatives of all Members. These Councils shall meet as necessary to carry out their functions.

6. The Council for Trade in Goods, the Council for Trade in Services and the Council for TRIPS shall establish subsidiary bodies as required. These subsidiary bodies shall establish their respective rules of procedure subject to the approval of their respective Councils.

7. The Ministerial Conference shall establish a Committee on Trade and Development, a Committee on Balance-of-Payments Restrictions and a Committee on Budget, Finance and Administration, which shall carry out the functions assigned to them by this Agreement and by the Multilateral Trade Agreements, and any additional functions assigned to them by the General Council, and may establish such additional Committees with such functions as it may deem appropriate. As part of its functions, the Committee on Trade and Development shall periodically review the special provisions in the Multilateral Trade Agreements in favour of the least-developed country Members and report to the General Council for appropriate action. Membership in these Committees shall be open to representatives of all Members.

8. The bodies provided for under the Plurilateral Trade Agreements shall carry out the functions assigned to them under those Agreements and shall operate within the institutional framework of the WTO. These bodies shall keep the General Council informed of their activities on a regular basis.

ARTICLE V

Relations with Other Organizations

1. The General Council shall make appropriate arrangements for effective cooperation with other intergovernmental organizations that have responsibilities related to those of the WTO.

2. The General Council may make appropriate arrangements for consultation and cooperation with non-governmental organizations concerned with matters related to those of the WTO.

ARTICLE VI

The Secretariat

1. There shall be a Secretariat of the WTO (hereinafter referred to as "the Secretariat") headed by a Director-General.

2. The Ministerial Conference shall appoint the Director-General and adopt regulations setting out the powers, duties, conditions of service and term of office of the Director-General.

3. The Director-General shall appoint the members of the staff of the Secretariat and determine their duties and conditions of service in accordance with regulations adopted by the Ministerial Conference.

4. The responsibilities of the Director-General and of the staff

of the Secretariat shall be exclusively international in character. In the discharge of their duties, the Director-General and the staff of the Secretariat shall not seek or accept instructions from any government or any other authority external to the WTO. They shall refrain from any action which might adversely reflect on their position as international officials. The Members of the WTO shall respect the international character of the responsibilities of the Director-General and of the staff of the Secretariat and shall not seek to influence them in the discharge of their duties.

ARTICLE VII

Budget and Contributions

1. The Director-General shall present to the Committee on Budget, Finance and Administration the annual budget estimate and financial statement of the WTO. The Committee on Budget, Finance and Administration shall review the annual budget estimate and the financial statement presented by the Director-General and make recommendations thereon to the General Council. The annual budget estimate shall be subject to approval by the General Council.

2. The Committee on Budget, Finance and Administration shall propose to the General Council financial regulations which shall include provisions setting out:

(a) the scale of contributions apportioning the expenses of the WTO among its Members; and

(b) the measures to be taken in respect of Members in arrears.

The financial regulations shall be based, as far as practicable, on the regulations and practices of GATT 1947.

3. The General Council shall adopt the financial regulations and the annual budget estimate by a two-thirds majority comprising more than half of the Members of the WTO.

4. Each Member shall promptly contribute to the WTO its share in the expenses of the WTO in accordance with the financial regulations adopted by the General Council.

ARTICLE VIII

Status of the WTO

1. The WTO shall have legal personality, and shall be accorded

by each of its Members such legal capacity as may be necessary for the exercise of its functions.

2. The WTO shall be accorded by each of its Members such privileges and immunities as are necessary for the exercise of its functions.

3. The officials of the WTO and the representatives of the Members shall similarly be accorded by each of its Members such privileges and immunities as are necessary for the independent exercise of their functions in connection with the WTO.

4. The privileges and immunities to be accorded by a Member to the WTO, its officials, and the representatives of its Members shall be similar to the privileges and immunities stipulated in the Convention on the Privileges and Immunities of the Specialized Agencies, approved by the General Assembly of the United Nations on 21 November 1947.

5. The WTO may conclude a headquarters agreement.

ARTICLE IX

Decision-Making

1. The WTO shall continue the practice of decision-making by consensus followed under GATT 1947.[1] Except as otherwise provided, where a decision cannot be arrived at by consensus, the matter at issue shall be decided by voting. At meetings of the Ministerial Conference and the General Council, each Member of the WTO shall have one vote. Where the European Communities exercise their right to vote, they shall have a number of votes equal to the number of their member States[2] which are Members of the WTO. Decisions of the Ministerial Conference and the General Council shall be taken by a majority of the votes cast, unless otherwise provided in this Agreement or in the relevant Multilateral Trade Agreement.[3]

2. The Ministerial Conference and the General Council shall have

---

1. The body concerned shall be deemed to have decided by consensus on a matter submitted for its consideration, if no Member, present at the meeting when the decision is taken, formally objects to the proposed decision.

2. The number of votes of the European Communities and their member States shall in no case exceed the number of the member States of the European Communities.

3. Decisions by the General Council when convened as the Dispute Settlement Body shall be taken only in accordance with the provisions of paragraph 4 of Article 2 of the Dispute Settlement Understanding.

the exclusive authority to adopt interpretations of this Agreement and of the Multilateral Trade Agreements. In the case of an interpretation of a Multilateral Trade Agreement in Annex 1, they shall exercise their authority on the basis of a recommendation by the Council overseeing the functioning of that Agreement. The decision to adopt an interpretation shall be taken by a three-fourths majority of the Members. This paragraph shall not be used in a manner that would undermine the amendment provisions in Article X.

3. In exceptional circumstances, the Ministerial Conference may decide to waive an obligation imposed on a Member by this Agreement or any of the Multilateral Trade Agreements, provided that any such decision shall be taken by three fourths[4] of the Members unless otherwise provided for in this paragraph.

(a) A request for a waiver concerning this Agreement shall be submitted to the Ministerial Conference for consideration pursuant to the practice of decision-making by consensus. The Ministerial Conference shall establish a time-period, which shall not exceed 90 days, to consider the request. If consensus is not reached during the time-period, any decision to grant a waiver shall be taken by three fourths[4] of the Members.

(b) A request for a waiver concerning the Multilateral Trade Agreements in Annexes 1A or 1B or 1C and their annexes shall be submitted initially to the Council for Trade in Goods, the Council for Trade in Services or the Council for TRIPS, respectively, for consideration during a time-period which shall not exceed 90 days. At the end of the time-period, the relevant Council shall submit a report to the Ministerial Conference.

4. A decision by the Ministerial Conference granting a waiver shall state the exceptional circumstances justifying the decision, the terms and conditions governing the application of the waiver, and the date on which the waiver shall terminate. Any waiver granted for a period of more than one year shall be reviewed by the Ministerial Conference not later than one year after it is granted, and

4. A decision to grant a waiver in respect of any obligation subject to a transition period or a period for staged implementation that the requesting Member has not performed by the end of the relevant period shall be taken only by consensus.

thereafter annually until the waiver terminates. In each review, the Ministerial Conference shall examine whether the exceptional circumstances justifying the waiver still exist and whether the terms and conditions attached to the waiver have been met. The Ministerial Conference, on the basis of the annual review, may extend, modify or terminate the waiver.

5. Decisions under a Plurilateral Trade Agreement, including any decisions on interpretations and waivers, shall be governed by the provisions of that Agreement.

ARTICLE X

Amendments

1. Any Member of the WTO may initiate a proposal to amend the provisions of this Agreement or the Multilateral Trade Agreements in Annex 1 by submitting such proposal to the Ministerial Conference. The Councils listed in paragraph 5 of Article IV may also submit to the Ministerial Conference proposals to amend the provisions of the corresponding Multilateral Trade Agreements in Annex 1 the functioning of which they oversee. Unless the Ministerial Conference decides on a longer period, for a period of 90 days after the proposal has been tabled formally at the Ministerial Conference any decision by the Ministerial Conference to submit the proposed amendment to the Members for acceptance shall be taken by consensus. Unless the provisions of paragraphs 2, 5 or 6 apply, that decision shall specify whether the provisions of paragraphs 3 or 4 shall apply. If consensus is reached, the Ministerial Conference shall forthwith submit the proposed amendment to the Members for acceptance. If consensus is not reached at a meeting of the Ministerial Conference within the established period, the Ministerial Conference shall decide by a two-thirds majority of the Members whether to submit the proposed amendment to the Members for acceptance. Except as provided in paragraphs 2, 5 and 6, the provisions of paragraph 3 shall apply to the proposed amendment, unless the Ministerial Conference decides by a three-fourths majority of the Members that the provisions of paragraph 4 shall apply.

2. Amendments to the provisions of this Article and to the provisions of the following Articles shall take effect only upon acceptance by all Members:

Article IX of this Agreement;

Articles I and II of GATT 1994;

Article II:1 of GATS;

Article 4 of the Agreement on TRIPS.

3. Amendments to provisions of this Agreement, or of the Multilateral Trade Agreements in Annexes 1A and 1C, other than those listed in paragraphs 2 and 6, of a nature that would alter the rights and obligations of the Members, shall take effect for the Members that have accepted them upon acceptance by two thirds of the Members and thereafter for each other Member upon acceptance by it. The Ministerial Conference may decide by a three-fourths majority of the Members that any amendment made effective under this paragraph is of such a nature that any Member which has not accepted it within a period specified by the Ministerial Conference in each case shall be free to withdraw from the WTO or to remain a Member with the consent of the Ministerial Conference.

4. Amendments to provisions of this Agreement or of the Multilateral Trade Agreements in Annexes 1A and 1C, other than those listed in paragraphs 2 and 6, of a nature that would not alter the rights and obligations of the Members, shall take effect for all Members upon acceptance by two thirds of the Members.

5. Except as provided in paragraph 2 above, amendments to Parts I, II and III of GATS and the respective annexes shall take effect for the Members that have accepted them upon acceptance by two thirds of the Members and thereafter for each Member upon acceptance by it. The Ministerial Conference may decide by a three-fourths majority of the Members that any amendment made effective under the preceding provision is of such a nature that any Member which has not accepted it within a period specified by the Ministerial Conference in each case shall be free to withdraw from the WTO or to remain a Member with the consent of the Ministerial Conference. Amendments to Parts IV, V and VI of GATS and the respective annexes shall take effect for all Members upon acceptance by two thirds of the Members.

6. Notwithstanding the other provisions of this Article, amendments to the Agreement on TRIPS meeting the requirements of paragraph 2 of Article 71 thereof may be adopted by the Ministerial Conference without further formal acceptance process.

7. Any Member accepting an amendment to this Agreement or

to a Multilateral Trade Agreement in Annex 1 shall deposit an instrument of acceptance with the Director-General of the WTO within the period of acceptance specified by the Ministerial Conference.

8. Any Member of the WTO may initiate a proposal to amend the provisions of the Multilateral Trade Agreements in Annexes 2 and 3 by submitting such proposal to the Ministerial Conference. The decision to approve amendments to the Multilateral Trade Agreement in Annex 2 shall be made by consensus and these amendments shall take effect for all Members upon approval by the Ministerial Conference. Decisions to approve amendments to the Multilateral Trade Agreement in Annex 3 shall take effect for all Members upon approval by the Ministerial Conference.

9. The Ministerial Conference, upon the request of the Members parties to a trade agreement, may decide exclusively by consensus to add that agreement to Annex 4. The Ministerial Conference, upon the request of the Members parties to a Plurilateral Trade Agreement, may decide to delete that Agreement from Annex 4.

10. Amendments to a Plurilateral Trade Agreement shall be governed by the provisions of that Agreement.

ARTICLE XI

Original Membership

1. The contracting parties to GATT 1947 as of the date of entry into force of this Agreement, and the European Communities, which accept this Agreement and the Multilateral Trade Agreements and for which Schedules of Concessions and Commitments are annexed to GATT 1994 and for which Schedules of Specific Commitments are annexed to GATS shall become original Members of the WTO.

2. The least-developed countries recognized as such by the United Nations will only be required to undertake commitments and concessions to the extent consistent with their individual development, financial and trade needs or their administrative and institutional capabilities.

ARTICLE XII

Accession

1. Any State or separate customs territory possessing full autonomy in the conduct of its external commercial relations and of

the other matters provided for in this Agreement and the Multilateral Trade Agreements may accede to this Agreement, on terms to be agreed between it and the WTO. Such accession shall apply to this Agreement and the Multilateral Trade Agreements annexed thereto.

2. Decisions on accession shall be taken by the Ministerial Conference. The Ministerial Conference shall approve the agreement on the terms of accession by a two-thirds majority of the Members of the WTO.

3. Accession to a Plurilateral Trade Agreement shall be governed by the provisions of that Agreement.

ARTICLE XIII

Non-Application of Multilateral Trade Agreements between Particular Members

1. This Agreement and the Multilateral Trade Agreements in Annexes 1 and 2 shall not apply as between any Member and any other Member if either of the Members, at the time either becomes a Member, does not consent to such application.

2. Paragraph 1 may be invoked between original Members of the WTO which were contracting parties to GATT 1947 only where Article XXXV of that Agreement had been invoked earlier and was effective as between those contracting parties at the time of entry into force for them of this Agreement.

3. Paragraph 1 shall apply between a Member and another Member which has acceded under Article XII only if the Member not consenting to the application has so notified the Ministerial Conference before the approval of the agreement on the terms of accession by the Ministerial Conference.

4. The Ministerial Conference may review the operation of this Article in particular cases at the request of any Member and make appropriate recommendations.

5. Non-application of a Plurilateral Trade Agreement between parties to that Agreement shall be governed by the provisions of that Agreement.

ARTICLE XIV

Acceptance, Entry into Force and Deposit

1. This Agreement shall be open for acceptance, by signature

or otherwise, by contracting parties to GATT 1947, and the European Communities, which are eligible to become original Members of the WTO in accordance with Article XI of this Agreement. Such acceptance shall apply to this Agreement and the Multilateral Trade Agreements annexed hereto. This Agreement and the Multilateral Trade Agreements annexed hereto shall enter into force on the date determined by Ministers in accordance with paragraph 3 of the Final Act Embodying the Results of the Uruguay Round of Multilateral Trade Negotiations and shall remain open for acceptance for a period of two years following that date unless the Ministers decide otherwise. An acceptance following the entry into force of this Agreement shall enter into force on the 30th day following the date of such acceptance.

2. A Member which accepts this Agreement after its entry into force shall implement those concessions and obligations in the Multilateral Trade Agreements that are to be implemented over a period of time starting with the entry into force of this Agreement as if it had accepted this Agreement on the date of its entry into force.

3. Until the entry into force of this Agreement, the text of this Agreement and the Multilateral Trade Agreements shall be deposited with the Director-General to the CONTRACTING PARTIES to GATT 1947. The Director-General shall promptly furnish a certified true copy of this Agreement and the Multilateral Trade Agreements, and a notification of each acceptance thereof, to each government and the European Communities having accepted this Agreement. This Agreement and the Multilateral Trade Agreements, and any amendments thereto, shall, upon the entry into force of this Agreement, be deposited with the Director-General of the WTO.

4. The acceptance and entry into force of a Plurilateral Trade Agreement shall be governed by the provisions of that Agreement. Such Agreements shall be deposited with the Director-General to the CONTRACTING PARTIES to GATT 1947. Upon the entry into force of this Agreement, such Agreements shall be deposited with the Director-General of the WTO.

ARTICLE XV

Withdrawal

1. Any Member may withdraw from this Agreement. Such withdrawal shall apply both to this Agreement and the Multilateral

Trade Agreements and shall take effect upon the expiration of six months from the date on which written notice of withdrawal is received by the Director-General of the WTO.

2. Withdrawal from a Plurilateral Trade Agreement shall be governed by the provisions of that Agreement.

ARTICLE XVI

Miscellaneous Provisions

1. Except as otherwise provided under this Agreement or the Multilateral Trade Agreements, the WTO shall be guided by the decisions, procedures and customary practices followed by the CONTRACTING PARTIES to GATT 1947 and the bodies established in the framework of GATT 1947.

2. To the extent practicable, the Secretariat of GATT 1947 shall become the Secretariat of the WTO, and the Director-General to the CONTRACTING PARTIES to GATT 1947, until such time as the Ministerial Conference has appointed a Director-General in accordance with paragraph 2 of Article VI of this Agreement, shall serve as Director-General of the WTO.

3. In the event of a conflict between a provision of this Agreement and a provision of any of the Multilateral Trade Agreements, the provision of this Agreement shall prevail to the extent of the conflict.

4. Each Member shall ensure the conformity of its laws, regulations and administrative procedures with its obligations as provided in the annexed Agreements.

5. No reservations may be made in respect of any provision of this Agreement. Reservations in respect of any of the provisions of the Multilateral Trade Agreements may only be made to the extent provided for in those Agreements. Reservations in respect of a provision of a Plurilateral Trade Agreement shall be governed by the provisions of that Agreement.

EXPLANATORY NOTES

The terms "country" or "countries" as used in this Agreement and the Multilateral Trade Agreements are to be understood to include any separate customs territory Member of the WTO.

In the case of a separate customs territory Member of the WTO, where an expression in this Agreement and the Multilateral Trade Agreements is qualified by the term "national", such expression shall be read as pertaining to that customs territory, unless otherwise specified.

6. This Agreement shall be registered in accordance with the provisions of Article 102 of the Charter of the United Nations.

DONE at Marrakesh this fifteenth day of April one thousand nine hundred and ninety-four, in a single copy, in the English, French and Spanish languages, each text being authentic.

LIST OF ANNEXES

ANNEX 1

ANNEX 1A:

MULTILATERAL AGREEMENTS ON TRADE IN GOODS

General Agreement on Tariffs and Trade 1994

Agreement on Agriculture

Agreement on the Application of Sanitary and Phytosanitary Measures

Agreement on Textiles and Clothing

Agreement on Technical Barriers to Trade

Agreement on Trade-Related Investment Measures

Agreement on Implementation of Article VI of the General Agreement on Tariffs and Trade 1994

Agreement on Implementation of Article VII of the General Agreement on Tariffs and Trade 1994

Agreement on Preshipment Inspection

Agreement on Rules of Origin

Agreement on Import Licensing Procedures

Agreement on Subsidies and Countervailing Measures

Agreement on Safeguards

ANNEX 1B:

General Agreement on Trade in Services and Annexes

ANNEX 1C:

Agreement on Trade-Related Aspects of Intellectual Property Rights

ANNEX 2

Understanding on Rules and Procedures Governing the Settlement of Disputes

ANNEX 3

Trade Policy Review Mechanism

ANNEX 4

Plurilateral Trade Agreements

4(a) Agreement on Trade in Civil Aircraft

4(b) Agreement on Government Procurement

4(c) International Dairy Agreement

4(d) International Bovine Meat Agreement

ANNEX 1

ANNEX 1A

MULTILATERAL AGREEMENTS ON TRADE IN GOODS

General interpretative note to Annex 1A:

In the event of conflict between a provision of the General Agreement on Tariffs and Trade 1994 and a provision of another agreement in Annex 1A to the Agreement Establishing the World Trade Organization (referred to in the agreements in Annex 1A as the "WTO Agreement"), the provision of the other agreement shall prevail to the extent of the conflict.

GENERAL AGREEMENT ON TARIFFS AND TRADE 1994

1.The General Agreement on Tariffs and Trade 1994 ("GATT 1994") shall consist of:

(a) the provisions in the General Agreement on Tariffs and Trade, dated 30 October 1947, annexed to the Final Act Adopted at the Conclusion of the Second Session of the Preparatory Committee of the United Nations Conference on Trade and Employment (excluding the Protocol of Provisional Application), as rectified, amended or modified by the terms of legal instruments which have entered into force before the date of entry into force of the WTO Agreement;

(b) the provisions of the legal instruments set forth below that have entered into force under the GATT 1947 before the date of entry into force of the WTO Agreement:

(i) protocols and certifications relating to tariff concessions;

(ii) protocols of accession (excluding the provisions (*a*) concerning provisional application and withdrawal of provisional application and (*b*) providing that Part II of GATT 1947 shall be applied provisionally to the fullest extent not inconsistent with legislation existing on the date of the Protocol);

(iii) decisions on waivers granted under Article XXV of GATT 1947 and still in force on the date of entry into force of the WTO Agreement[1];

(iv) other decisions of the CONTRACTING PARTIES to GATT 1947;

(c) the Understandings set forth below:

(i) Understanding on the Interpretation of Article II:1(b) of the General Agreement on Tariffs and Trade 1994;

(ii) Understanding on the Interpretation of Article XVII of the General Agreement on Tariffs and Trade 1994;

(iii) Understanding on Balance-of-Payments Provisions of the General Agreement on Tariffs and Trade 1994;

(iv) Understanding on the Interpretation of Article XXIV of the General Agreement on Tariffs and Trade 1994;

(v) Understanding in Respect of Waivers of Obligations under the General Agreement on Tariffs and Trade 1994;

(vi) Understanding on the Interpretation of Article XXVIII of the General Agreement on Tariffs and Trade 1994; and

(d) the Marrakesh Protocol to GATT 1994.

2. Explanatory Notes

(a) The references to "contracting party" in the provisions of GATT 1994 shall be deemed to read "Member". The references to "less-developed contracting party" and "developed contracting party" shall be deemed to read "developing country Member" and

1. The waivers covered by this provisin are listed in footnote 7 on pages 11 and 12 in Part II of document MTN/FA of 15 December 1993 qnd in MTN/FACorr. 6 of 21 March 1994. The Ministerial Conference shall establish at its first session a revised list of waivers covered by this provision that adds any waivers granted under GATT 1947 after 15 December 1993 and before the date of entry into force of the WTO Agreement, and deletes the waivers which will have expired by that time.

"developed country Member". The references to "Executive Secretary" shall be deemed to read "Director-General of the WTO"

(b) The references to the CONTRACTING PARTIES acting jointly in Articles XV:1, XV:2, XV:8, XXXVIII and the Notes *Ad* Article XII and XVIII; and in the provisions on special exchange agreements in Articles XV:2, XV:3, XV:6, XV:7 and XV:9 of GATT 1994 shall be deemed to be references to the WTO. The other functions that the provisions of GATT 1994 assign to the CONTRACTING PARTIES acting jointly shall be allocated by the Ministerial Conference.

(c) (i) The text of GATT 1994 shall be authentic in English, French and Spanish.

(ii) The text of GATT 1994 in the French language shall be subject to the rectifications of terms indicated in Annex A to document MTN.TNC/41.

(iii) The authentic text of GATT 1994 in the Spanish language shall be the text in Volume IV of the Basic Instruments and Selected Documents series, subject to the rectifications of terms indicated in Annex B to document MTN.TNC/41.

3. (a) The provisions of Part II of GATT 1994 shall not apply to measures taken by a Member under specific mandatory legislation, enacted by that Member before it became a contracting party to GATT 1947, that prohibits the use, sale or lease of foreign-built or foreign-reconstructed vessels in commercial applications between points in national waters or the waters of an exclusive economic zone. This exemption applies to: (*a*) the continuation or prompt renewal of a non-conforming provision of such legislation; and (*b*) the amendment to a non-conforming provision of such legislation to the extent that the amendment does not decrease the conformity of the provision with Part II of GATT 1947. This exemption is limited to measures taken under legislation described above that is notified and specified prior to the date of entry into force of the WTO Agreement. If such legislation is subsequently modified to decrease its conformity with Part II of GATT 1994, it will no longer qualify for coverage under this paragraph.

(b) The Ministerial Conference shall review this exemption not later than five years after the date of entry into force of the WTO

Agreement and thereafter every two years for as long as the exemption is in force for the purpose of examining whether the conditions which created the need for the exemption still prevail.

(c) A Member whose measures are covered by this exemption shall annually submit a detailed statistical notification consisting of a five-year moving average of actual and expected deliveries of relevant vessels as well as additional information on the use, sale, lease or repair of relevant vessels covered by this exemption.

(d) A Member that considers that this exemption operates in such a manner as to justify a reciprocal and proportionate limitation on the use, sale, lease or repair of vessels constructed in the territory of the Member invoking the exemption shall be free to introduce such a limitation subject to prior notification to the Ministerial Conference.

(e) This exemption is without prejudice to solutions concerning specific aspects of the legislation covered by this exemption negotiated in sectoral agreements or in other fora.

GENERAL AGREEMENT ON TARIFFS AND TRADE

TEXT OF THE GENERAL AGREEMENT

PREFACE

The General Agreement on Tariffs and Trade came into force on 1 January 1948. This booklet contains the complete text of the General Agreement together with all amendments which have become effective since its entry into force. The text is identical to that published, since 1969, as Volume IV in the series Basic Instruments and Selected Documents. A guide to the legal sources of the provisions of the Agreement is provided in an appendix. An Analytical Index, containing notes on the drafting, interpretation and application of the articles of the Agreement has been prepared and published by the secretariat. A second publication, complementary to this one, contains the text of the agreements reached as a result of the Tokyo Round of Multilateral Trade Negotiations (1973-1979).

The General Agreement is applied "provisionally" by all contracting parties. The original contracting parties, and also those former territories of Belgium, France, the Netherlands and the United Kingdom which, after attaining independence, acceded to the General Agreement under Article XXVI:5(*c*), apply the GATT under the Protocol of Provisional Application, the text of which is reproduced in this volume. Chile applies the General Agreement under a Special Protocol of September 1948. The contracting parties which have acceded since 1948 apply the General Agreement under their respective Protocols of Accession.

For the convenience of the reader, **asterisks** mark the portions of the text which should be read in conjunction with notes and supplementary provisions in Annex I to the Agreement. In accordance with Article XXXIV, Annexes A to I are an integral part of the Agreement. The Schedules of tariff concessions annexed to the General Agreement (not here reproduced) are also, in accordance with Article II:7, an integral part of the Agreement.

By the Decision of 23 March 1965, the CONTRACTING PARTIES changed the title of the head of the GATT secretariat from "Executive Secretary" to "Director-General". However, in the absence of an amendment to the General Agreement to take account of this change, the title "Executive Secretary" has been retained in the text of Articles XVIII:12(*e*), XXIII:2 and XXVI:4, 5 and 6. The Decision of 23 March 1965 provides that the duties and powers conferred upon the Executive Secretary by the General Agreement "shall be exercised by the person holding the position of Director-General, who shall, for this purpose, also hold the position of Executive Secretary".

TABLE OF CONTENTS

THE GENERAL AGREEMENT ON TARIFFS AND TRADE 1947

The Governments of the COMMONWEALTH OF AUSTRALIA, the KKINGDOM OF BELGIUM, the UNITED STATES OF BRAZIL, BURMA, CANADA, CEYLON, the REPUBLIC OF CHILE, the REPUBLIC OF CHINA, the REPUBLIC OF CUBA, the CZECHOSLOVAK REPUBLIC, the FRENCH REPUBLIC, INDIA, LEBANON, the GRAND-DUCHY OF LUXEMBURG, the KINGDOM OF THE NETHERLANDS, NEW ZEALAND, the KINGDOM OF NORWAY, PAKISTAN, SOUTHERN RHODESIA, SYRIA, the UNION OF SOUTH AFRICA, the UNITED KINGDOM OF GREAT BRITAIN AND NORTHERN IRELAND, and the UNITED STATES OF AMERICA:

Recognizing that their relations in the field of trade and economic endeavour should be conducted with a view to raising standards of living, ensuring full employment and a large and steadily growing volume of real income and effective demand, developing the full use of the resources of the world and expanding the production and exchange of goods,

Being desirous of contributing to these objectives by entering into reciprocal and mutually advantageous arrangements directed to the substantial reduction of tariffs and other barriers to trade and to the elimination of discriminatory treatment in international commerce,

Have through their Representatives agreed as follows:

PART I

ARTICLE I

General Most-Favoured-Nation Treatment

1. With respect to customs duties and charges of any kind imposed on or in connection with importation or exportation or imposed on the international transfer of payments for imports or exports, and with respect to the method of levying such duties and charges, and with respect to all rules and formalities in connection with importation and exportation, and with respect to all matters referred to in paragraphs 2 and 4 of Article III,* any advantage, favour, privilege or immunity granted by any contracting party to any product originating in or destined for any other country shall be accorded immediately and unconditionally to the like product originating in or destined for the territories of all other contracting parties.

2. The provisions of paragraph 1 of this Article shall not require the elimination of any preferences in respect of import duties or charges which do not exceed the levels provided for in paragraph 4 of this Article and which fall within the following descriptions:

(*a*) Preferences in force exclusively between two or more of the territories listed in Annex A, subject to the conditions set forth therein;

(*b*) Preferences in force exclusively between two or more territories which on July 1, 1939, were connected by common sovereignty or relations of protection or suzerainty and which are listed in Annexes B, C and D, subject to the conditions set forth therein;

(*c*) Preferences in force exclusively between the United States of America and the Republic of Cuba;

(*d*) Preferences in force exclusively between neighbouring countries listed in Annexes E and F.

3. The provisions of paragraph 1 shall not apply to preferences between the countries formerly a part of the Ottoman Empire and detached from it on July 24, 1923, provided such preferences are approved under paragraph 5† of Article XXV, which shall be applied in this respect in the light of paragraph 1 of Article XXIX.

4. The margin of preference* on any product in respect of which a preference is permitted under paragraph 2 of this Article but is not specifically set forth as a maximum margin of preference in the appropriate Schedule annexed to this Agreement shall not exceed:

(*a*) in respect of duties or charges on any product described in such Schedule, the difference between the most-favoured-nation and preferential rates provided for therein; if no preferential rate is provided for, the preferential rate shall for the purposes of this paragraph be taken to be that in force on April 10, 1947, and, if no most-favoured-nation rate is provided for, the margin shall not exceed the difference between the most-favoured-nation and preferential rates existing on April 10, 1947;

(*b*) in respect of duties or charges on any product not described in the appropriate Schedule, the difference between the most-favoured-nation and preferential rates existing on April 10, 1947.

---

† The authentic text erroneously reads "sub-paragraph 5 (a)".

In the case of the contracting parties named in Annex G, the date of April 10, 1947, referred to in sub-paragraph (*a*) and (*b*) of this paragraph shall be replaced by the respective dates set forth in that Annex.

ARTICLE II

Schedules of Concessions

1. (*a*) Each contracting party shall accord to the commerce of the other contracting parties treatment no less favourable than that provided for in the appropriate Part of the appropriate Schedule annexed to this Agreement.

(*b*) The products described in Part I of the Schedule relating to any contracting party, which are the products of territories of other contracting parties, shall, on their importation into the territory to which the Schedule relates, and subject to the terms, conditions or qualifications set forth in that Schedule, be exempt from ordinary customs duties in excess of those set forth and provided therein. Such products shall also be exempt from all other duties or charges of any kind imposed on or in connection with the importation in excess of those imposed on the date of this Agreement or those directly and mandatorily required to be imposed thereafter by legislation in force in the importing territory on that date.

(*c*) The products described in Part II of the Schedule relating to any contracting party which are the products of territories entitled under Article I to receive preferential treatment upon importation into the territory to which the Schedule relates shall, on their importation into such territory, and subject to the terms, conditions or qualifications set forth in that Schedule, be exempt from ordinary customs duties in excess of those set forth and provided for in Part II of that Schedule. Such products shall also be exempt from all other duties or charges of any kind imposed on or in connection with importation in excess of those imposed on the date of this Agreement or those directly or mandatorily required to be imposed thereafter by legislation in force in the importing territory on that date. Nothing in this Article shall prevent any contracting party from maintaining its requirements existing on the date of this Agreement as to the eligibility of goods for entry at preferential rates of duty.

2. Nothing in this Article shall prevent any contracting party from imposing at any time on the importation of any product:

(*a*) a charge equivalent to an internal tax imposed consistently with the provisions of paragraph 2 of Article III* in respect of the like domestic product or in respect of an article from which the imported product has been manufactured or produced in whole or in part;

(*b*) any anti-dumping or countervailing duty applied consistently with the provisions of Article VI;*

(*c*) fees or other charges commensurate with the cost of services rendered.

3. No contracting party shall alter its method of determining dutiable value or of converting currencies so as to impair the value of any of the concessions provided for in the appropriate Schedule annexed to this Agreement.

4. If any contracting party establishes, maintains or authorizes, formally or in effect, a monopoly of the importation of any product described in the appropriate Schedule annexed to this Agreement, such monopoly shall not, except as provided for in that Schedule or as otherwise agreed between the parties which initially negotiated the concession, operate so as to afford protection on the average in excess of the amount of protection provided for in that Schedule. The provisions of this paragraph shall not limit the use by contracting parties of any form of assistance to domestic producers permitted by other provisions of this Agreement.*

5. If any contracting party considers that a product is not receiving from another contracting party the treatment which the first contracting party believes to have been contemplated by a concession provided for in the appropriate Schedule annexed to this Agreement, it shall bring the matter directly to the attention of the other contracting party. If the latter agrees that the treatment contemplated was that claimed by the first contracting party, but declares that such treatment cannot be accorded because a court or other proper authority has ruled to the effect that the product involved cannot be classified under the tariff laws of such contracting party so as to permit the treatment contemplated in this Agreement, the two contracting parties, together with any other contracting parties substantially interested, shall enter promptly into further negotiations with a view to a compensatory adjustment of the matter.

6. (*a*) The specific duties and charges included in the Schedules

relating to contracting parties members of the International Monetary Fund, and margins of preference in specific duties and charges maintained by such contracting parties, are expressed in the appropriate currency at the par value accepted or provisionally recognized by the Fund at the date of this Agreement. Accordingly, in case this par value is reduced consistently with the Articles of Agreement of the International Monetary Fund by more than twenty per centum, such specific duties and charges and margins of preference may be adjusted to take account of such reduction; *provided* that the CONTRACTING PARTIES (*i.e.*, the contracting parties acting jointly as provided for in Article XXV) concur that such adjustments will not impair the value of the concessions provided for in the appropriate Schedule or elsewhere in this Agreement, due account being taken of all factors which may influence the need for, or urgency of, such adjustments.

(*b*) Similar provisions shall apply to any contracting party not a member of the Fund, as from the date on which such contracting party becomes a member of the Fund or enters into a special exchange agreement in pursuance of Article XV.

7. The Schedules annexed to this Agreement are hereby made an integral part of Part I of this Agreement.

PART II

ARTICLE III*

National Treatment on Internal Taxation and Regulation

1. The contracting parties recognize that internal taxes and other internal charges, and laws, regulations and requirements affecting the internal sale, offering for sale, purchase, transportation, distribution or use of products, and internal quantitative regulations requiring the mixture, processing or use of products in specified amounts or proportions, should not be applied to imported or domestic products so as to afford protection to domestic production.*

2. The products of the territory of any contracting party imported into the territory of any other contracting party shall not be subject, directly or indirectly, to internal taxes or other internal charges of any kind in excess of those applied, directly or indirectly, to like domestic products. Moreover, no contracting party shall otherwise apply internal taxes or other internal charges to imported

or domestic products in a manner contrary to the principles set forth in paragraph 1.*

3. With respect to any existing internal tax which is inconsistent with the provisions of paragraph 2, but which is specifically authorized under a trade agreement, in force on April 10, 1947, in which the import duty on the taxed product is bound against increase, the contracting party imposing the tax shall be free to postpone the application of the provisions of paragraph 2 to such tax until such time as it can obtain release from the obligations of such trade agreement in order to permit the increase of such duty to the extent necessary to compensate for the elimination of the protective element of the tax.

4. The products of the territory of any contracting party imported into the territory of any other contracting party shall be accorded treatment no less favourable than that accorded to like products of national origin in respect of all laws, regulations and requirements affecting their internal sale, offering for sale, purchase, transportation, distribution or use. The provisions of this paragraph shall not prevent the application of differential internal transportation charges which are based exclusively on the economic operation of the means of transport and not on the nationality of the product.

5. No contracting party shall establish or maintain any internal quantitative regulation relating to the mixture, processing or use of products in specified amounts or proportions which requires, directly or indirectly, that any specified amount or proportion of any product which is the subject of the regulation must be supplied from domestic sources. Moreover, no contracting party shall otherwise apply internal quantitative regulations in a manner contrary to the principles set forth in paragraph 1.*

6. The provisions of paragraph 5 shall not apply to any internal quantitative regulation in force in the territory of any contracting party on July 1, 1939, April 10, 1947, or March 24, 1948, at the option of that contracting party; *Provided* that any such regulation which is contrary to the provisions of paragraph 5 shall not be modified to the detriment of imports and shall be treated as a customs duty for the purpose of negotiation.

7. No internal quantitative regulation relating to the mixture, processing or use of products in specified amounts or proportions

shall be applied in such a manner as to allocate any such amount or proportion among external sources of supply.

8. (*a*) The provisions of this Article shall not apply to laws, regulations or requirements governing the procurement by governmental agencies of products purchased for governmental purposes and not with a view to commercial resale or with a view to use in the production of goods for commercial sale.

(*b*) The provisions of this Article shall not prevent the payment of subsidies exclusively to domestic producers, including payments to domestic producers derived from the proceeds of internal taxes or charges applied consistently with the provisions of this Article and subsidies effected through governmental purchases of domestic products.

9. The contracting parties recognize that internal maximum price control measures, even though conforming to the other provisions of this Article, can have effects prejudicial to the interests of contracting parties supplying imported products. Accordingly, contracting parties applying such measures shall take account of the interests of exporting contracting parties with a view to avoiding to the fullest practicable extent such prejudicial effects.

10. The provisions of this Article shall not prevent any contracting party from establishing or maintaining internal quantitative regulations relating to exposed cinematograph films and meeting the requirements of Article IV.

ARTICLE IV

Special Provisions relating to Cinematograph Films

If any contracting party establishes or maintains internal quantitative regulations relating to exposed cinematograph films, such regulations shall take the form of screen quotas which shall conform to the following requirements:

(*a*) Screen quotas may require the exhibition of cinematograph films of national origin during a specified minimum proportion of the total screen time actually utilized, over a specified period of not less than one year, in the commercial exhibition of all films of whatever origin, and shall be computed on the basis of screen time per theatre per year or the equivalent thereof;

(*b*) With the exception of screen time reserved for films of national origin under a screen quota, screen time including that released by administrative action from screen time reserved for films of national origin, shall not be allocated formally or in effect among sources of supply;

(*c*) Notwithstanding the provisions of sub-paragraph (*b*) of this Article, any contracting party may maintain screen quotas conforming to the requirements of sub-paragraph (*a*) of this Article which reserve a minimum proportion of screen time for films of a specified origin other than that of the contracting party imposing such screen quotas; *Provided* that no such minimum proportion of screen time shall be increased above the level in effect on April 10, 1947;

(*d*) Screen quotas shall be subject to negotiation for their limitation, liberalization or elimination.

ARTICLE V

Freedom of Transit

1. Goods (including baggage), and also vessels and other means of transport, shall be deemed to be in transit across the territory of a contracting party when the passage across such territory, with or without trans-shipment, warehousing, breaking bulk, or change in the mode of transport, is only a portion of a complete journey beginning and terminating beyond the frontier of the contracting party across whose territory the traffic passes. Traffic of this nature is termed in this article "traffic in transit".

2. There shall be freedom of transit through the territory of each contracting party, via the routes most convenient for international transit, for traffic in transit to or from the territory of other contracting parties. No distinction shall be made which is based on the flag of vessels, the place of origin, departure, entry, exit or destination, or on any circumstances relating to the ownership of goods, of vessels or of other means of transport.

3. Any contracting party may require that traffic in transit through its territory be entered at the proper custom house, but, except in cases of failure to comply with applicable customs laws and regulations, such traffic coming from or going to the territory

of other contracting parties shall not be subject to any unnecessary delays or restrictions and shall be exempt from customs duties and from all transit duties or other charges imposed in respect of transit, except charges for transportation or those commensurate with administrative expenses entailed by transit or with the cost of services rendered.

4. All charges and regulations imposed by contracting parties on traffic in transit to or from the territories of other contracting parties shall be reasonable, having regard to the conditions of the traffic.

5. With respect to all charges, regulations and formalities in connection with transit, each contracting party shall accord to traffic in transit to or from the territory of any other contracting party treatment no less favourable than the treatment accorded to traffic in transit to or from any third country.*

6. Each contracting party shall accord to products which have been in transit through the territory of any other contracting party treatment no less favourable than that which would have been accorded to such products had they been transported from their place of origin to their destination without going through the territory of such other contracting party. Any contracting party shall, however, be free to maintain its requirements of direct consignment existing on the date of this Agreement, in respect of any goods in regard to which such direct consignment is a requisite condition of eligibility for entry of the goods at preferential rates of duty or has relation to the contracting party's prescribed method of valuation for duty purposes.

7. The provisions of this Article shall not apply to the operation of aircraft in transit, but shall apply to air transit of goods (including baggage).

ARTICLE VI

Anti-dumping and Countervailing Duties

1. The contracting parties recognize that dumping, by which products of one country are introduced into the commerce of another country at less than the normal value of the products, is to be condemned if it causes or threatens material injury to an established industry in the territory of a contracting party or materially retards the establishment of a domestic industry. For the purposes of this

Article, a product is to be considered as being introduced into the commerce of an importing country at less than its normal value, if the price of the product exported from one country to another

(*a*) is less than the comparable price, in the ordinary course of trade, for the like product when destined for consumption in the exporting country, or,

(*b*) in the absence of such domestic price, is less than either

(i) the highest comparable price for the like product for export to any third country in the ordinary course of trade, or

(ii) the cost of production of the product in the country of origin plus a reasonable addition for selling cost and profit.

Due allowance shall be made in each case for differences in conditions and terms of sale, for differences in taxation, and for other differences affecting price comparability.*

2. In order to offset or prevent dumping, a contracting party may levy on any dumped product an anti-dumping duty not greater in amount than the margin of dumping in respect of such product. For the purposes of this Article, the margin of dumping is the price difference determined in accordance with the provisions of paragraph 1.*

3. No countervailing duty shall be levied on any product of the territory of any contracting party imported into the territory of another contracting party in excess of an amount equal to the estimated bounty or subsidy determined to have been granted, directly or indirectly, on the manufacture, production or export of such product in the country of origin or exportation, including any special subsidy to the transportation of a particular product. The term "countervailing duty" shall be understood to mean a special duty levied for the purpose of offsetting any bounty or subsidy bestowed, directly, or indirectly, upon the manufacture, production or export of any merchandise.*

4. No product of the territory of any contracting party imported into the territory of any other contracting party shall be subject to anti-dumping or countervailing duty by reason of the exemption of such product from duties or taxes borne by the like product when

destined for consumption in the country of origin or exportation, or by reason of the refund of such duties or taxes.

5. No product of the territory of any contracting party imported into the territory of any other contracting party shall be subject to both anti-dumping and countervailing duties to compensate for the same situation of dumping or export subsidization.

6. (*a*) No contracting party shall levy any anti-dumping or countervailing duty on the importation of any product of the territory of another contracting party unless it determines that the effect of the dumping or subsidization, as the case may be, is such as to cause or threaten material injury to an established domestic industry, or is such as to retard materially the establishment of a domestic industry.

(*b*) The CONTRACTING PARTIES may waive the requirement of sub-paragraph (*a*) of this paragraph so as to permit a contracting party to levy an anti-dumping or countervailing duty on the importation of any product for the purpose of offsetting dumping or subsidization which causes or threatens material injury to an industry in the territory of another contracting party exporting the product concerned to the territory of the importing contracting party. The CONTRACTING PARTIES shall waive the requirements of sub-paragraph (*a*) of this paragraph, so as to permit the levying of a countervailing duty, in cases in which they find that a subsidy is causing or threatening material injury to an industry in the territory of another contracting party exporting the product concerned to the territory of the importing contracting party.*

(*c*) In exceptional circumstances, however, where delay might cause damage which would be difficult to repair, a contracting party may levy a countervailing duty for the purpose referred to in sub-paragraph (*b*) of this paragraph without the prior approval of the CONTRACTING PARTIES; *Provided* that such action shall be reported immediately to the CONTRACTING PARTIES and that the countervailing duty shall be withdrawn promptly if the CONTRACTING PARTIES disapprove.

7. A system for the stabilization of the domestic price or of the return to domestic producers of a primary commodity, independently of the movements of export prices, which results at times in the sale of the commodity for export at a price lower than the comparable price charged for the like commodity to buyers in

the domestic market, shall be presumed not to result in material injury within the meaning of paragraph 6 if it is determined by consultation among the contracting parties substantially interested in the commodity concerned that:

(*a*) the system has also resulted in the sale of the commodity for export at a price higher than the comparable price charged for the like commodity to buyers in the domestic market, and

(*b*) the system is so operated, either because of the effective regulation of production, or otherwise, as not to stimulate exports unduly or otherwise seriously prejudice the interests of other contracting parties.

ARTICLE VII

Valuation for Customs Purposes

1. The contracting parties recognize the validity of the general principles of valuation set forth in the following paragraphs of this Article, and they undertake to give effect to such principles, in respect of all products subject to duties or other charges* or restrictions on importation and exportation based upon or regulated in any manner by value. Moreover, they shall, upon a request by another contracting party review the operation of any of their laws or regulations relating to value for customs purposes in the light of these principles. The CONTRACTING PARTIES may request from contracting parties reports on steps taken by them in pursuance of the provisions of this Article.

2. (*a*) The value for customs purposes of imported merchandise should be based on the actual value of the imported merchandise on which duty is assessed, or of like merchandise, and should not be based on the value of merchandise of national origin or on arbitrary or fictitious values.*

(*b*) "Actual value" should be the price at which, at a time and place determined by the legislation of the country of importation, such or like merchandise is sold or offered for sale in the ordinary course of trade under fully competitive conditions. To the extent to which the price of such or like merchandise is governed by the quantity in a particular transaction, the price to be considered should uniformly be related to either (i) comparable quantities, or (ii) quantities not less favourable to importers than those in which the greater volume of the merchandise is sold in the trade between the countries of exportation and importation.*

(*c*) When the actual value is not ascertainable in accordance with sub-paragraph (*b*) of this paragraph, the value for customs purposes should be based on the nearest ascertainable equivalent of such value.*

3. The value for customs purposes of any imported product should not include the amount of any internal tax, applicable within the country of origin or export, from which the imported product has been exempted or has been or will be relieved by means of refund.

4. (*a*) Except as otherwise provided for in this paragraph, where it is necessary for the purposes of paragraph 2 of this Article for a contracting party to convert into its own currency a price expressed in the currency of another country, the conversion rate of exchange to be used shall be based, for each currency involved, on the par value as established pursuant to the Articles of Agreement of the International Monetary Fund or on the rate of exchange recognized by the Fund, or on the par value established in accordance with a special exchange agreement entered into pursuant to Article XV of this Agreement.

(*b*) Where no such established par value and no such recognized rate of exchange exist, the conversion rate shall reflect effectively the current value of such currency in commercial transactions.

(*c*) The CONTRACTING PARTIES, in agreement with the International Monetary Fund, shall formulate rules governing the conversion by contracting parties of any foreign currency in respect of which multiple rates of exchange are maintained consistently with the Articles of Agreement of the International Monetary Fund. Any contracting party may apply such rules in respect of such foreign currencies for the purposes of paragraph 2 of this Article as an alternative to the use of par values. Until such rules are adopted by the CONTRACTING PARTIES, any contracting party may employ, in respect of any such foreign currency, rules of conversion for the purposes of paragraph 2 of this Article which are designed to reflect effectively the value of such foreign currency in commercial transactions.

(*d*) Nothing in this paragraph shall be construed to require any contracting party to alter the method of converting currencies for customs purposes which is applicable in its territory on the date of this Agreement, if such alteration would have the effect of increasing generally the amounts of duty payable.

5. The bases and methods for determining the value of products subject to duties or other charges or restrictions based upon or regulated in any manner by value should be stable and should be given sufficient publicity to enable traders to estimate, with a reasonable degree of certainty, the value for customs purposes.

ARTICLE VIII

Fees and Formalities connected with Importation and Exportation*

1. (*a*) All fees and charges of whatever character (other than import and export duties and other than taxes within the purview of Article III) imposed by contracting parties on or in connection with importation or exportation shall be limited in amount to the approximate cost of services rendered and shall not represent an indirect protection to domestic products or a taxation of imports or exports for fiscal purposes.

(*b*) The contracting parties recognize the need for reducing the number and diversity of fees and charges referred to in sub-paragraph (*a*).

(*c*) The contracting parties also recognize the need for minimizing the incidence and complexity of import and export formalities and for decreasing and simplifying import and export documentation requirements.*

2. A contracting party shall, upon request by another contracting party or by the CONTRACTING PARTIES, review the operation of its laws and regulations in the light of the provisions of this Article.

3. No contracting party shall impose substantial penalties for minor breaches of customs regulations or procedural requirements. In particular, no penalty in respect of any omission or mistake in customs documentation which is easily rectifiable and obviously made without fraudulent intent or gross negligence shall be greater than necessary to serve merely as a warning.

4. The provisions of this Article shall extend to fees, charges,

formalities and requirements imposed by governmental authorities in connection with importation and exportation, including those relating to:

(*a*) consular transactions, such as consular invoices and certificates;

(*b*) quantitative restrictions;

(*c*) licensing;

(*d*) exchange control;

(*e*) statistical services;

(*f*) documents, documentation and certification;

(*g*) analysis and inspection; and

(*h*) quarantine, sanitation and fumigation.

ARTICLE IX

Marks of Origin

1. Each contracting party shall accord to the products of the territories of other contracting parties treatment with regard to marking requirements no less favourable than the treatment accorded to like products of any third country.

2. The contracting parties recognize that, in adopting and enforcing laws and regulations relating to marks of origin, the difficulties and inconveniences which such measures may cause to the commerce and industry of exporting countries should be reduced to a minimum, due regard being had to the necessity of protecting consumers against fraudulent or misleading indications.

3. Whenever it is administratively practicable to do so, contracting parties should permit required marks of origin to be affixed at the time of importation.

4. The laws and regulations of contracting parties relating to the marking of imported products shall be such as to permit compliance without seriously damaging the products, or materially reducing their value, or unreasonably increasing their cost.

5. As a general rule, no special duty or penalty should be imposed by any contracting party for failure to comply with marking requirements prior to importation unless corrective marking is unreasonably delayed or deceptive marks have been affixed or the required marking has been intentionally omitted.

6. The contracting parties shall co-operate with each other with a view to preventing the use of trade names in such manner as to misrepresent the true origin of a product, to the detriment of such distinctive regional or geographical names of products of the territory of a contracting party as are protected by its legislation. Each contracting party shall accord full and sympathetic consideration to such requests or representations as may be made by any other contracting party regarding the application of the undertaking set forth in the preceding sentence to names of products which have been communicated to it by the other contracting party.

ARTICLE X

Publication and Administration of Trade Regulations

1. Laws, regulations, judicial decisions and administrative rulings of general application, made effective by any contracting party, pertaining to the classification or the valuation of products for customs purposes, or to rates of duty, taxes or other charges, or to requirements, restrictions or prohibitions on imports or exports or on the transfer of payments therefor, or affecting their sale, distribution, transportation, insurance, warehousing inspection, exhibition, processing, mixing or other use, shall be published promptly in such a manner as to enable governments and traders to become acquainted with them. Agreements affecting international trade policy which are in force between the government or a governmental agency of any contracting party and the government or governmental agency of any other contracting party shall also be published. The provisions of this paragraph shall not require any contracting party to disclose confidential information which would impede law enforcement or otherwise be contrary to the public interest or would prejudice the legitimate commercial interests of particular enterprises, public or private.

2. No measure of general application taken by any contracting party effecting an advance in a rate of duty or other charge on imports under an established and uniform practice, or imposing a new or more burdensome requirement, restriction or prohibition on imports, or on the transfer of payments therefor, shall be enforced before such measure has been officially published.

3. (*a*) Each contracting party shall administer in a uniform, impartial and reasonable manner all its laws, regulations, decisions and rulings of the kind described in paragraph 1 of this Article.

(*b*) Each contracting party shall maintain, or institute as soon as practicable, judicial, arbitral or administrative tribunals or procedures for the purpose, *inter alia*, of the prompt review and correction of administrative action relating to customs matters. Such tribunals or procedures shall be independent of the agencies entrusted with administrative enforcement and their decisions shall be implemented by, and shall govern the practice of, such agencies unless an appeal is lodged with a court or tribunal of superior jurisdiction within the time prescribed for appeals to be lodged by importers; *Provided* that the central administration of such agency may take steps to obtain a review of the matter in another proceeding if there is good cause to believe that the decision is inconsistent with established principles of law or the actual facts.

(*c*) The provisions of sub-paragraph (*b*) of this paragraph shall not require the elimination or substitution of procedures in force in the territory of a contracting party on the date of this Agreement which in fact provide for an objective and impartial review of administrative action even though such procedures are not fully or formally independent of the agencies entrusted with administrative enforcement. Any contracting party employing such procedures shall, upon request, furnish the CONTRACTING PARTIES with full information thereon in order that they may determine whether such procedures conform to the requirements of this sub-paragraph.

ARTICLE XI*

General Elimination of Quantitative Restrictions

1. No prohibitions or restrictions other than duties, taxes or other charges, whether made effective through quotas, import or export licences or other measures, shall be instituted or maintained by any contracting party on the importation of any product of the territory of any other contracting party or on the exportation or sale for export of any product destined for the territory of any other contracting party.

2. The provisions of paragraph 1 of this Article shall not extend to the following:

(*a*) Export prohibitions or restrictions temporarily applied to prevent or relieve critical shortages of foodstuffs or other products essential to the exporting contracting party;

(*b*) Import and export prohibitions or restrictions necessary to the application of standards or regulations for the classification, grading or marketing of commodities in international trade;

(*c*) Import restrictions on any agricultural or fisheries product, imported in any form,* necessary to the enforcement of governmental measures which operate:

(i) to restrict the quantities of the like domestic product permitted to be marketed or produced, or, if there is no substantial domestic production of the like product, of a domestic product for which the imported product can be directly substituted; or

(ii) to remove a temporary surplus of the like domestic product, or, if there is no substantial domestic production of the like product, of a domestic product for which the imported product can be directly substituted, by making the surplus available to certain groups of domestic consumers free of charge or at prices below the current market level; or

(iii) to restrict the quantities permitted to be produced of any animal product the production of which is directly dependent, wholly or mainly, on the imported commodity, if the domestic production of that commodity is relatively negligible.

Any contracting party applying restrictions on the importation of any product pursuant to sub-paragraph (*c*) of this paragraph shall give public notice of the total quantity or value of the product permitted to be imported during a specified future period and of any change in such quantity or value. Moreover, any restrictions applied under (i) above shall not be such as will reduce the total of imports relative to the total of domestic production, as compared with the proportion which might reasonably be expected to rule between the two in the absence of restrictions. In determining this proportion, the contracting party shall pay due regard to the proportion prevailing during a previous representative period and to any special factors* which may have affected or may be affecting the trade in the product concerned.

ARTICLE XII*

Restrictions to Safeguard the Balance of Payments

1. Notwithstanding the provisions of paragraph 1 of Article XI, any contracting party, in order to safeguard its external financial

position and its balance of payments, may restrict the quantity or value of merchandise permitted to be imported, subject to the provisions of the following paragraphs of this Article.

2. (*a*) Import restrictions instituted, maintained or intensified by a contracting party under this Article shall not exceed those necessary:

(i) to forestall the imminent threat of, or to stop, a serious decline in its monetary reserves, or

(ii) in the case of a contracting party with very low monetary reserves, to achieve a reasonable rate of increase in its reserves.

Due regard shall be paid in either case to any special factors which may be affecting the reserves of such contracting party or its need for reserves, including, where special external credits or other resources are available to it, the need to provide for the appropriate use of such credits or resources.

(*b*) Contracting parties applying restrictions under sub-paragraph (*a*) of this paragraph shall progressively relax them as such conditions improve, maintaining them only to the extent that the conditions specified in that sub-paragraph still justify their application. They shall eliminate the restrictions when conditions would no longer justify their institution or maintenance under that sub-paragraph.

3. (*a*) Contracting parties undertake, in carrying out their domestic policies, to pay due regard to the need for maintaining or restoring equilibrium in their balance of payments on a sound and lasting basis and to the desirability of avoiding an uneconomic employment of productive resources. They recognize that, in order to achieve these ends, it is desirable so far as possible to adopt measures which expand rather than contract international trade.

(*b*) Contracting parties applying restrictions under this Article may determine the incidence of the restrictions on imports of different products or classes of products in such a way as to give priority to the importation of those products which are more essential.

(*c*) Contracting parties applying restrictions under this Article undertake:

(i) to avoid unnecessary damage to the commercial or economic interests of any other contracting party;*

(ii) not to apply restrictions so as to prevent unreasonably the importation of any description of goods in minimum commercial quantities the exclusion of which would impair regular channels of trade; and

(iii) not to apply restrictions which would prevent the importations of commercial samples or prevent compliance with patent, trade mark, copyright, or similar procedures.

(*d*) The contracting parties recognize that, as a result of domestic policies directed towards the achievement and maintenance of full and productive employment or towards the development of economic resources, a contracting party may experience a high level of demand for imports involving a threat to its monetary reserves of the sort referred to in paragraph 2 (*a*) of this Article. Accordingly, a contracting party otherwise complying with the provisions of this Article shall not be required to withdraw or modify restrictions on the ground that a change in those policies would render unnecessary restrictions which it is applying under this Article.

4. (*a*) Any contracting party applying new restrictions or raising the general level of its existing restrictions by a substantial intensification of the measures applied under this Article shall immediately after instituting or intensifying such restrictions (or, in circumstances in which prior consultation is practicable, before doing so) consult with the CONTRACTING PARTIES as to the nature of its balance of payments difficulties, alternative corrective measures which may be available, and the possible effect of the restrictions on the economies of other contracting parties.

(*b*) On a date to be determined by them,* the CONTRACTING PARTIES shall review all restrictions still applied under this Article on that date. Beginning one year after that date, contracting parties applying import restrictions under this Article shall enter into consultations of the type provided for in sub-paragraph (*a*) of this paragraph with the CONTRACTING PARTIES annually.

(*c*) (i) If, in the course of consultations with a contracting party under sub-paragraph (*a*) or (*b*) above, the CONTRACTING PARTIES find that the restrictions are not consistent with provisions of this Article or with those of Article XIII (subject to the provisions of Article XIV), they shall indicate the nature of the inconsistency and may advise that the restrictions be suitably modified.

(ii) If, however, as a result of the consultations, the CONTRACTING PARTIES determine that the restrictions are being applied in a manner involving an inconsistency of a serious nature with the provisions of this Article or with those of Article XIII (subject to the provisions of Article XIV) and that damage to the trade of any contracting party is caused or threatened thereby, they shall so inform the contracting party applying the restrictions and shall make appropriate recommendations for securing conformity with such provisions within the specified period of time. If such contracting party does not comply with these recommendations within the specified period, the CONTRACTING PARTIES may release any contracting party the trade of which is adversely affected by the restrictions from such obligations under this Agreement towards the contracting party applying the restrictions as they determine to be appropriate in the circumstances.

(*d*) The CONTRACTING PARTIES shall invite any contracting party which is applying restrictions under this Article to enter into consultations with them at the request of any contracting party which can establish a *prima facie* case that the restrictions are inconsistent with the provisions of this Article or with those of Article XIII (subject to the provisions of Article XIV) and that its trade is adversely affected thereby. However, no such invitation shall be issued unless the CONTRACTING PARTIES have ascertained that direct discussions between the contracting parties concerned have not been successful. If, as a result of the consultations with the CONTRACTING PARTIES, no agreement is reached and they determine that the restrictions are being applied inconsistently with such provisions, and that damage to the trade of the contracting party initiating the procedure is caused or threatened thereby, they shall recommend the withdrawal or modification of the restrictions. If the restrictions are not withdrawn or modified within such time as the CONTRACTING PARTIES may prescribe, they may release the contracting party initiating the procedure from such obligations under this Agreement towards the contracting party applying the restrictions as they determine to be appropriate in the circumstances.

(*e*) In proceeding under this paragraph, the CONTRACTING PARTIES shall have due regard to any special external factors adversely affecting the export trade of the contracting party applying the restrictions.*

(*f*) Determinations under this paragraph shall be rendered expeditiously and, if possible, within sixty days of the initiation of the consultations.

5. If there is a persistent and widespread application of import restrictions under this Article, indicating the existence of a general disequilibrium which is restricting international trade, the CONTRACTING PARTIES shall initiate discussions to consider whether other measures might be taken, either by those contracting parties the balance of payments of which are under pressure or by those the balance of payments of which are tending to be exceptionally favourable, or by any appropriate intergovernmental organization, to remove the underlying causes of the disequilibrium. On the invitation of the CONTRACTING PARTIES, contracting parties shall participate in such discussions.

ARTICLE XIII*

Non-discriminatory Administration of Quantitative Restrictions

1. No prohibition or restriction shall be applied by any contracting party on the importation of any product of the territory of any other contracting party or on the exportation of any product destined for the territory of any other contracting party, unless the importation of the like product of all third countries or the exportation of the like product to all third countries is similarly prohibited or restricted.

2. In applying import restrictions to any product, contracting parties shall aim at a distribution of trade in such product approaching as closely as possible the shares which the various contracting parties might be expected to obtain in the absence of such restrictions and to this end shall observe the following provisions:

(*a*) Wherever practicable, quotas representing the total amount of permitted imports (whether allocated among supplying countries or not) shall be fixed, and notice given of their amount in accordance with paragraph 3 (*b*) of this Article;

(*b*) In cases in which quotas are not practicable, the restrictions may be applied by means of import licences or permits without a quota;

(*c*) Contracting parties shall not, except for purposes of

operating quotas allocated in accordance with sub-paragraph (*d*) of this paragraph, require that import licences or permits be utilized for the importation of the product concerned from a particular country or source;

(*d*) In cases in which a quota is allocated among supplying countries the contracting party applying the restrictions may seek agreement with respect to the allocation of shares in the quota with all other contracting parties having a substantial interest in supplying the product concerned. In cases in which this method is not reasonably practicable, the contracting party concerned shall allot to contracting parties having a substantial interest in supplying the product shares based upon the proportions, supplied by such contracting parties during a previous representative period, of the total quantity or value of imports of the product, due account being taken of any special factors which may have affected or may be affecting the trade in the product. No conditions or formalities shall be imposed which would prevent any contracting party from utilizing fully the share of any such total quantity or value which has been allotted to it, subject to importation being made within any prescribed period to which the quota may relate.*

3. (*a*) In cases in which import licences are issued in connection with import restrictions, the contracting party applying the restrictions shall provide, upon the request of any contracting party having an interest in the trade in the product concerned, all relevant information concerning the administration of the restrictions, the import licences granted over a recent period and the distribution of such licences among supplying countries; *Provided* that there shall be no obligation to supply information as to the names of importing or supplying enterprises.

(*b*) In the case of import restrictions involving the fixing of quotas, the contracting party applying the restrictions shall give public notice of the total quantity or value of the product or products which will be permitted to be imported during a specified future period and of any change in such quantity or value. Any supplies of the product in question which were *en route* at the time at which public notice was given shall not be excluded from entry; *Provided* that they may be counted so far as practicable, against the quantity permitted to be imported in the period in question, and also, where necessary, against the quantities permitted to be imported in the next following period or periods; and *Provided* further that if any contracting party customarily exempts from such restrictions products entered for consumption or withdrawn from warehouse for consumption during a period of thirty days after the day of such public notice, such practice shall be considered full compliance with this sub-paragraph.

(*c*) In the case of quotas allocated among supplying countries, the contracting party applying the restrictions shall promptly inform all other contracting parties having an interest in supplying the product concerned of the shares in the quota currently allocated, by quantity or value, to the various supplying countries and shall give public notice thereof.

4. With regard to restrictions applied in accordance with paragraph 2 (*d*) of this Article or under paragraph 2 (*c*) of Article XI, the selection of a representative period for any product and the appraisal of any special factors* affecting the trade in the product shall be made initially by the contracting party applying the restriction; *Provided* that such contracting party shall, upon the request of any other contracting party having a substantial interest in supplying that product or upon the request of the CONTRACTING PARTIES, consult promptly with the other contracting party or the CONTRACTING PARTIES regarding the need for an adjustment of the proportion determined or of the base period selected, or for the reappraisal of the special factors involved, or for the elimination of conditions, formalities or any other provisions established unilaterally relating to the allocation of an adequate quota or its unrestricted utilization.

5. The provisions of this Article shall apply to any tariff quota instituted or maintained by any contracting party, and, in so far as applicable, the principles of this Article shall also extend to export restrictions.

ARTICLE XIV*

Exceptions to the Rule of Non-discrimination

1. A contracting party which applies restrictions under Article XII or under Section B of Article XVIII may, in the application of

such restrictions, deviate from the provisions of Article XIII in a manner having equivalent effect to restrictions on payments and transfers for current international transactions which that contracting party may at that time apply under Article VIII or XIV of the Articles of Agreement of the International Monetary Fund, or under analogous provisions of a special exchange agreement entered into pursuant to paragraph 6 of Article XV.*

2. A contracting party which is applying import restrictions under Article XII or under Section B of Article XVIII may, with the consent of the CONTRACTING PARTIES, temporarily deviate from the provisions of Article XIII in respect of a small part of its external trade where the benefits to the contracting party or contracting parties concerned substantially outweigh any injury which may result to the trade of other contracting parties.*

3. The provisions of Article XIII shall not preclude a group of territories having a common quota in the International Monetary Fund from applying against imports from other countries, but not among themselves, restrictions in accordance with the provisions of Article XII or of Section B of Article XVIII on condition that such restrictions are in all other respects consistent with the provisions of Article XIII.

4. A contracting party applying import restrictions under Article XII or under Section B of Article XVIII shall not be precluded by Articles XI to XV or Section B of Article XVIII of this Agreement from applying measures to direct its exports in such a manner as to increase its earnings of currencies which it can use without deviation from the provisions of Article XIII.

5. A contracting party shall not be precluded by Articles XI to XV, inclusive, or by Section B of Article XVIII, of this Agreement from applying quantitative restrictions:

(*a*) having equivalent effect to exchange restrictions authorized under Section 3 (*b*) of Article VII of the Articles of Agreement of the International Monetary Fund, or

(*b*) under the preferential arrangements provided for in Annex A of this Agreement, pending the outcome of the negotiations referred to therein.

ARTICLE XV
EXCHANGE ARRANGEMENTS

1. The CONTRACTING PARTIES shall seek co-operation with the International Monetary Fund to the end that the CONTRACTING PARTIES and the Fund may pursue a co-ordinated policy with regard to exchange questions within the jurisdiction of the Fund and questions of quantitative restrictions and other trade measures within the jurisdiction of the CONTRACTING PARTIES.

2. In all cases in which the CONTRACTING PARTIES are called upon to consider or deal with problems concerning monetary reserves, balances of payments or foreign exchange arrangements, they shall consult fully with the International Monetary Fund. In such consultations, the CONTRACTING PARTIES shall accept all findings of statistical and other facts presented by the Fund relating to foreign exchange, monetary reserves and balances of payments, and shall accept the determination of the Fund as to whether action by a contracting party in exchange matters is in accordance with the Articles of Agreement of the International Monetary Fund, or with the terms of a special exchange agreement between that contracting party and the CONTRACTING PARTIES. The CONTRACTING PARTIES in reaching their final decision in cases involving the criteria set forth in paragraph 2 (*a*) of Article XII or in paragraph 9 of Article XVIII, shall accept the determination of the Fund as to what constitutes a serious decline in the contracting party's monetary reserves, a very low level of its monetary reserves or a reasonable rate of increase in its monetary reserves, and as to the financial aspects of other matters covered in consultation in such cases.

3. The CONTRACTING PARTIES shall seek agreement with the Fund regarding procedures for consultation under paragraph 2 of this Article.

4. Contracting parties shall not, by exchange action, frustrate* the intent of the provisions of this Agreement, nor, by trade action, the intent of the provisions of the Articles of Agreement of the International Monetary Fund.

5. If the CONTRACTING PARTIES consider, at any time, that exchange restrictions on payments and transfers in connection with imports are being applied by a contracting party in a manner inconsistent with the exceptions provided for in this Agreement for quantitative restrictions, they shall report thereon to the Fund.

6. Any contracting party which is not a member of the Fund shall, within a time to be determined by the CONTRACTING PARTIES after consultation with the Fund, become a member of the Fund, or, failing that, enter into a special exchange agreement with the CONTRACTING PARTIES. A contracting party which ceases to be a member of the Fund shall forthwith enter into a special exchange agreement with the CONTRACTING PARTIES. Any special exchange agreement entered into by a contracting party under this paragraph shall thereupon become part of its obligations under this Agreement.

7. (*a*) A special exchange agreement between a contracting party and the CONTRACTING PARTIES under paragraph 6 of this Article shall provide to the satisfaction of the CONTRACTING PARTIES that the objectives of this Agreement will not be frustrated as a result of action in exchange matters by the contracting party in question.

(*b*) The terms of any such agreement shall not impose obligations on the contracting party in exchange matters generally more restrictive than those imposed by the Articles of Agreement of the International Monetary Fund on members of the Fund.

8. A contracting party which is not a member of the Fund shall furnish such information within the general scope of section 5 of Article VIII of the Articles of Agreement of the International Monetary Fund as the CONTRACTING PARTIES may require in order to carry out their functions under this Agreement.

9. Nothing in this Agreement shall preclude:

(*a*) the use by a contracting party of exchange controls or exchange restrictions in accordance with the Articles of Agreement of the International Monetary Fund or with that contracting party's special exchange agreement with the CONTRACTING PARTIES, or

(*b*) the use by a contracting party of restrictions or controls in imports or exports, the sole effect of which, additional to the effects permitted under Articles XI, XII, XIII and XIV, is to make effective such exchange controls or exchange restrictions.

ARTICLE XVI*

SUBSIDIES

Section A - Subsidies in General

1. If any contracting party grants or maintains any subsidy,

including any form of income or price support, which operates directly or indirectly to increase exports of any product from, or to reduce imports of any product into, its territory, it shall notify the CONTRACTING PARTIES in writing of the extent and nature of the subsidization, of the estimated effect of the subsidization on the quantity of the affected product or products imported into or exported from its territory and of the circumstances making the subsidization necessary. In any case in which it is determined that serious prejudice to the interests of any other contracting party is caused or threatened by any such subsidization, the contracting party granting the subsidy shall, upon request, discuss with the other contracting party or parties concerned, or with the CONTRACTING PARTIES, the possibility of limiting the subsidization.

Section B - Additional Provisions on Export Subsidies*

2. The contracting parties recognize that the granting by a contracting party of a subsidy on the export of any product may have harmful effects for other contracting parties, both importing and exporting, may cause undue disturbance to their normal commercial interests, and may hinder the achievement of the objectives of this Agreement.

3. Accordingly, contracting parties should seek to avoid the use of subsidies on the export of primary products. If, however, a contracting party grants directly or indirectly any form of subsidy which operates to increase the export of any primary product from its territory, such subsidy shall not be applied in a manner which results in that contracting party having more than an equitable share of world export trade in that product, account being taken of the shares of the contracting parties in such trade in the product during a previous representative period, and any special factors which may have affected or may be affecting such trade in the product.*

4. Further, as from 1 January 1958 or the earliest practicable date thereafter, contracting parties shall cease to grant either directly or indirectly any form of subsidy on the export of any product other than a primary product which subsidy results in the sale of such product for export at a price lower than the comparable price charged for the like product to buyers in the domestic market. Until 31 December 1957 no contracting party shall extend the scope of any such subsidization beyond that existing on 1 January 1955 by the introduction of new, or the extension of existing, subsidies.*

5. The CONTRACTING PARTIES shall review the operation of the provisions of this Article from time to time with a view to examining its effectiveness, in the light of actual experience, in promoting the objectives of this Agreement and avoiding subsidization seriously prejudicial to the trade or interests of contracting parties.

ARTICLE XVII

State Trading Enterprises

1.* (*a*) Each contracting party undertakes that if it establishes or maintains a State enterprise, wherever located, or grants to any enterprise, formally or in effect, exclusive or special privileges,* such enterprise shall, in its purchases or sales involving either imports or exports, act in a manner consistent with the general principles of non-discriminatory treatment prescribed in this Agreement for governmental measures affecting imports or exports by private traders.

(*b*) The provisions of sub-paragraph (*a*) of this paragraph shall be understood to require that such enterprises shall, having due regard to the other provisions of this Agreement, make any such purchases or sales solely in accordance with commercial considerations,* including price, quality, availability, marketability, transportation and other conditions of purchase or sale, and shall afford the enterprises of the other contracting parties adequate opportunity, in accordance with customary business practice, to compete for participation in such purchases or sales.

(*c*) No contracting party shall prevent any enterprise (whether or not an enterprise described in sub-paragraph (*a*) of this paragraph) under its jurisdiction from acting in accordance with the principles of sub-paragraphs (*a*) and (*b*) of this paragraph.

2. The provisions of paragraph 1 of this Article shall not apply to imports of products for immediate or ultimate consumption in governmental use and not otherwise for resale or use in the production of goods* for sale. With respect to such imports, each contracting party shall accord to the trade of the other contracting parties fair and equitable treatment.

3. The contracting parties recognize that enterprises of the kind described in paragraph 1 (*a*) of this Article might be operated so as to create serious obstacles to trade; thus negotiations on a reciprocal and mutually advantageous basis designed to limit or reduce such obstacles are of importance to the expansion of international trade.*

4. (*a*) Contracting parties shall notify the CONTRACTING PARTIES of the products which are imported into or exported from their territories by enterprises of the kind described in paragraph 1 (*a*) of this Article.

(*b*) A contracting party establishing, maintaining or authorizing an import monopoly of a product, which is not the subject of a concession under Article II, shall, on the request of another contracting party having a substantial trade in the product concerned, inform the CONTRACTING PARTIES of the import mark-up* on the product during a recent representative period, or, when it is not possible to do so, of the price charged on the resale of the product.

(*c*) The CONTRACTING PARTIES may, at the request of a contracting party which has reason to believe that its interest under this Agreement are being adversely affected by the operations of an enterprise of the kind described in paragraph 1 (*a*), request the contracting party establishing, maintaining or authorizing such enterprise to supply information about its operations related to the carrying out of the provisions of this Agreement.

(*d*) The provisions of this paragraph shall not require any contracting party to disclose confidential information which would impede law enforcement or otherwise be contrary to the public interest or would prejudice the legitimate commercial interests of particular enterprises.

ARTICLE XVIII*

Governmental Assistance to Economic Development

1. The contracting parties recognize that the attainment of the objectives of this Agreement will be facilitated by the progressive development of their economies, particularly of those contracting parties the economies of which can only support low standards of living* and are in the early stages of development.*

2. The contracting parties recognize further that it may be necessary for those contracting parties, in order to implement programmes and policies of economic development designed to raise the general standard of living of their people, to take protective or other measures affecting imports, and that such measures are justified in so far as they facilitate the attainment of the objectives of this Agreement. They agree, therefore, that those contracting parties should enjoy additional facilities to enable them (*a*) to maintain sufficient

flexibility in their tariff structure to be able to grant the tariff protection required for the establishment of a particular industry* and (*b*) to apply quantitative restrictions for balance of payments purposes in a manner which takes full account of the continued high level of demand for imports likely to be generated by their programmes of economic development.

3. The contracting parties recognize finally that, with those additional facilities which are provided for in Sections A and B of this Article, the provisions of this Agreement would normally be sufficient to enable contracting parties to meet the requirements of their economic development. They agree, however, that there may be circumstances where no measure consistent with those provisions is practicable to permit a contracting party in the process of economic development to grant the governmental assistance required to promote the establishment of particular industries* with a view to raising the general standard of living of its people. Special procedures are laid down in Sections C and D of this Article to deal with those cases.

4. (*a*) Consequently, a contracting party, the economy of which can only support low standards of living* and is in the early stages of development,* shall be free to deviate temporarily from the provisions of the other Articles of this Agreement, as provided in Sections A, B and C of this Article.

(*b*) A contracting party, the economy of which is in the process of development, but which does not come within the scope of sub-paragraph (*a*) above, may submit applications to the CONTRACTING PARTIES under Section D of this Article.

5. The contracting parties recognize that the export earnings of contracting parties, the economies of which are of the type described in paragraph 4 (*a*) and (*b*) above and which depend on exports of a small number of primary commodities, may be seriously reduced by a decline in the sale of such commodities. Accordingly, when the exports of primary commodities by such a contracting party are seriously affected by measures taken by another contracting party, it may have resort to the consultation provisions of Article XXII of this Agreement.

6. The CONTRACTING PARTIES shall review annually all measures applied pursuant to the provisions of Sections C and D of this Article.

SECTION A

7. (*a*) If a contracting party coming within the scope of paragraph 4 (*a*) of this Article considers it desirable, in order to promote the establishment of a particular industry* with a view to raising the general standard of living of its people, to modify or withdraw a concession included in the appropriate Schedule annexed to this Agreement, it shall notify the CONTRACTING PARTIES to this effect and enter into negotiations with any contracting party with which such concession was initially negotiated, and with any other contracting party determined by the CONTRACTING PARTIES to have a substantial interest therein. If agreement is reached between such contracting parties concerned, they shall be free to modify or withdraw concessions under the appropriate Schedules to this Agreement in order to give effect to such agreement, including any compensatory adjustments involved.

(*b*) If agreement is not reached within sixty days after the notification provided for in sub-paragraph (*a*) above, the contracting party which proposes to modify or withdraw the concession may refer the matter to the CONTRACTING PARTIES which shall promptly examine it. If they find that the contracting party which proposes to modify or withdraw the concession has made every effort to reach an agreement and that the compensatory adjustment offered by it is adequate, that contracting party shall be free to modify or withdraw the concession if, at the same time, it gives effect to the compensatory adjustment. If the CONTRACTING PARTIES do not find that the compensation offered by a contracting party proposing to modify or withdraw the concession is adequate, but find that it has made every reasonable effort to offer adequate compensation, that contracting party shall be free to proceed with such modification or withdrawal. If such action is taken, any other contracting party referred to in sub-paragraph (*a*) above shall be free to modify or withdraw substantially equivalent concessions initially negotiated with the contracting party which has taken the action.*

SECTION B

8. The contracting parties recognize that contracting parties coming within the scope of paragraph 4 (*a*) of this Article tend, when they are in rapid process of development, to experience balance of payments difficulties arising mainly from efforts to expand their

internal markets as well as from the instability in their terms of trade.

9. In order to safeguard its external financial position and to ensure a level of reserves adequate for the implementation of its programme of economic development, a contracting party coming within the scope of paragraph 4 (*a*) of this Article may, subject to the provisions of paragraphs 10 to 12, control the general level of its imports by restricting the quantity or value of merchandise permitted to be imported; *Provided* that the import restrictions instituted, maintained or intensified shall not exceed those necessary:

(*a*) to forestall the threat of, or to stop, a serious decline in its monetary reserves, or

(*b*) in the case of a contracting party with inadequate monetary reserves, to achieve a reasonable rate of increase in its reserves.

Due regard shall be paid in either case to any special factors which may be affecting the reserves of the contracting party or its need for reserves, including, where special external credits or other resources are available to it, the need to provide for the appropriate use of such credits or resources.

10. In applying these restrictions, the contracting party may determine their incidence on imports of different products or classes of products in such a way as to give priority to the importation of those products which are more essential in the light of its policy of economic development; *Provided* that the restrictions are so applied as to avoid unnecessary damage to the commercial or economic interests of any other contracting party and not to prevent unreasonably the importation of any description of goods in minimum commercial quantities the exclusion of which would impair regular channels of trade; and *Provided* further that the restrictions are not so applied as to prevent the importation of commercial samples or to prevent compliance with patent, trade mark, copyright or similar procedures.

11. In carrying out its domestic policies, the contracting party concerned shall pay due regard to the need for restoring equilibrium in its balance of payments on a sound and lasting basis and to the desirability of assuring an economic employment of productive resources. It shall progressively relax any restrictions applied under

this Section as conditions improve, maintaining them only to the extent necessary under the terms of paragraph 9 of this Article and shall eliminate them when conditions no longer justify such maintenance; *Provided* that no contracting party shall be required to withdraw or modify restrictions on the ground that a change in its development policy would render unnecessary the restrictions which it is applying under this Section.*

12. (*a*) Any contracting party applying new restrictions or raising the general level of its existing restrictions by a substantial intensification of the measures applied under this Section, shall immediately after instituting or intensifying such restrictions (or, in circumstances in which prior consultation is practicable, before doing so) consult with the CONTRACTING PARTIES as to the nature of its balance of payments difficulties, alternative corrective measures which may be available, and the possible effect of the restrictions on the economies of other contracting parties.

(*b*) On a date to be determined by them* the CONTRACTING PARTIES shall review all restrictions still applied under this Section on that date. Beginning two years after that date, contracting parties applying restrictions under this Section shall enter into consultations of the type provided for in sub-paragraph (*a*) above with the CONTRACTING PARTIES at intervals of approximately, but not less than, two years according to a programme to be drawn up each year by the CONTRACTING PARTIES; *Provided* that no consultation under this sub-paragraph shall take place within two years after the conclusion of a consultation of a general nature under any other provision of this paragraph.

(*c*) (i) If, in the course of consultations with a contracting party under sub-paragraph (*a*) or (*b*) of this paragraph, the CONTRACTING PARTIES find that the restrictions are not consistent with the provisions of this Section or with those of Article XIII (subject to the provisions of Article XIV), they shall indicate the nature of the inconsistency and may advise that the restrictions be suitably modified.

(ii) If, however, as a result of the consultations, the CONTRACTING PARTIES determine that the restrictions are being applied in a manner involving an inconsistency of a serious nature with the provisions of this Section or with those of Article XIII (subject to the provisions of Article XIV) and that damage to the trade of any contracting party is caused or threatened thereby, they shall so inform the contracting party applying the restrictions and shall make appropriate recommendations for securing conformity with such provisions within a specified period. If such contracting party does not comply with these recommendations within the specified period, the CONTRACTING PARTIES may release any contracting party the trade of which is adversely affected by the restrictions from such obligations under this Agreement towards the contracting party applying the restrictions as they determine to be appropriate in the circumstances.

(*d*) The CONTRACTING PARTIES shall invite any contracting party which is applying restrictions under this Section to enter into consultations with them at the request of any contracting party which can establish a *prima facie* case that the restrictions are inconsistent with the provisions of this Section or with those of Article XIII (subject to the provisions of Article XIV) and that its trade is adversely affected thereby. However, no such invitation shall be issued unless the CONTRACTING PARTIES have ascertained that direct discussions between the contracting parties concerned have not been successful. If, as a result of the consultations with the CONTRACTING PARTIES no agreement is reached and they determine that the restrictions are being applied inconsistently with such provisions, and that damage to the trade of the contracting party initiating the procedure is caused or threatened thereby, they shall recommend the withdrawal or modification of the restrictions. If the restrictions are not withdrawn or modified within such time as the CONTRACTING PARTIES may prescribe, they may release the contracting party initiating the procedure from such obligations under this Agreement towards the contracting party applying the restrictions as they determine to be appropriate in the circumstances.

(*e*) If a contracting party against which action has been taken in accordance with the last sentence of sub-paragraph (*c*) (ii) or (*d*) of this paragraph, finds that the release of obligations authorized by the CONTRACTING PARTIES adversely affects the operation of its programme and policy of economic development, it shall be free, not later than sixty days after such action is taken, to give written notice to the Executive Secretary[1] to the CONTRACTING PARTIES of its intention to withdraw from this Agreement and such withdrawal shall

1. See Preface.

take effect on the sixtieth day following the day on which the notice is received by him.

(*f*) In proceeding under this paragraph, the CONTRACTING PARTIES shall have due regard to the factors referred to in paragraph 2 of this Article. Determinations under this paragraph shall be rendered expeditiously and, if possible, within sixty days of the initiation of the consultations.

SECTION C

13. If a contracting party coming within the scope of paragraph 4 (*a*) of this Article finds that governmental assistance is required to promote the establishment of a particular industry* with a view to raising the general standard of living of its people, but that no measure consistent with the other provisions of this Agreement is practicable to achieve that objective, it may have recourse to the provisions and procedures set out in this Section.*

14. The contracting party concerned shall notify the CONTRACTING PARTIES of the special difficulties which it meets in the achievement of the objective outlined in paragraph 13 of this Article and shall indicate the specific measure affecting imports which it proposes to introduce in order to remedy these difficulties. It shall not introduce that measure before the expiration of the time-limit laid down in paragraph 15 or 17, as the case may be, or if the measure affects imports of a product which is the subject of a concession included in the appropriate Schedule annexed to this Agreement, unless it has secured the concurrence of the CONTRACTING PARTIES in accordance with provisions of paragraph 18; *Provided* that, if the industry receiving assistance has already started production, the contracting party may, after informing the CONTRACTING PARTIES, take such measures as may be necessary to prevent, during that period, imports of the product or products concerned from increasing substantially above a normal level.*

15. If, within thirty days of the notification of the measure, the CONTRACTING PARTIES do not request the contracting party concerned to consult with them,* that contracting party shall be free to deviate from the relevant provisions of the other Articles of this Agreement to the extent necessary to apply the proposed measure.

16. If it is requested by the CONTRACTING PARTIES to do so,* the contracting party concerned shall consult with them as to the

purpose of the proposed measure, as to alternative measures which may be available under this Agreement, and as to the possible effect of the measure proposed on the commercial and economic interests of other contracting parties. If, as a result of such consultation, the CONTRACTING PARTIES agree that there is no measure consistent with the other provisions of this Agreement which is practicable in order to achieve the objective outlined in paragraph 13 of this Article, and concur* in the proposed measure, the contracting party concerned shall be released from its obligations under the relevant provisions of the other Articles of this Agreement to the extent necessary to apply that measure.

17. If, within ninety days after the date of the notification of the proposed measure under paragraph 14 of this Article, the CONTRACTING PARTIES have not concurred in such measure, the contracting party concerned may introduce the measure proposed after informing the CONTRACTING PARTIES.

18. If the proposed measure affects a product which is the subject of a concession included in the appropriate Schedule annexed to this Agreement, the contracting party concerned shall enter into consultations with any other contracting party with which the concession was initially negotiated, and with any other contracting party determined by the CONTRACTING PARTIES to have a substantial interest therein. The CONTRACTING PARTIES shall concur* in the measure if they agree that there is no measure consistent with the other provisions of this Agreement which is practicable in order to achieve the objective set forth in paragraph 13 of this Article, and if they are satisfied:

(*a*) that agreement has been reached with such other contracting parties as a result of the consultations referred to above, or

(*b*) if no such agreement has been reached within sixty days after the notification provided for in paragraph 14 has been received by the CONTRACTING PARTIES, that the contracting party having recourse to this Section has made all reasonable efforts to reach an agreement and that the interests of other contracting parties are adequately safeguarded.*

The contracting party having recourse to this Section shall thereupon be released from its obligations under the relevant provisions of the other Articles of this Agreement to the extent necessary to permit it to apply the measure.

19. If a proposed measure of the type described in paragraph 13 of this Article concerns an industry the establishment of which has in the initial period been facilitated by incidental protection afforded by restrictions imposed by the contracting party concerned for balance of payments purposes under the relevant provisions of this Agreement, that contracting party may resort to the provisions and procedures of this Section; *Provided* that it shall not apply the proposed measure without the concurrence* of the CONTRACTING PARTIES.*

20. Nothing in the preceding paragraphs of this Section shall authorize any deviation from the provisions of Articles I, II and XIII of this Agreement. The provisos to paragraph 10 of this Article shall also be applicable to any restriction under this Section.

21. At any time while a measure is being applied under paragraph 17 of this Article any contracting party substantially affected by it may suspend the application to the trade of the contracting party having recourse to this Section of such substantially equivalent concessions or other obligations under this Agreement the suspension of which the CONTRACTING PARTIES do not disapprove;* *Provided* that sixty days' notice of such suspension is given to the CONTRACTING PARTIES not later than six months after the measure has been introduced or changed substantially to the detriment of the contracting party affected. Any such contracting party shall afford adequate opportunity for consultation in accordance with the provisions of Article XXII of this Agreement.

SECTION D

22. A contracting party coming within the scope of sub-paragraph 4 (*b*) of this Article desiring, in the interest of the development of its economy, to introduce a measure of the type described in paragraph 13 of this Article in respect of the establishment of a particular industry* may apply to the CONTRACTING PARTIES for approval of such measure. The CONTRACTING PARTIES shall promptly consult with such contracting party and shall, in making their decision, be guided by the considerations set out in paragraph 16. If the CONTRACTING PARTIES concur* in the proposed measure the contracting party concerned shall be released from its obligations under the relevant provisions of the other Articles of this Agreement to the extent necessary to permit it to apply the measure. If the

proposed measure affects a product which is the subject of a concession included in the appropriate Schedule annexed to this Agreement, the provisions of paragraph 18 shall apply.*

23. Any measure applied under this Section shall comply with the provisions of paragraph 20 of this Article.

ARTICLE XIX

Emergency Action on Imports of Particular Products

1. (*a*) If, as a result of unforeseen developments and of the effect of the obligations incurred by a contracting party under this Agreement, including tariff concessions, any product is being imported into the territory of that contracting party in such increased quantities and under such conditions as to cause or threaten serious injury to domestic producers in that territory of like or directly competitive products, the contracting party shall be free, in respect of such product, and to the extent and for such time as may be necessary to prevent or remedy such injury, to suspend the obligation in whole or in part or to withdraw or modify the concession.

(*b*) If any product, which is the subject of a concession with respect to a preference, is being imported into the territory of a contracting party in the circumstances set forth in sub-paragraph (*a*) of this paragraph, so as to cause or threaten serious injury to domestic producers of like or directly competitive products in the territory of a contracting party which receives or received such preference, the importing contracting party shall be free, if that other contracting party so requests, to suspend the relevant obligation in whole or in part or to withdraw or modify the concession in respect of the product, to the extent and for such time as may be necessary to prevent or remedy such injury.

2. Before any contracting party shall take action pursuant to the provisions of paragraph 1 of this Article, it shall give notice in writing to the CONTRACTING PARTIES as far in advance as may be practicable and shall afford the CONTRACTING PARTIES and those contracting parties having a substantial interest as exporters of the product concerned an opportunity to consult with it in respect of the proposed action. When such notice is given in relation to a concession with respect to a preference, the notice shall name the contracting party which has requested the action. In critical circumstances, where delay would cause damage which it would be

difficult to repair, action under paragraph 1 of this Article may be taken provisionally without prior consultation, on the condition that consultation shall be effected immediately after taking such action.

3. (*a*) If agreement among the interested contracting parties with respect to the action is not reached, the contracting party which proposes to take or continue the action shall, nevertheless, be free to do so, and if such action is taken or continued, the affected contracting parties shall then be free, not later than ninety days after such action is taken, to suspend, upon the expiration of thirty days from the day on which written notice of such suspension is received by the CONTRACTING PARTIES, the application to the trade of the contracting party taking such action, or, in the case envisaged in paragraph 1 (*b*) of this Article, to the trade of the contracting party requesting such action, of such substantially equivalent concessions or other obligations under this Agreement the suspension of which the CONTRACTING PARTIES do not disapprove.

(*b*) Notwithstanding the provisions of sub-paragraph (*a*) of this paragraph, where action is taken under paragraph 2 of this Article without prior consultation and causes or threatens serious injury in the territory of a contracting party to the domestic producers of products affected by the action, that contracting party shall, where delay would cause damage difficult to repair, be free to suspend, upon the taking of the action and throughout the period of consultation, such concessions or other obligations as may be necessary to prevent or remedy the injury.

ARTICLE XX

General Exceptions

Subject to the requirement that such measures are not applied in a manner which would constitute a means of arbitrary or unjustifiable discrimination between countries where the same conditions prevail, or a disguised restriction on international trade, nothing in this Agreement shall be construed to prevent the adoption or enforcement by any contracting party of measures:

(*a*) necessary to protect public morals;

(*b*) necessary to protect human, animal or plant life or health;

(*c*) relating to the importations or exportations of gold or silver;

(*d*) necessary to secure compliance with laws or regulations which are not inconsistent with the provisions of this Agreement, including those relating to customs enforcement, the enforcement of monopolies operated under paragraph 4 of Article II and Article XVII, the protection of patents, trade marks and copyrights, and the prevention of deceptive practices;

(*e*) relating to the products of prison labour;

(*f*) imposed for the protection of national treasures of artistic, historic or archaeological value;

(*g*) relating to the conservation of exhaustible natural resources if such measures are made effective in conjunction with restrictions on domestic production or consumption;

(*h*) undertaken in pursuance of obligations under any intergovernmental commodity agreement which conforms to criteria submitted to the CONTRACTING PARTIES and not disapproved by them or which is itself so submitted and not so disapproved;*

(*i*) involving restrictions on exports of domestic materials necessary to ensure essential quantities of such materials to a domestic processing industry during periods when the domestic price of such materials is held below the world price as part of a governmental stabilization plan; *Provided* that such restrictions shall not operate to increase the exports of or the protection afforded to such domestic industry, and shall not depart from the provisions of this Agreement relating to non-discrimination;

(*j*) essential to the acquisition or distribution of products in general or local short supply; *Provided* that any such measures shall be consistent with the principle that all contracting parties are entitled to an equitable share of the international supply of such products, and that any such measures, which are inconsistent with the other provisions of the Agreement shall be discontinued as soon as the conditions giving rise to them have ceased to exist. The CONTRACTING PARTIES shall review the need for this sub-paragraph not later than 30 June 1960.

ARTICLE XXI

Security Exceptions

Nothing in this Agreement shall be construed

(*a*) to require any contracting party to furnish any information the disclosure of which it considers contrary to its essential security interests; or

(*b*) to prevent any contracting party from taking any action which it considers necessary for the protection of its essential security interests

(i) relating to fissionable materials or the materials from which they are derived;

(ii) relating to the traffic in arms, ammunition and implements of war and to such traffic in other goods and materials as is carried on directly or indirectly for the purpose of supplying a military establishment;

(iii) taken in time of war or other emergency in international relations; or

(*c*) to prevent any contracting party from taking any action in pursuance of its obligations under the United Nations Charter for the maintenance of international peace and security.

ARTICLE XXII

Consultation

1. Each contracting party shall accord sympathetic consideration to, and shall afford adequate opportunity for consultation regarding, such representations as may be made by another contracting party with respect to any matter affecting the operation of this Agreement.

2. The CONTRACTING PARTIES may, at the request of a contracting party, consult with any contracting party or parties in respect of any matter for which it has not been possible to find a satisfactory solution through consultation under paragraph 1.

ARTICLE XXIII

Nullification or Impairment

1. If any contracting party should consider that any benefit accruing to it directly or indirectly under this Agreement is being

nullified or impaired or that the attainment of any objective of the Agreement is being impeded as the result of

(*a*) the failure of another contracting party to carry out its obligations under this Agreement, or

(*b*) the application by another contracting party of any measure, whether or not it conflicts with the provisions of this Agreement, or

(*c*) the existence of any other situation, the contracting party may, with a view to the satisfactory adjustment of the matter, make written representations or proposals to the other contracting party or parties which it considers to be concerned. Any contracting party thus approached shall give sympathetic consideration to the representations or proposals made to it.

2. If no satisfactory adjustment is effected between the contracting parties concerned within a reasonable time, or if the difficulty is of the type described in paragraph 1 (*c*) of this Article, the matter may be referred to the CONTRACTING PARTIES. The CONTRACTING PARTIES shall promptly investigate any matter so referred to them and shall make appropriate recommendations to the contracting parties which they consider to be concerned, or give a ruling on the matter, as appropriate. The CONTRACTING PARTIES may consult with contracting parties, with the Economic and Social Council of the United Nations and with any appropriate inter-governmental organization in cases where they consider such consultation necessary. If the CONTRACTING PARTIES consider that the circumstances are serious enough to justify such action, they may authorize a contracting party or parties to suspend the application to any other contracting party or parties of such concessions or other obligations under this Agreement as they determine to be appropriate in the circumstances. If the application to any contracting party of any concession or other obligation is in fact suspended, that contracting party shall then be free, not later than sixty days after such action is taken, to give written notice to the Executive Secretary[1] to the CONTRACTING PARTIES of its intention to withdraw from this Agreement and such withdrawal shall take effect upon the sixtieth day following the day on which such notice is received by him.

1. See Preface.

PART III

ARTICLE XXIV

Territorial Application — Frontier Traffic — Customs Unionsand Free-trade Areas

1. The provisions of this Agreement shall apply to the metropolitan customs territories of the contracting parties and to any other customs territories in respect of which this Agreement has been accepted under Article XXVI or is being applied under Article XXXIII or pursuant to the Protocol of Provisional Application. Each such customs territory shall, exclusively for the purposes of the territorial application of this Agreement, be treated as though it were a contracting party; *Provided* that the provisions of this paragraph shall not be construed to create any rights or obligations as between two or more customs territories in respect of which this Agreement has been accepted under Article XXVI or is being applied under Article XXXIII or pursuant to the Protocol of Provisional Application by a single contracting party.

2. For the purposes of this Agreement a customs territory shall be understood to mean any territory with respect to which separate tariffs or other regulations of commerce are maintained for a substantial part of the trade of such territory with other territories.

3. The provisions of this Agreement shall not be construed to prevent:

(*a*) Advantages accorded by any contracting party to adjacent countries in order to facilitate frontier traffic;

(*b*) Advantages accorded to the trade with the Free Territory of Trieste by countries contiguous to that territory, provided that such advantages are not in conflict with the Treaties of Peace arising out of the Second World War.

4. The contracting parties recognize the desirability of increasing freedom of trade by the development, through voluntary agreements, of closer integration between the economies of the countries parties to such agreements. They also recognize that the purpose of a customs union or of a free-trade area should be to facilitate trade between the constituent territories and not to raise barriers to the trade of other contracting parties with such territories.

5. Accordingly, the provisions of this Agreement shall not prevent, as between the territories of contracting parties, the formation of a customs union or of a free-trade area or the adoption of an interim agreement necessary for the formation of a customs union or of a free-trade area; *Provided* that:

(*a*) with respect to a customs union, or an interim agreement leading to a formation of a customs union, the duties and other regulations of commerce imposed at the institution of any such union or interim agreement in respect of trade with contracting parties not parties to such union or agreement shall not on the whole be higher or more restrictive than the general incidence of the duties and regulations of commerce applicable in the constituent territories prior to the formation of such union or the adoption of such interim agreement, as the case may be;

(*b*) with respect to a free-trade area, or an interim agreement leading to the formation of a free-trade area, the duties and other regulations of commerce maintained in each if the constituent territories and applicable at the formation of such free-trade area or the adoption of such interim agreement to the trade of contracting parties not included in such area or not parties to such agreement shall not be higher or more restrictive than the corresponding duties and other regulations of commerce existing in the same constituent territories prior to the formation of the free-trade area, or interim agreement as the case may be; and

(*c*) any interim agreement referred to in sub-paragraphs (*a*) and (*b*) shall include a plan and schedule for the formation of such a customs union or of such a free-trade area within a reasonable length of time.

6. If, in fulfilling the requirements of sub-paragraph 5 (*a*), a contracting party proposes to increase any rate of duty inconsistently with the provisions of Article II, the procedure set forth in Article XXVIII shall apply. In providing for compensatory adjustment, due account shall be taken of the compensation already afforded by the reduction brought about in the corresponding duty of the other constituents of the union.

7. (*a*) Any contracting party deciding to enter into a customs union or free-trade area, or an interim agreement leading to the formation of such a union or area, shall promptly notify the CONTRACTING PARTIES and shall make available to them such information regarding the proposed union or area as will enable them to make such reports and recommendations to contracting parties as they may deem appropriate.

(*b*) If, after having studied the plan and schedule included in an interim agreement referred to in paragraph 5 in consultation with the parties to that agreement and taking due account of the information made available in accordance with the provisions of sub-paragraph (*a*), the CONTRACTING PARTIES find that such agreement is not likely to result in the formation of a customs union or of a free-trade area within the period contemplated by the parties to the agreement or that such period is not a reasonable one, the CONTRACTING PARTIES shall make recommendations to the parties to the agreement. The parties shall not maintain or put into force, as the case may be, such agreement if they are not prepared to modify it in accordance with these recommendations.

(*c*) Any substantial change in the plan or schedule referred to in paragraph 5 (*c*) shall be communicated to the CONTRACTING PARTIES, which may request the contracting parties concerned to consult with them if the change seems likely to jeopardize or delay unduly the formation of the customs union or of the free-trade area.

8. For the purposes of this Agreement:

(*a*) A customs union shall be understood to mean the substitution of a single customs territory for two or more customs territories, so that

(i) duties and other restrictive regulations of commerce (except, where necessary, those permitted under Articles XI, XII, XIII, XIV, XV and XX) are eliminated with respect to substantially all the trade between the constituent territories of the union or at least with respect to substantially all the trade in products originating in such territories, and,

(ii) subject to the provisions of paragraph 9, substantially the same duties and other regulations of commerce are applied by each of the members of the union to the trade of territories not included in the union;

(*b*) A free-trade area shall be understood to mean a group of two or more customs territories in which the duties and other restrictive regulations of commerce (except, where necessary, those permitted under Articles XI, XII, XIII, XIV, XV and XX) are eliminated on substantially all the trade between the constituent territories in products originating in such territories.

9. The preferences referred to in paragraph 2 of Article I shall not be affected by the formation of a customs union or of a free-trade area but may be eliminated or adjusted by means of negotiations with contracting parties affected.* This procedure of negotiations with affected contracting parties shall, in particular, apply to the elimination of preferences required to conform with the provisions of paragraph 8 (*a*)(i) and paragraph 8 (*b*).

10. The CONTRACTING PARTIES may by a two-thirds majority approve proposals which do not fully comply with the requirements of paragraphs 5 to 9 inclusive, provided that such proposals lead to the formation of a customs union or a free-trade area in the sense of this Article.

11. Taking into account the exceptional circumstances arising out of the establishment of India and Pakistan as independent States and recognizing the fact that they have long constituted an economic unit, the contracting parties agree that the provisions of this Agreement shall not prevent the two countries from entering into special arrangements with respect to the trade between them, pending the establishment of their mutual trade relations on a definitive basis.*

12. Each contracting party shall take such reasonable measures as may be available to it to ensure observance of the provisions of this Agreement by the regional and local governments and authorities within its territories.

ARTICLE XXV

Joint Action by the Contracting Parties

1. Representatives of the contracting parties shall meet from time to time for the purpose of giving effect to those provisions of this Agreement which involve joint action and, generally, with a view to facilitating the operation and furthering the objectives of this Agreement. Wherever reference is made in this Agreement to the contracting parties acting jointly they are designated as the CONTRACTING PARTIES.

2. The Secretary-General of the United Nations is requested to convene the first meeting of the CONTRACTING PARTIES, which shall take place not later than March 1, 1948.

3. Each contracting party shall be entitled to have one vote at all meetings of the CONTRACTING PARTIES.

4. Except as otherwise provided for in this Agreement, decisions of the CONTRACTING PARTIES shall be taken by a majority of the votes cast.

5. In exceptional circumstances not elsewhere provided for in this Agreement, the CONTRACTING PARTIES may waive an obligation imposed upon a contracting party by this Agreement; *Provided* that any such decision shall be approved by a two-thirds majority of the votes cast and that such majority shall comprise more than half of the contracting parties. The CONTRACTING PARTIES may also by such a vote

(i) define certain categories of exceptional circumstances to which other voting requirements shall apply for the waiver of obligations, and

(ii) prescribe such criteria as may be necessary for the application of this paragraph.†

ARTICLE XXVI

Acceptance, Entry into Force and Registration

1. The date of this Agreement shall be 30 October 1947.

2. This Agreement shall be open for acceptance by any contracting party which, on 1 March 1955, was a contracting party or was negotiating with a view to accession to this Agreement.

3. This Agreement, done in a single English original and a single French original, both texts authentic, shall be deposited with the Secretary-General of the United Nations, who shall furnish certified copies thereof to all interested governments.

4. Each government accepting this Agreement shall deposit an instrument of acceptance with the Executive Secretary[1] to the CONTRACTING PARTIES, who will inform all interested governments of the date of deposit of each instrument of acceptance and of the day

† The authentic text erroneously reads "sub-paragraph".

on which this Agreement enters into force under paragraph 6 of this Article.

5. (*a*) Each government accepting this Agreement does so in respect of its metropolitan territory and of the other territories for which it has international responsibility, except such separate customs territories as it shall notify to the Executive Secretary[1] to the CONTRACTING PARTIES at the time of its own acceptance.

(*b*) Any government, which has so notified the Executive Secretary[1] under the exceptions in sub-paragraph (*a*) of this paragraph, may at any time give notice to the Executive Secretary[1] that its acceptance shall be effective in respect of any separate customs territory or territories so excepted and such notice shall take effect on the thirtieth day following the day on which it is received by the Executive Secretary.[1]

(*c*) If any of the customs territories, in respect of which a contracting party has accepted this Agreement, possesses or acquires full autonomy in the conduct of its external commercial relations and of the other matters provided for in this Agreement, such territory shall, upon sponsorship through a declaration by the responsible contracting party establishing the above-mentioned fact, be deemed to be a contracting party.

6. This Agreement shall enter into force, as among the governments which have accepted it, on the thirtieth day following the day on which instruments of acceptance have been deposited with Executive Secretary[1] to the CONTRACTING PARTIES on behalf of governments named in Annex H, the territories of which account for 85 per centum of the total external trade of the territories of such governments, computed in accordance with the applicable column of percentages set forth therein, The instrument of acceptance of each other government shall take effect on the thirtieth day following the day on which such instrument has been deposited.

7. The United Nations is authorized to effect registration of this Agreement as soon as it enters into force.

ARTICLE XXVII

Withholding or Withdrawal of Concessions

Any contracting party shall at any time be free to withhold or

1. See Preface.

to withdraw in whole or in part any concession, provided for in the appropriate Schedule annexed to this Agreement, in respect of which such contracting party determines that it was initially negotiated with a government which has not become, or has ceased to be, a contracting party. A contracting party taking such action shall notify the CONTRACTING PARTIES and, upon request, consult with contracting parties which have a substantial interest in the product concerned.

ARTICLE XXVIII*

Modification of Schedules

1. On the first day of each three-year period, the first period beginning on 1 January 1958 (or on the first day of any other period* that may be specified by the CONTRACTING PARTIES by two-thirds of the votes cast) a contracting party (hereafter in this Article referred to as the "applicant contracting party") may, by negotiation and agreement with any contracting party with which such concession was initially negotiated and with any other contracting party determined by the CONTRACTING PARTIES to have a principal supplying interest* (which two preceding categories of contracting parties, together with the applicant contracting party, are in this Article hereinafter referred to as the "contracting parties primarily concerned"), and subject to consultation with any other contracting party determined by the CONTRACTING PARTIES to have a substantial interest* in such concession, modify or withdraw a concession* included in the appropriate schedule annexed to this Agreement.

2. In such negotiations and agreement, which may include provision for compensatory adjustment with respect to other products, the contracting parties concerned shall endeavour to maintain a general level of reciprocal and mutually advantageous concessions not less favourable to trade than that provided for in this Agreement prior to such negotiations.

3. (*a*) If agreement between the contracting parties primarily concerned cannot be reached before 1 January 1958 or before the expiration of a period envisaged in paragraph 1 of this Article, the contracting party which proposes to modify or withdraw the concession shall, nevertheless, be free to do so and if such action is taken any contracting party with which such concession was initially negotiated, any contracting party determined under paragraph 1 to have a principal supplying interest and any contracting party

determined under paragraph 1 to have a substantial interest shall then be free not later than six months after such action is taken, to withdraw, upon the expiration of thirty days from the day on which written notice of such withdrawal is received by the CONTRACTING PARTIES, substantially equivalent concessions initially negotiated with the applicant contracting party.

(*b*) If agreement between the contracting parties primarily concerned is reached but any other contracting party determined under paragraph 1 of this Article to have a substantial interest is not satisfied, such other contracting party shall be free, not later than six months after action under such agreement is taken, to withdraw, upon the expiration of thirty days from the day on which written notice of such withdrawal is received by the CONTRACTING PARTIES, substantially equivalent concessions initially negotiated with the applicant contracting party.

4. The CONTRACTING PARTIES may, at any time, in special circumstances, authorize* a contracting party to enter into negotiations for modification or withdrawal of a concession included in the appropriate Schedule annexed to this Agreement subject to the following procedures and conditions:

(*a*) Such negotiations* and any related consultations shall be conducted in accordance with the provisions of paragraph 1 and 2 of this Article.

(*b*) If agreement between the contracting parties primarily concerned is reached in the negotiations, the provisions of paragraph 3 (*b*) of this Article shall apply.

(*c*) If agreement between the contracting parties primarily concerned is not reached within a period of sixty days* after negotiations have been authorized, or within such longer period as the CONTRACTING PARTIES may have prescribed, the applicant contracting party may refer the matter to the CONTRACTING PARTIES.

(*d*) Upon such reference, the CONTRACTING PARTIES shall promptly examine the matter and submit their views to the contracting parties primarily concerned with the aim of achieving a settlement. If a settlement is reached, the provisions of paragraph 3 (*b*) shall apply as if agreement between the contracting parties primarily concerned had been reached. If no settlement is reached between the contracting parties primarily concerned, the applicant contracting party shall be free to modify or withdraw the concession, unless the CONTRACTING PARTIES determine that the applicant contracting party has unreasonably failed to offer adequate compensation.* If such action is taken, any contracting party with which the concession was initially negotiated, any contracting party determined under paragraph 4 (*a*) to have a principal supplying interest and any contracting party determined under paragraph 4 (*a*) to have a substantial interest, shall be free, not later than six months after such action is taken, to modify or withdraw, upon the expiration of thirty days from the day on which written notice of such withdrawal is received by the CONTRACTING PARTIES, substantially equivalent concessions initially negotiated with applicant contracting party.

5. Before 1 January 1958 and before the end of any period envisaged in paragraph 1 a contracting party may elect by notifying the CONTRACTING PARTIES to reserve the right, for the duration of the next period, to modify the appropriate Schedule in accordance with the procedures of paragraph 1 to 3. If a contracting party so elects, other contracting parties shall have the right, during the same period, to modify or withdraw, in accordance with the same procedures, concessions initially negotiated with that contracting party.

ARTICLE XXVIII BIS

Tariff Negotiations

1. The contracting parties recognize that customs duties often constitute serious obstacles to trade; thus negotiations on a reciprocal and mutually advantageous basis, directed to the substantial reduction of the general level of tariffs and other charges on imports and exports and in particular to the reduction of such high tariffs as discourage the importation even of minimum quantities, and conducted with due regard to the objectives of this Agreement and the varying needs of individual contracting parties, are of great importance to the expansion of international trade. The CONTRACTING PARTIES may therefore sponsor such negotiations from time to time.

2. (*a*) Negotiations under this Article may be carried out on a selective product-by-product basis or by the application of such multilateral procedures as may be accepted by the contracting parties concerned. Such negotiations may be directed towards the reduction of duties, the binding of duties at then existing levels or undertakings that individual duties or the average duties on specified categories of products shall not exceed specified levels. The binding against increase of low duties or of duty-free treatment shall, in principle, be recognized as a concession equivalent in value to the reduction of high duties.

(*b*) The contracting parties recognize that in general the success of multilateral negotiations would depend on the participation of all contracting parties which conduct a substantial proportion of their external trade with one another.

3. Negotiations shall be conducted on a basis which affords adequate opportunity to take into account:

(*a*) the needs of individual contracting parties and individual industries;

(*b*) the needs of less-developed countries for a more flexible use of tariff protection to assist their economic development and the special needs of these countries to maintain tariffs for revenue purposes; and

(*c*) all other relevant circumstances, including the fiscal,* developmental, strategic and other needs of the contracting parties concerned.

ARTICLE XXIX

The Relation of this Agreement to the Havana Charter

1. The contracting parties undertake to observe to the fullest extent of their executive authority the general principles of Chapters I to VI inclusive and of Chapter IX of the Havana Charter pending their acceptance of it in accordance with their constitutional procedures.*

2. Part II of this Agreement shall be suspended on the day on which the Havana Charter enters into force.

3. If by September 30, 1949, the Havana Charter has not entered into force, the contracting parties shall meet before December

31, 1949, to agree whether this Agreement shall be amended, supplemented or maintained.

4. If at any time the Havana Charter should cease to be in force, the CONTRACTING PARTIES shall meet as soon as practicable thereafter to agree whether this Agreement shall be supplemented, amended or maintained. Pending such agreement, Part II of this Agreement shall again enter into force; *Provided* that the provisions of Part II other than Article XXIII shall be replaced, *mutatis mutandis,* in the form in which they then appeared in the Havana Charter; and *Provided* further that no contracting party shall be bound by any provisions which did not bind it at the time when the Havana Charter ceased to be in force.

5. If any contracting party has not accepted the Havana Charter by the date upon which it enters into force, the CONTRACTING PARTIES shall confer to agree whether, and if so in what way, this Agreement in so far as it affects relations between such contracting party and other contracting parties, shall be supplemented or amended. Pending such agreement the provisions of Part II of this Agreement shall, notwithstanding the provisions of paragraph 2 of this Article, continue to apply as between such contracting party and other contracting parties.

6. Contracting parties which are Members of the International Trade Organization shall not invoke the provisions of this Agreement so as to prevent the operation of any provision of the Havana Charter. The application of the principle underlying this paragraph to any contracting party which is not a Member of the International Trade Organization shall be the subject of an agreement pursuant to paragraph 5 of this Article.

ARTICLE XXX

Amendments

1. Except where provision for modification is made elsewhere in this Agreement, amendments to the provisions of Part I of this Agreement or the provisions of Article XXIX or of this Article shall become effective upon acceptance by all the contracting parties, and other amendments to this Agreement shall become effective, in respect of those contracting parties which accept them, upon acceptance by two-thirds of the contracting parties and thereafter for each other contracting party upon acceptance by it.

2. Any contracting party accepting an amendment to this Agreement shall deposit an instrument of acceptance with the Secretary-General of the United Nations within such period as the CONTRACTING PARTIES may specify. The CONTRACTING PARTIES may decide that any amendment made effective under this Article is of such a nature that any contracting party which has not accepted it within a period specified by the CONTRACTING PARTIES shall be free to withdraw from this Agreement, or to remain a contracting party with the consent of the CONTRACTING PARTIES.

ARTICLE XXXI

Withdrawal

Without prejudice to the provisions of paragraph 12 of Article XVIII, of Article XXIII or of paragraph 2 of Article XXX, any contracting party may withdraw from this Agreement, or may separately withdraw on behalf of any of the separate customs territories for which it has international responsibility and which at the time possesses full autonomy in the conduct of its external commercial relations and of the other matters provided for in this Agreement. The withdrawal shall take effect upon the expiration of six months from the day on which written notice of withdrawal is received by the Secretary-General of the United Nations.

ARTICLE XXXII

Contracting Parties

1. The contracting parties to this Agreement shall be understood to mean those governments which are applying the provisions of this Agreement under Articles XXVI or XXXIII or pursuant to the Protocol of Provisional Application.

2. At any time after the entry into force of this Agreement pursuant to paragraph 6 of Article XXVI, those contracting parties which have accepted this Agreement pursuant to paragraph 4 of Article XXVI may decide that any contracting party which has not so accepted it shall cease to be a contracting party.

ARTICLE XXXIII

Accession

A government not party to this Agreement, or a government acting on behalf of a separate customs territory possessing full autonomy in the conduct of its external commercial relations and of the other matters provided for in this Agreement, may accede to this Agreement, on its own behalf or on behalf of that territory, on terms to be agreed between such government and the CONTRACTING PARTIES. Decisions of the CONTRACTING PARTIES under this paragraph shall be taken by a two-thirds majority.

ARTICLE XXXIV

Annexes

The annexes to this Agreement are hereby made an integral part of this Agreement.

ARTICLE XXXV

Non-application of the Agreement between Particular Contracting Parties

1. This Agreement, or alternatively Article II of this Agreement, shall not apply as between any contracting party and any other contracting party if:

(*a*) the two contracting parties have not entered into tariff negotiations with each other, and

(*b*) either of the contracting parties, at the time either becomes a contracting party, does not consent to such application.

2. The CONTRACTING PARTIES may review the operation of this Article in particular cases at the request of any contracting party and make appropriate recommendations.

PART IV*

TRADE AND DEVELOPMENT

ARTICLE XXXVI

Principles and Objectives

1.* The contracting parties,

(*a*) recalling that the basic objectives of this Agreement include the raising of standards of living and the progressive development of the economies of all contracting parties, and considering that the attainment of these objectives is particularly urgent for less-developed contracting parties;

(*b*) considering that export earnings of the less-developed contracting parties can play a vital part in their economic development and that the extent of this contribution depends on the prices paid by the less-developed contracting parties for essential imports, the volume of their exports, and the prices received for these exports;

(*c*) noting, that there is a wide gap between standards of living in less-developed countries and in other countries;

(*d*) recognizing that individual and joint action is essential to further the development of the economies of less-developed contracting parties and to bring about a rapid advance in the standards of living in these countries;

(*e*) recognizing that international trade as a means of achieving economic and social advancement should be governed by such rules and procedures — and measures in conformity with such rules and procedures — as are consistent with the objectives set forth in this Article;

(*f*) noting that the CONTRACTING PARTIES may enable less-developed contracting parties to use special measures to promote their trade and development;

agree as follows.

2. There is need for a rapid and sustained expansion of the export earnings of the less-developed contracting parties.

3. There is need for positive efforts designed to ensure that less-developed contracting parties secure a share in the growth in international trade commensurate with the needs of their economic development.

4. Given the continued dependence of many less-developed contracting parties on the exportation of a limited range of primary products,* there is need to provide in the largest possible measure more favourable and acceptable conditions of access to world markets for these products, and wherever appropriate to devise measures designed to stabilize and improve conditions of world markets in these products, including in particular measures designed to attain stable, equitable and remunerative prices, thus permitting an expansion of world trade and demand and a dynamic and steady growth of the real export earnings of these countries so as to provide them with expanding resources for their economic development.

5. The rapid expansion of the economies of the less-developed contracting parties will be facilitated by a diversification* of the structure of their economies and the avoidance of an excessive dependence on the export of primary products. There is, therefore, need for increased access in the largest possible measure to markets under favourable conditions for processed and manufactured products currently or potentially of particular export interest to less-developed contracting parties.

6. Because of the chronic deficiency in the export proceeds and other foreign exchange earnings of less-developed contracting parties, there are important inter-relationships between trade and financial assistance to development. There is, therefore, need for close and continuing collaboration between the CONTRACTING PARTIES and the international lending agencies so that they can contribute most effectively to alleviating the burdens these less-developed contracting parties assume in the interest of their economic development.

7. There is need for appropriate collaboration between the CONTRACTING PARTIES, other intergovernmental bodies and the organs and agencies of the United Nations system, whose activities relate to the trade and economic development of less-developed countries.

8. The developed contracting parties do not expect reciprocity for commitments made by them in trade negotiations to reduce or remove tariffs and other barriers to the trade of less-developed contracting parties.*

9. The adoption of measures to give effect to these principles and objectives shall be a matter of conscious and purposeful effort on the part of the contracting parties both individually and jointly.

ARTICLE XXXVII

Commitments

1. The developed contracting parties shall to the fullest extent possible — that is, except when compelling reasons, which may include legal reasons, make it impossible — give effect to the following provisions:

(*a*) accord high priority to the reduction and elimination of barriers to products currently or potentially of particular export interest to less-developed contracting parties, including customs duties and other restrictions which differentiate unreasonably between such products in their primary and in their processed forms;*

(*b*) refrain from introducing, or increasing the incidence of, customs duties or non-tariff import barriers on products currently or potentially of particular export interest to less-developed contracting parties; and

(*c*) (i) refrain from imposing new fiscal measures, and

(ii) in any adjustments of fiscal policy accord high priority to the reduction and elimination of fiscal measures,

which would hamper, or which hamper, significantly the growth of consumption of primary products, in raw or processed form, wholly or mainly produced in the territories of less-developed contracting parties, and which are applied specifically to those products.

2. (*a*) Whenever it is considered that effect is not being given to any of the provisions of sub-paragraph (*a*), (*b*) or (*c*) of paragraph 1, the matter shall be reported to the CONTRACTING PARTIES either by the contracting party not so giving effect to the relevant provisions or by any other interested contracting party.

(*b*) (i) The CONTRACTING PARTIES shall, if requested so to do by any interested contracting party, and without prejudice to any bilateral consultations that may be undertaken, consult with the contracting party concerned and all interested contracting parties with respect to the matter with a view to reaching solutions satisfactory to all contracting parties concerned in order to further the objectives set forth in Article XXXVI. In the course of these consultations, the reasons given in cases where effect was not being given to the provisions of sub-paragraph (*a*), (*b*) or (*c*) of paragraph 1 shall be examined.

(ii) As the implementation of the provisions of sub-paragraph (*a*), (*b*) or (*c*) of paragraph 1 by individual contracting parties may in some cases be more readily achieved where action is taken jointly with other developed contracting parties, such consultation might, where appropriate, be directed towards this end.

(iii) The consultations by the CONTRACTING PARTIES might also, in appropriate cases, be directed towards agreement on joint action designed to further the objectives of this Agreement as envisaged in paragraph 1 of Article XXV.

3. The developed contracting parties shall:

(*a*) make every effort, in cases where a government directly or indirectly determines the resale price of products wholly or mainly produced in the territories of less-developed contracting parties, to maintain trade margins at equitable levels;

(*b*) give active consideration to the adoption of other measures* designed to provide greater scope for the development of imports from less-developed contracting parties and collaborate in appropriate international action to this end;

(*c*) have special regard to the trade interests of less-developed contracting parties when considering the application of other measures permitted under this Agreement to meet particular problems and explore all possibilities of constructive remedies before applying such measures where they would affect essential interests of those contracting parties.

4. Less-developed contracting parties agree to take appropriate action in implementation of the provisions of Part IV for the benefit of the trade of other less-developed contracting parties, in so far as such action is consistent with their individual present and future development, financial and trade needs taking into account past trade developments as well as the trade interests of less-developed contracting parties as a whole.

5. In the implementation of the commitments set forth in paragraph 1 to 4 each contracting party shall afford to any other interested contracting party or contracting parties full and prompt opportunity for consultations under the normal procedures of this Agreement with respect to any matter or difficulty which may arise.

ARTICLE XXXVIII

Joint Action

1. The contracting parties shall collaborate jointly, with the

framework of this Agreement and elsewhere, as appropriate, to further the objectives set forth in Article XXXVI.

2. In particular, the CONTRACTING PARTIES shall:

(*a*) where appropriate, take action, including action through international arrangements, to provide improved and acceptable conditions of access to world markets for primary products of particular interest to less-developed contracting parties and to devise measures designed to stabilize and improve conditions of world markets in these products including measures designed to attain stable, equitable and remunerative prices for exports of such products;

(*b*) seek appropriate collaboration in matters of trade and development policy with the United Nations and its organs and agencies, including any institutions that may be created on the basis of recommendations by the United Nations Conference on Trade and Development;

(*c*) collaborate in analysing the development plans and policies of individual less-developed contracting parties and in examining trade and aid relationships with a view to devising concrete measures to promote the development of export potential and to facilitate access to export markets for the products of the industries thus developed and, in this connection, seek appropriate collaboration with governments and international organizations, and in particular with organizations having competence in relation to financial assistance for economic development, in systematic studies of trade and aid relationships in individual less-developed contracting parties aimed at obtaining a clear analysis of export potential, market prospects and any further action that may be required;

(*d*) keep under continuous review the development of world trade with special reference to the rate of growth of the trade of less-developed contracting parties and make such recommendations to contracting parties as may, in the circumstances, be deemed appropriate;

(*e*) collaborate in seeking feasible methods to expand trade for the purpose of economic development, through international harmonization and adjustment of national policies and regulations, through technical and commercial standards affecting production, transportation and marketing, and through export promotion by the establishment of facilities for the increased flow of trade information and the development of market research; and

(*f*) establish such institutional arrangements as may be necessary to further the objectives set forth in Article XXXVI and to give effect to the provision of this Part.

ANNEX A

List of Territories referred to in Paragraph 2 (a) of Article I

United Kingdom of Great Britain and Northern Ireland
Dependent territories of the United Kingdom of Great Britain and Northern Ireland
Canada
Commonwealth of Australia
Dependent territories of the Commonwealth of Australia
New Zealand
Dependent territories of New Zealand
Union of South Africa including South West Africa
Ireland
India (as on April 10, 1947)
Newfoundland
Southern Rhodesia
Burma
Ceylon

Certain of the territories listed above have two or more preferential rates in force for certain products. Any such territory may, by agreement with the other contracting parties which are principal suppliers of such products at the most-favoured-nation rate, substitute for such preferential rates a single preferential rate which shall not on the whole be less Xfavourable to suppliers at the most-favoured-nation rate than the preferences in force prior to such substitūtion.

The imposition of an equivalent margin of tariff preference to replace a margin of preference in an internal tax existing on April 10, 1947 exclusively between two or more of the territories listed in this Annex or to replace the preferential quantitative arrangements described in the following paragraph, shall not be deemed to constitute an increase in a margin of tariff preference.

The preferential arrangements referred to in paragraph 5 (*b*) of Article XIV are those existing in the United Kingdom on 10 April 1947, under contractual agreements with the Governments of Canada, Australia and New Zealand, in respect of chilled and frozen beef and veal, frozen mutton and lamb, chilled and frozen pork and bacon. It is the intention, without prejudice to any action taken under sub-paragraph (*h*)† of Article XX, that these arrangements shall be eliminated or replaced by tariff preferences, and that negotiations to this end shall take place as soon as practicable among the countries substantially concerned or involved.

The film hire tax in force in New Zealand on 10 April 1947, shall, for the purposes of this Agreement, be treated as a customs duty under Article I. The renters' film quota in force in New Zealand on April 10, 1947, shall, for the purposes of this Agreement, be treated as a screen quota under Article IV.

The Dominions of India and Pakistan have not been mentioned separately in the above list since they had not come into existence as such on the base date of April 10, 1947.

ANNEX B

List of Territories of the French Union referred to in Paragraph 2 (*b*) of Article I

France
French Equatorial Africa (Treaty Basin of the Congo[1] and other territories)
French West Africa
Cameroons under French Trusteeship[1]
French Somali Coast and Dependencies
French Establishments in Oceania
French Establishments in the Condominium of the New Hebrides[1]
Indo-China
Madagascar and Dependencies
Morocco (French zone)[1]
New Caledonia and Dependencies

† The authentic text erroneously reads "part I (h)".

1. For imports into Metropolitan France and Territories of the French Union.

Saint-Pierre and Miquelon
Togo under French Trusteeship[1]
Tunisia

ANNEX C

List of Territories referred to in Paragraph 2 (*b*) of Article I As respects the Customs Union of Belgium, Luxemburg and the Netherlands

The Economic Union of Belgium and Luxemburg
Belgian Congo
Ruanda Urundi
Netherlands
New Guinea
Surinam
Netherlands Antilles
Republic of Indonesia

For imports into the territories constituting the Customs Union only.

ANNEX D

List of Territories referred to in Paragraph 2 (*b*) of Article I as respects the United States of America

United States of America (customs territory)

Dependent territories of the United States of America

Republic of the Philippines

The imposition of an equivalent margin of tariff preference to replace a margin of preference in an internal tax existing on 10 April, 1947, exclusively between two or more of the territories listed in this Annex shall not be deemed to constitute an increase in a margin of tariff preference.

ANNEX E

List of Territories covered by Preferential Arrangements between Chile and Neighbouring Countries referred to in Paragraph 2 (*d*) of Article I

Preferences in force exclusively between Chile on the one hand, and

1. Argentina

1. For imports into Metropolitan France and Territories of the French Union.

2. Bolivia
3. Peru

on the other hand.

ANNEX F

List of Territories covered by Preferential Arrangements between Lebanon and Syria and Neighbouring Countries referred to in Paragraph 2 (*d*) of Article I

Preferences in force exclusively between the Lebano-Syrian Customs Union, on the one hand, and

1. Palestine
2. Transjordan

on the other hand.

ANNEX G

Dates establishing Maximum Margins of Preference referred to in Paragraph 4† of Article I

Australia	October 15, 1946
Canada	July 1, 1939
France	January 1, 1939
Lebano-Syrian Customs Union	November 30, 1938
Union of South Africa	July 1, 1938
Southern Rhodesia	May 1, 1941

ANNEX H

Percentage Shares of Total External Trade to be used for the Purpose of Making the Determination referred to in Article XXVI

(based on the average of 1949-1953)

If, prior to the accession of the Government of Japan to the General Agreement, the present Agreement has been accepted by contracting parties the external trade of which under Column I accounts for the percentage of such trade specified in paragraph 6 of Article XXVI, column I shall be applicable for the purposes of that paragraph. If the present Agreement has not been so accepted prior to the accession of the Government of Japan, column II shall be applicable for the purposes of that paragraph.

† The authentic text erroneously reads "paragraph 3".

	Column I (Contracting parties on 1 March 1955)	*Column II* (Contracting parties on 1 March 1955 and Japan)
Australia	3.1	3.0
Austria	0.9	0.8
Belgium-Luxemburg	4.3	4.2
Brazil	2.5	2.4
Burma	0.3	0.3
Canada	6.7	6.5
Ceylon	0.5	0.5
Chile	0.6	0.6
Cuba	1.1	1.1
Czechoslovakia	1.4	1.4
Denmark	1.4	1.4
Dominican Republic	0.1	0.1
Finland	1.0	1.0
France	8.7	8.5
Germany, Federal Republic of	5.3	5.2
Greece	0.4	0.4
Haiti	0.1	0.1
India	2.4	2.4
Indonesia	1.3	1.3
Italy	2.9	2.8
Netherlands, Kingdom of the	4.7	4.6
New Zealand	1.0	1.0
Nicaragua	0.1	0.1
Norway	1.1	1.1
Pakistan	0.9	0.8
Peru	0.4	0.4
Rhodesia and Nyasaland	0.6	0.6
Sweden	2.5	2.4
Turkey	0.6	0.6
Union of South Africa	1.8	1.8
United Kingdom	20.3	19.8
United States of America	20.6	20.1
Uruguay	0.4	0.4
Japan	—	2.3
	100.0	100.0

Note: These percentages have been computed taking into account the trade of all territories in respect of which the General Agreement on Tariffs and Trade is applied.

ANNEX I

Notes and Supplementary Provisions

Ad Article I

Paragraph 1

The obligations incorporated in paragraph 1 of Article I by reference to paragraphs 2 and 4 of Article III and those incorporated in paragraph 2 (*b*) of Article II by reference to Article VI shall be considered as falling within Part II for the purposes of the Protocol of Provisional Application.

The cross-references, in the paragraph immediately above and in paragraph 1 of Article I, to paragraphs 2 and 4 of Article III shall only apply after Article III has been modified by the entry into force of the amendment provided for in the Protocol Modifying Part II and Article XXVI of the General Agreement on Tariffs and Trade, dated September 14, 1948.[1]

Paragraph 4

The term "margin of preference" means the absolute difference between the most-favoured-nation rate of duty and the preferential rate of duty for the like product, and not the proportionate relation between those rates. As examples:

(1) If the most-favoured-nation rate were 36 per cent *ad valorem* and the preferential rate were 24 per cent *ad valorem*, the margin of preference would be 12 per cent *ad valorem,* and not one-third of the most-favoured-nation rate;

(2) If the most-favoured-nation rate were 36 per cent *ad valorem* and the preferential rate were expressed as two-thirds of the most-favoured-nation rate, the margin of preference would be 12 per cent *ad valorem*;

(3) If the most-favoured-nation rate were 2 francs per kilogramme and the preferential rate were 1.50 francs per kilogramme, the margin of preference would be 0.50 franc per kilogramme.

The following kinds of customs action, taken in accordance with

1. This Protocol entered into force on 14 December 1948.

established uniform procedures, would not be contrary to a general binding of margins of preference:

(i) The re-application to an imported product of a tariff classification or rate of duty, properly applicable to such product, in cases in which the application of such classification or rate to such product was temporarily suspended or inoperative on April 10, 1947; and

(ii) The classification of a particular product under a tariff item other than that under which importations of that product were classified on April 10, 1947, in cases in which the tariff law clearly contemplates that such product may be classified under more than one tariff item.

Ad Article II

Paragraph 2 (a)

The cross-reference, in paragraph 2 (*a*) of Article II, to paragraph 2 of Article III shall only apply after Article III has been modified by the entry into force of the amendment provided for in the Protocol Modifying Part II and Article XXVI of the General Agreement on Tariffs and Trade, dated September 14, 1948.[1]

Paragraph 2 (b)

See the note relating to paragraph 1 of Article I.

Paragraph 4

Except where otherwise specifically agreed between the contracting parties which initially negotiated the concession, the provisions of this paragraph will be applied in the light of the provisions of Article 31 of the Havana Charter.

Ad Article III

Any internal tax or other internal charge, or any law, regulation or requirement of the kind referred to in paragraph 1 which applies to an imported product and to the like domestic product and is collected or enforced in the case of the imported product at the time or point of importation, is nevertheless to be regarded as an internal tax or other internal charge, or a law, regulation or requirement of the kind referred to in paragraph 1, and is accordingly subject to the provisions of Article III.

1. This Protocol entered into force on 14 December 1948.

Paragraph 1

The application of paragraph 1 to internal taxes imposed by local governments and authorities with the territory of a contracting party is subject to the provisions of the final paragraph of Article XXIV. The term "reasonable measures" in the last-mentioned paragraph would not require, for example, the repeal of existing national legislation authorizing local governments to impose internal taxes which, although technically inconsistent with the letter of Article III, are not in fact inconsistent with its spirit, if such repeal would result in a serious financial hardship for the local governments or authorities concerned. With regard to taxation by local governments or authorities which is inconsistent with both the letter and spirit of Article III, the term "reasonable measures" would permit a contracting party to eliminate the inconsistent taxation gradually over a transition period, if abrupt action would create serious administrative and financial difficulties.

Paragraph 2

A tax conforming to the requirements of the first sentence of paragraph 2 would be considered to be inconsistent with the provisions of the second sentence only in cases where competition was involved between, on the one hand, the taxed product and, on the other hand, a directly competitive or substitutable product which was not similarly taxed.

Paragraph 5

Regulations consistent with the provisions of the first sentence of paragraph 5 shall not be considered to be contrary to the provisions of the second sentence in any case in which all of the products subject to the regulations are produced domestically in substantial quantities. A regulation cannot be justified as being consistent with the provisions of the second sentence on the ground that the proportion or amount allocated to each of the products which are the subject of the regulation constitutes an equitable relationship between imported and domestic products.

Ad Article V

Paragraph 5

With regard to transportation charges, the principle laid down in paragraph 5 refers to like products being transported on the same route under like conditions.

Ad Article VI

Paragraph 1

1. Hidden dumping by associated houses (that is, the sale by an importer at a price below that corresponding to the price invoiced by an exporter with whom the importer is associated, and also below the price in the exporting country) constitutes a form of price dumping with respect to which the margin of dumping may be calculated on the basis of the price at which the goods are resold by the importer.

2. It is recognized that, in the case of imports from a country which has a complete or substantially complete monopoly of its trade and where all domestic prices are fixed by the State, special difficulties may exist in determining price comparability for the purposes of paragraph 1, and in such cases importing contracting parties may find it necessary to take into account the possibility that a strict comparison with domestic prices in such a country may not always be appropriate.

Paragraphs 2 and 3

1. As in many other cases in customs administration, a contracting party may require reasonable security (bond or cash deposit) for the payment of anti-dumping or countervailing duty pending final determination of the facts in any case of suspected dumping or subsidization.

2. Multiple currency practices can in certain circumstances constitute a subsidy to exports which may be met by countervailing duties under paragraph 3 or can constitute a form of dumping by means of a partial depreciation of a country's currency which may be met by action under paragraph 2. By "multiple currency practices" is meant practices by governments or sanctioned by governments.

Paragraph 6 (b)

Waivers under the provisions of this sub-paragraph shall be granted only on application by the contracting party proposing to levy an anti-dumping or countervailing duty, as the case may be.

Ad Article VII

Paragraph 1

The expression "or other charges" is not to be regarded as

including internal taxes or equivalent charges imposed on or in connection with imported products.

Paragraph 2

1. It would be in conformity with Article VII to presume that "actual value" may be represented by the invoice price, plus any non-included charges for legitimate costs which are proper elements of "actual value" and plus any abnormal discount or other reduction from the ordinary competitive price.

2. It would be in conformity with Article VII, paragraph 2 (*b*), for a contracting party to construe the phrase "in the ordinary course of trade ... under fully competitive conditions", as excluding any transaction wherein the buyer and seller are not independent of each other and price is not the sole consideration.

3. The standard of "fully competitive conditions" permits a contracting party to exclude from consideration prices involving special discounts limited to exclusive agents.

4. The wording of sub-paragraphs (*a*) and (*b*) permits a contracting party to determine the value for customs purposes uniformly either (1) on the basis of a particular exporter's prices of the imported merchandise, or (2) on the basis of the general price level of like merchandise.

Ad Article VIII

1. While Article VIII does not cover the use of multiple rates of exchange as such, paragraphs 1 and 4 condemn the use of exchange taxes or fees as a device for implementing multiple currency practices; if, however, a contracting party is using multiple currency exchange fees for balance of payments reasons with the approval of the International Monetary Fund, the provisions of paragraph 9 (*a*) of Article XV fully safeguard its position.

2. It would be consistent with paragraph 1 if, on the importation of products from the territory of a contracting party into the territory of another contracting party, the production of certificates of origin should only be required to the extent that is strictly indispensable.

Ad Articles XI, XII, XIII, XIV and XVIII

Throughout Articles XI, XII, XIII, XIV and XVIII, the terms "import restrictions" or "export restrictions" include restrictions made effective through state-trading operations.

Ad Article XI

Paragraph 2 (c)

The term "in any form" in this paragraph covers the same products when in an early stage of processing and still perishable, which compete directly with the fresh product and if freely imported would tend to make the restriction on the fresh product ineffective.

Paragraph 2, last sub-paragraph

The term "special factors" includes changes in relative productive efficiency as between domestic and foreign producers, or as between different foreign producers, but not changes artificially brought about by means not permitted under the Agreement.

Ad Article XII

The CONTRACTING PARTIES shall make provision for the utmost secrecy in the conduct of any consultation under the provisions of this Article.

Paragraph 3 (c)(i)

Contracting parties applying restrictions shall endeavour to avoid causing serious prejudice to exports of a commodity on which the economy of a contracting party is largely dependent.

Paragraph 4 (b)

It is agreed that the date shall be within ninety days after the entry into force of the amendments of this Article effected by the Protocol Amending the Preamble and Parts II and III of this Agreement. However, should the CONTRACTING PARTIES find that conditions were not suitable for the application of the provisions of this sub-paragraph at the time envisaged, they may determine a later date; *Provided* that such date is not more than thirty days after such time as the obligations of Article VIII, Sections 2, 3 and 4, of the Articles of Agreement of the International Monetary Fund become applicable to contracting parties, members of the Fund, the combined foreign trade of which constitutes at least fifty per centum of the aggregate foreign trade of all contracting parties.

Paragraph 4 (e)

It is agreed that paragraph 4 (*e*) does not add any new criteria for the imposition or maintenance of quantitative restrictions for balance of payments reasons. It is solely intended to ensure that all external factors such as changes in the terms of trade, quantitative restrictions, excessive tariffs and subsidies, which may be contributing to the balance of payments difficulties of the contracting party applying restrictions, will be fully taken into account.

Ad Article XIII

Paragraph 2 (d)

No mention was made of "commercial considerations" as a rule for the allocation of quotas because it was considered that its application by governmental authorities might not always be practicable. Moreover, in cases where it is practicable, a contracting party could apply these considerations in the process of seeking agreement, consistently with the general rule laid down in the opening sentence of paragraph 2.

Paragraph 4

See note relating to "special factors" in connection with the last sub-paragraph of paragraph 2 of Article XI.

Ad Article XIV

Paragraph 1

The provisions of this paragraph shall not be so construed as to preclude full consideration by the CONTRACTING PARTIES, in the consultations provided for in paragraph 4 of Article XII and in paragraph 12 of Article XVIII, of the nature, effects and reasons for discrimination in the field of import restrictions.

Paragraph 2

One of the situations contemplated in paragraph 2 is that of a contracting party holding balances acquired as a result of current transactions which it finds itself unable to use without a measure of discrimination.

Ad Article XV

Paragraph 4

The word "frustrate" is intended to indicate, for example, that infringements of the letter of any Article of this Agreement by exchange action shall not be regarded as a violation of that Article if, in practice, there is no appreciable departure from the intent of the Article. Thus, a contracting party which, as part of its exchange control operated in accordance with the Articles of Agreement of the International Monetary Fund, requires payment to be received for its exports in its own currency or in the currency of one or more members of the International Monetary Fund will not thereby be deemed to contravene Article XI or Article XIII. Another example would be that of a contracting party which specifies on an import licence the country from which the goods may be imported, for the purpose not of introducing any additional element of discrimination in its import licensing system but of enforcing permissible exchange controls.

Ad Article XVI

The exemption of an exported product from duties or taxes borne by the like product when destined for domestic consumption, or the remission of such duties or taxes in amounts not in excess of those which have accrued, shall not be deemed to be a subsidy.

Section B

1. Nothing in Section B shall preclude the use by a contracting party of multiple rates of exchange in accordance with the Articles of Agreement of the International Monetary Fund.

2. For the purposes of Section B, a "primary product" is understood to be any product of farm, forest or fishery, or any mineral, in its natural form or which has undergone such processing as is customarily required to prepare it for marketing in substantial volume in international trade.

Paragraph 3

1. The fact that a contracting party has not exported the product in question during the previous representative period would not in itself preclude that contracting party from establishing its right to obtain a share of the trade in the product concerned.

2. A system for the stabilization of the domestic price or of the return to domestic producers of a primary product independently of the movements of export prices, which results at times in the sale of the product for export at a price lower than the comparable price charged for the like product to buyers in the domestic market, shall be considered not to involve a subsidy on exports within the meaning of paragraph 3 if the CONTRACTING PARTIES determine that:

(*a*) the system has also resulted, or is so designed as to result, in the sale of the product for export at a price higher than the comparable price charged for the like product to buyers in the domestic market; and

(*b*) the system is so operated, or is designed so to operate, either because of the effective regulation of production or otherwise, as not to stimulate exports unduly or otherwise seriously to prejudice the interests of other contracting parties.

Notwithstanding such determination by the CONTRACTING PARTIES, operations under such a system shall be subject to the provisions of paragraph 3 where they are wholly or partly financed out of government funds in addition to the funds collected from producers in respect of the product concerned.

Paragraph 4

The intention of paragraph 4 is that the contracting parties should seek before the end of 1957 to reach agreement to abolish all remaining subsidies as from 1 January 1958; or, failing this, to reach agreement to extend the application of the standstill until the earliest date thereafter by which they can expect to reach such agreement.

Ad Article XVII

Paragraph 1

The operations of Marketing Boards, which are established by contracting parties and are engaged in purchasing or selling, are subject to the provisions of sub-paragraphs (*a*) and (*b*).

The activities of Marketing Boards which are established by contracting parties and which do not purchase or sell but lay down regulations covering private trade are governed by the relevant Articles of this Agreement.

The charging by a state enterprise of different prices for its sales of a product in different markets is not precluded by the provisions of this Article, provided that such different prices are charged for commercial reasons, to meet conditions of supply and demand in export markets.

Paragraph 1 (a)

Governmental measures imposed to insure standards of quality and efficiency in the operation of external trade, or privileges granted for the exploitation of national natural resources but which do not empower the government to exercise control over the trading activities of the enterprise in question, do not constitute "exclusive or special privileges".

Paragraph 1 (b)

A country receiving a "tied loan" is free to take this loan into account as a "commercial consideration" when purchasing requirements abroad.

Paragraph 2

The term "goods" is limited to products as understood in commercial practice, and is not intended to include the purchase or sale of services.

Paragraph 3

Negotiations which contracting parties agree to conduct under this paragraph may be directed towards the reduction of duties and other charges on imports and exports or towards the conclusion of any other mutually satisfactory arrangement consistent with the provisions of this Agreement. (See paragraph 4 of Article II and the note to that paragraph.)

Paragraph 4 (b)

The term "import mark-up" in this paragraph shall represent the margin by which the price charged by the import monopoly for the imported product (exclusive of internal taxes within the purview of Article III, transportation, distribution, and other expenses incident to the purchase, sale or further processing, and a reasonable margin of profit) exceeds the landed cost.

Ad Article XVIII

The CONTRACTING PARTIES and the contracting parties concerned shall preserve the utmost secrecy in respect of matters arising under this Article.

Paragraphs 1 and 4

1. When they consider whether the economy of a contracting party "can only support low standards of living", the CONTRACTING PARTIES shall take into consideration the normal position of that economy and shall not base their determination on exceptional circumstances such as those which may result from the temporary

existence of exceptionally favourable conditions for the staple export product or products of such contracting party.

2. The phrase "in the early stages of development" is not meant to apply only to contracting parties which have just started their economic development, but also to contracting parties the economies of which are undergoing a process of industrialization to correct an excessive dependence on primary production.

Paragraphs 2, 3, 7, 13 and 22

The reference to the establishment of particular industries shall apply not only to the establishment of a new industry, but also to the establishment of a new branch of production in an existing industry and to the substantial transformation of an existing industry, and to the substantial expansion of an existing industry supplying a relatively small proportion of the domestic demand. It shall also cover the reconstruction of an industry destroyed or substantially damaged as a result of hostilities or natural disasters.

Paragraph 7 (b)

A modification or withdrawal, pursuant to paragraph 7 (*b*), by a contracting party, other than the applicant contracting party, referred to in paragraph 7 (*a*), shall be made within six months of the day on which the action is taken by the applicant contracting party, and shall become effective on the thirtieth day following the day on which such modification or withdrawal has been notified to the CONTRACTING PARTIES.

Paragraph 11

The second sentence in paragraph 11 shall not be interpreted to mean that a contracting party is required to relax or remove restrictions if such relaxation or removal would thereupon produce conditions justifying the intensification or institution, respectively, of restrictions under paragraph 9 of Article XVIII.

Paragraph 12 (b)

The date referred to in paragraph 12 (*b*) shall be the date determined by the CONTRACTING PARTIES in accordance with the provisions of paragraph 4 (*b*) of Article XII of this Agreement.

Paragraphs 13 and 14

It is recognized that, before deciding on the introduction of a measure and notifying the CONTRACTING PARTIES in accordance with paragraph 14, a contracting party may need a reasonable period of time to assess the competitive position of the industry concerned.

Paragraphs 15 and 16

It is understood that the CONTRACTING PARTIES shall invite a contracting party proposing to apply a measure under Section C to consult with them pursuant to paragraph 16 if they are requested to do so by a contracting party the trade of which would be appreciably affected by the measure in question.

Paragraphs 16, 18, 19 and 22

1. It is understood that the CONTRACTING PARTIES may concur in a proposed measure subject to specific conditions or limitations. If the measure as applied does not conform to the terms of the concurrence it will to that extent be deemed a measure in which the CONTRACTING PARTIES have not concurred. In cases in which the CONTRACTING PARTIES have concurred in a measure for a specified period, the contracting party concerned, if it finds that the maintenance of the measure for a further period of time is required to achieve the objective for which the measure was originally taken, may apply to the CONTRACTING PARTIES for an extension of that period in accordance with the provisions and procedures of Section C or D, as the case may be.

2. It is expected that the CONTRACTING PARTIES will, as a rule, refrain from concurring in a measure which is likely to cause serious prejudice to exports of a commodity on which the economy of a contracting party is largely dependent.

Paragraph 18 and 22

The phrase "that the interests of other contracting parties are adequately safeguarded" is meant to provide latitude sufficient to permit consideration in each case of the most appropriate method of safeguarding those interests. The appropriate method may, for instance, take the form of an additional concession to be applied by the contracting party having recourse to Section C or D during such time as the deviation from the other Articles of the Agreement would remain in force or of the temporary suspension by any other contracting party referred to in paragraph 18 of a concession substantially equivalent to the impairment due to the introduction of the measure in question. Such contracting party would have the right to safeguard its interests through such a temporary suspension of a concession; *Provided* that this right will not be exercised when, in the case of a measure imposed by a contracting party coming within the scope of paragraph 4 (*a*), the CONTRACTING PARTIES have determined that the extent of the compensatory concession proposed was adequate.

Paragraph 19

The provisions of paragraph 19 are intended to cover the cases where an industry has been in existence beyond the "reasonable period of time" referred to in the note to paragraphs 13 and 14, and should not be so construed as to deprive a contracting party coming within the scope of paragraph 4 (*a*) of Article XVIII, of its right to resort to the other provisions of Section C, including paragraph 17, with regard to a newly established industry even though it has benefited from incidental protection afforded by balance of payments import restrictions.

Paragraph 21

Any measure taken pursuant to the provisions of paragraph 21 shall be withdrawn forthwith if the action taken in accordance with paragraph 17 is withdrawn or if the CONTRACTING PARTIES concur in the measure proposed after the expiration of the ninety-day time limit specified in paragraph 17.

Ad Article XX

Sub-paragraph (h)

The exception provided for in this sub-paragraph extends to any commodity agreement which conforms to the principles approved by the Economic and Social Council in its resolution 30 (IV) of 28 March 1947.

Ad Article XXIV

Paragraph 9

It is understood that the provisions of Article I would require that, when a product which has been imported into the territory of a member of a customs union or free-trade area at a preferential rate of duty is re-exported to the territory of another member of such union or area, the latter member should collect a duty equal to the difference between the duty already paid and any higher duty that would be payable if the product were being imported directly into its territory.

Paragraph 11

Measures adopted by India and Pakistan in order to carry out definitive trade arrangements between them, once they have been agreed upon, might depart from particular provisions of this Agreement, but these measures would in general be consistent with the objectives of the Agreement.

Ad Article XXVIII

The CONTRACTING PARTIES and each contracting party concerned should arrange to conduct the negotiations and consultations with the greatest possible secrecy in order to avoid premature disclosure of details of prospective tariff changes. The CONTRACTING PARTIES shall be informed immediately of all changes in national tariffs resulting from recourse to this Article.

Paragraph 1

1. If the CONTRACTING PARTIES specify a period other than a three-year period, a contracting party may act pursuant to paragraph 1 or paragraph 3 of Article XXVIII on the first day following the expiration of such other period and, unless the CONTRACTING PARTIES have again specified another period, subsequent periods will be three-year periods following the expiration of such specified period.

2. The provision that on 1 January 1958, and on other days determined pursuant to paragraph 1, a contracting party "may ... modify or withdraw a concession" means that on such day, and on the first day after the end of each period, the legal obligation of such contracting party under Article II is altered; it does not mean that the changes in its customs tariff should necessarily be made effective on that day. If a tariff change resulting from negotiations undertaken pursuant to this Article is delayed, the entry into force of any compensatory concessions may be similarly delayed.

3. Not earlier than six months, nor later than three months, prior to 1 January 1958, or to the termination date of any subsequent period, a contracting party wishing to modify or withdraw any concession embodied in the appropriate Schedule, should notify the CONTRACTING PARTIES to this effect. The CONTRACTING PARTIES shall

then determine the contracting party or contracting parties with which the negotiations or consultations referred to in paragraph 1 shall take place. Any contracting party so determined shall participate in such negotiations or consultations with the applicant contracting party with the aim of reaching agreement before the end of the period. Any extension of the assured life of the Schedules shall relate to the Schedules as modified after such negotiations, in accordance with paragraphs 1, 2, and 3 of Article XXVIII. If the CONTRACTING PARTIES are arranging for multilateral tariff negotiations to take place within the period of six months before 1 January 1958, or before any other day determined pursuant to paragraph 1, they shall include in the arrangements for such negotiations suitable procedures for carrying out the negotiations referred to in this paragraph.

4. The object of providing for the participation in the negotiation of any contracting party with a principle supplying interest, in addition to any contracting party with which the concession was originally negotiated, is to ensure that a contracting party with a larger share in the trade affected by the concession than a contracting party with which the concession was originally negotiated shall have an effective opportunity to protect the contractual right which it enjoys under this Agreement.

On the other hand, it is not intended that the scope of the negotiations should be such as to make negotiations and agreement under Article XXVIII unduly difficult nor to create complications in the application of this Article in the future to concessions which result from negotiations thereunder. Accordingly, the CONTRACTING PARTIES should only determine that a contracting party has a principal supplying interest if that contracting party has had, over a reasonable period of time prior to the negotiations, a larger share in the market of the applicant contracting party than a contracting party with which the concession was initially negotiated or would, in the judgement of the CONTRACTING PARTIES, have had such a share in the absence of discriminatory quantitative restrictions maintained by the applicant contracting party. It would therefore not be appropriate for the CONTRACTING PARTIES to determine that more than one contracting party, or in those exceptional cases where there is near equality more than two contracting parties, had a principal supplying interest.

5. Notwithstanding the definition of a principal supplying interest in note 4 to paragraph 1, the CONTRACTING PARTIES may exceptionally

determine that a contracting party has a principal supplying interest if the concession in question affects trade which constitutes a major part of the total exports of such contracting party.

6. It is not intended that provision for participation in the negotiations of any contracting party with a principal supplying interest, and for consultation with any contracting party having a substantial interest in the concession which the applicant contracting party is seeking to modify or withdraw, should have the effect that it should have to pay compensation or suffer retaliation greater than the withdrawal or modification sought, judged in the light of the conditions of trade at the time of the proposed withdrawal or modification, making allowance for any discriminatory quantitative restrictions maintained by the applicant contracting party.

7. The expression "substantial interest" is not capable of a precise definition and accordingly may present difficulties for the CONTRACTING PARTIES. It is, however, intended to be construed to cover only those contracting parties which have, or in the absence of discriminatory quantitative restrictions affecting their exports could reasonably be expected to have, a significant share in the market of the contracting party seeking to modify or withdraw the concession.

Paragraph 4

1. Any request for authorization to enter into negotiations shall be accompanied by all relevant statistical and other data. A decision on such request shall be made within thirty days of its submission.

2. It is recognized that to permit certain contracting parties, depending in large measure on a relatively small number of primary commodities and relying on the tariff as an important aid for furthering diversification of their economies or as an important source of revenue, normally to negotiate for the modification or withdrawal of concessions only under paragraph 1 of Article XXVIII, might cause them at such time to make modifications or withdrawals which in the long run would prove unnecessary. To avoid such a situation the CONTRACTING PARTIES shall authorize any such contracting party, under paragraph 4, to enter into negotiations unless they consider this would result in, or contribute substantially towards, such an increase in tariff levels as to threaten the stability of the Schedules to this Agreement or lead to undue disturbance of international trade.

3. It is expected that negotiations authorized under paragraph 4 for modification or withdrawal of a single item, or a very small group of items, could normally be brought to a conclusion in sixty days. It is recognized, however, that such a period will be inadequate for cases involving negotiations for the modification or withdrawal of a larger number of items and in such cases, therefore, it would be appropriate for the CONTRACTING PARTIES to prescribe a longer period.

4. The determination referred to in paragraph 4 (*d*) shall be made by the CONTRACTING PARTIES within thirty days of the submission of the matter to them unless the applicant contracting party agrees to a longer period.

5. In determining under paragraph 4 (*d*) whether an applicant contracting party has unreasonably failed to offer adequate compensation, it is understood that the CONTRACTING PARTIES will take due account of the special position of a contracting party which has bound a high proportion of its tariffs at very low rates of duty and to this extent has less scope than other contracting parties to make compensatory adjustment.

Ad Article XXVIII bis

Paragraph 3

It is understood that the reference to fiscal needs would include the revenues aspect of duties and particularly duties imposed primarily for revenue purpose, or duties imposed on products which can be substituted for products subject to revenue duties to prevent the avoidance of such duties.

Ad Article XXIX

Paragraph 1

Chapters VII and VIII of the Havana Charter have been excluded from paragraph 1 because they generally deal with the organization, functions and procedures of the International Trade Organization.

Ad Part IV

The words "developed contracting parties" and the words "less-developed contracting parties" as used in Part IV are to be understood to refer to developed and less-developed countries which are parties to the General Agreement on Tariffs and Trade.

Ad Article XXXVI

Paragraph 1

This Article is based upon the objectives set forth in Article I as it will be amended by Section A of paragraph 1 of the Protocol Amending Part I and Articles XXIX and XXX when that Protocol enters into force.[1]

Paragraph 4

The term "primary products" includes agricultural products, *vide* paragraph 2 of the note *ad* Article XVI, Section B.

Paragraph 5

A diversification programme would generally include the intensification of activities for the processing of primary products and the development of manufacturing industries, taking into account the situation of the particular contracting party and the world outlook for production and consumption of different commodities.

Paragraph 8

It is understood that the phrase "do not expect reciprocity" means, in accordance with the objectives set forth in this Article, that the less-developed contracting parties should not be expected, in the course of trade negotiations, to make contributions which are inconsistent with their individual development, financial and trade needs, taking into consideration past trade developments.

This paragraph would apply in the event of action under Section A of Article XVIII, Article XXVIII, Article XXVIII *bis* (Article XXIX after the amendment set forth in Section A of paragraph 1 of the Protocol Amending Part I and Articles XXIX and XXX shall have become effective), Article XXXIII, or any other procedure under this Agreement.

Ad Article XXXVII

Paragraph 1 (a)

This paragraph would apply in the event of negotiations for reduction or elimination of tariffs or other restrictive regulations of commerce under Articles XXVIII, XXVIII *bis* (XXIX after the amendment set forth in Section A of paragraph 1 of the Protocol

---

1. This Protocol was abandoned on 1 January 1968.

Amending Part I and Articles XXIX and XXX shall have become effective¦), and Article XXXIII, as well as in connection with other action to effect such reduction or elimination which contracting parties may be able to undertake.

Paragraph 3 (b)

The other measures referred to in this paragraph might include steps to promote domestic structural changes, to encourage the consumption of particular products, or to introduce measures of trade promotion.

PROTOCOL OF PROVISIONAL APPLICATION OF THE GENERAL AGREEMENT ON TARIFFS AND TRADE

1. The Governments of the COMMONWEALTH OF AUSTRALIA, the KINGDOM OF BELGIUM (in respect of its metropolitan territory), CANADA, the FRENCH REPUBLIC (in respect of its metropolitan territory), the GRAND-DUCHY OF LUXEMBURG, the KINGDOM OF THE NETHERLANDS (in respect of its metropolitan territory), the UNITED KINGDOM OF GREAT BRITAIN AND NORTHERN IRELAND (in respect of its metropolitan territory), and the UNITED STATES OF AMERICA undertake, provided that this Protocol shall have been signed on behalf of all the foregoing Governments not later than 15 November 1947, to apply provisionally on and after 1 January 1948:

(*a*) Parts I and III of the General Agreement on Tariffs and Trade, and

(*b*) Part II of that Agreement to the fullest extent not inconsistent with existing legislation.

2. The foregoing Governments shall make effective such provisional application of the General Agreement, in respect of any of their territories other than their metropolitan territories, on or after 1 January 1948, upon the expiration of thirty days from the day on which notice of such application is received by the Secretary-General of the United Nations.

3. Any other government signatory to this Protocol shall make effective such provisional application of the General Agreement, on or after 1 January 1948, upon the expiration of thirty days from the day of signature of this Protocol on behalf of such Government.

4. This Protocol shall remain open for signature at the

Headquarters of the United Nations (*a*) until 15 November 1947, on behalf of any government named in paragraph 1 of this Protocol which has not signed it on this day, and (*b*) until 30 June 1948, on behalf of any other Government signatory to the Final Act adopted at the conclusion of the Second Session of the Preparatory Committee of the United Nations Conference on Trade and Employment which has not signed it on this day.

5. Any government applying this Protocol shall be free to withdraw such application, and such withdrawal shall take effect upon the expiration of sixty days from the day on which written notice of such withdrawal is received by the Secretary-General of the United Nations.

6. The original of this Protocol shall be deposited with the Secretary-General of the United Nations, who will furnish certified copies thereof to all interested Governments.

In WITNESS WHEREOF the respective Representatives, after having communicated their full powers, found to be in good and due form, have signed the Protocol.

DONE at Geneva, in a single copy, in the English and the French languages, both texts authentic, this thirtieth day of October one thousand nine hundred and forty-seven.

APPENDIX

The first section of this Appendix gives the source (legal instruments) of the various provisions of the GATT, other than schedules, their effective date and their respective citations in the United Nations *Treaty Series* (UNTS) or in GATT publications.

The second section contains a key to the abbreviated titles used in the first section, together with their citations. Column 4 refers to provisions in Part I of the General Agreement and indicates where they have been qualified, for instance, with regard to territorial application or the maintenance of preferences. Column 5 refers to provisions in Part II of the General Agreement, and indicates where they have been qualified, e.g. with regard to dates of application. Column 6 refers to different applicable dates with regard to paragraph 1 of Article II. Column 7 refers to different applicable dates with regard to Article V:6, Article VII:4 (*d*), Article X:3 (*c*). Column 8 refers to different termination periods for withdrawal from the Agreement.

I. SOURCE AND EFFECTIVE DATE OF GATT PROVISIONS

GATT provision	*Source*	*Effective*	*Citation*
1	2	3	4
Title	GATT	1 Jan. 1948	55 UNTS 194
Preamble	GATT	1 Jan. 1948	55 UNTS 194
Part I	GATT	1 Jan. 1948	55 UNTS 196
Article 1	GATT	1 Jan. 1948	55 UNTS 196
Par. 1	Cross reference to Art. III modified by 1948 Pt. I Prot., par. 1, sec. A(i)	24 Sept. 1952	138 UNTS 336
Par. 2	Cross reference to subsquent par. modified by 1948 Pt. I Prot., par. 1, sec. A(ii)	24 Sept. 1952	138 UNTS 336
	Provisions in supplementary agreements permitting additional tariff preferences are listed in Col. 4 of key in section II		
Par. 3	1948 Pt. I Prot., par. 1, sec. A(iii)	24 Sept. 1952	138 UNTS 336
Par. 4	Par. No. modified by 1948 Pt. 1 Prot., par. 1, sec. A(iii)	24 Sept. 1952	138 UNTS 336
	Provisions in supplementary agreements providing different base dates are listed in Col. 4 of key in section II		
Article II	GATT	1 Jan. 1948	55 UNTS 200
Par. 1	Provisions in supplementary agreements providing different dates applicable to certain concessions are listed in Col. 6 of key in section II		
Par. 2 Subpar. (*a*)	Cross reference to Art. III modified by 1948 Pt.	24 Sept. 1952	138 UNTS 336
	Provisions in supplementary agreements providing different dates concerning currency conversion		
	Methods are listed in Col. 7 of key in Section II		
Par. 6 Subpar. (a)	Provisions in supplementary		

Contd.

GATT provision	*Source*	*Effective*	*Citation*
1	2	3	4
	agreements listed in Col. 6 of key in section II		
Part II		1 Jan. 1948	55 UNTS 204
Article III		14 Dec. 1948	62 UNTS 82
Ariticle IV	GATT	1 Jan. 1948	55 UNTS 208
Article V	Provisions in supplementary agreements qualifying application of this part are listed in Col. 5 of key in section II	1 Jan. 1948	55 UNTS 208
Par. 6			
Article VI		14 Dec. 1948	62 UNTS 86
Par. 6	1948 Pt. II Prot., par. 1, sec. A.	7 Oct. 1957	278 UNTS 170
Article VII	GATT	1 Jan. 1948	55 UNTs 216
Par. 1	GATT	7 Oct. 1957	278 UNTS 172
Par. 2 Subpar. (*b*)	Provisions in supplementary agreements providing different dates concerning consignment requirements are listed in Col. 7 of key in section II	7 Oct. 1957	278 UNTS 172
Par. 4 Subpar. (*a*) and (*b*)		7 Oct. 1957	278 UNTS 172
Subpar. (*d*)			
	1948 Pt. II Prot., par. 1, sec. B		
	1955 Pt. II Prot., par. 1, sec. D		
	GATT		
	Former qualification deleted from first sentence by 1955 Pt. II Prot., par. 1, sec. E(i)		
	Modified by 1955 Pt. II Prot., par. 1, sec. E(iii)		
Article VIII	GATT	1 Jan. 1948	55 UNTS 218
Title	1955 Pt. II Prot., par. 1, sec. F(i)	7 Oct. 1957	278 UNTS 174
Par. 1 and 2	1955 Pt. II Prot., par. 1, sec. F(ii)	7 Oct. 1957	278 UNTS 174

Contd.

GATT provision	*Source*	*Effective*	*Citation*
1	2	3	4
Article IX	GATT	1 Jan. 1948	55 UNTS 220
Par. 2	1955 Pt. II Prot., par. 1, sec. G(i)	7 Oct. 1957	278 UNTS 174
Par. 3 to 6	Par. No. modified by 1955 Pt. II Prot., par. 1, sec. G(ii)	7 Oct. 1957	278 UNTS 174
Article X	GATT	1 Jan. 1948	55 UNTS 222
Par. 3 Subpar. (*c*)	Provisions in supplementary agreements providing different dates concering procedures are listed in Col. 7 of key in section II		
Article XI	GATT	1 Jan. 1948	55 UNTS 224
	Former par. 3 deleted by 1955 Pt. II Prot., par. 1, sec. H	7 Oct. 1957	278 UNTS 174
Article XII	1955 Pt. II Prot., par. 1, sec. I	7 Oct. 1957	278 UNTS 174
Article XIII	GATT	1 Jan. 1948	55 UNTS 234
Par. 5	Former reference to Art. III deleted by 1948 Pt. II Prot., par. 1, sec. C	14 Dec. 1948	62 UNTS 90
Article XIV	1955 Pt. II Prot., par. 1, sec. J(i)	15 Feb. 1961	278 UNTS 180
Par. 1			
Par. 2 to 5	1955 Pt. II Prot., par. 1, sec. J(ii)	7 Oct. 1957	278 UNTS 180
Article XV	GATT	1 Jan. 1948	55 UNTs 246
Par. 2	Reference to Art. XVIII added by 1955 Pt. II Prot., par. 1, sec. K	7 Oct. 1957	278 UNTS 182
Par. 9	Opening clause modified by 1948 Pt. II, Prot., par. 1, sec. D	14 Dec. 1948	62 UNTS 90
Article XVI	GATT	1 Jan. 1948	55 UNTS 250
Sec. A			
Title	Section designation and title added by 1955 Pt. II Prot., par. 1, sec. L (i)	7 Oct. 1957	278 UNTS 182
Par. 1	Par. No. added by 1955 Pt. II Prot., par. 1, sec. L (ii)	7 Oct. 1957	278 UNTS 182

Contd.

GATT provision	*Source*	*Effective*	*Citation*
1	2	3	4
Sec. B	1955 Pt. II Prot., par. 1, sec. L (ii)	7 Oct. 1957	278 UNTS 182
Par. 2	Opening words modified by 1955 Rectif. P.-V., Art. I, sec. B, par. 4	7 Oct. 1957	278 UNTS 248
Par. 4	Effective date of prohibition provided for in 1960 Art. XVI:4 Prohib. Decl., par. 1	14 Nov. 1962	445 UNTS 294
	Reference to domestic market modified by 1955 Rectif. P.-V., Art. I, sec. B, par. 4	7 Oct. 1957	287 UNTS 248
Article XVII	GATT	1 Jan. 1948	55 UNTS 250
Title	Modified by 1955 Pt. II Prot., par 1, sec. M(i)	7 Oct. 1957	278 UNTS 184
Par. 3 and 4	1955 Pt. II Prot., par. 1, sec. M(ii)	7 Oct. 1957	278 UNTS 184
Article XVIII	1955 Pt. II Prot., par. 1, sec. N	7 Oct., 1957	278 UNTS 186
Article XIX	GATT	1 Jan. 1948	55 UNTS 258
Par. 3	Language of suspension rights modified by 1955 Pt. II Prot., par. 1, sec. O	7 Oct. 1957	278 UNTS 200
Article XX	GATT	1 Jan. 1948	55 UNTS 262
	Former Pt. II and No. of Pt. I deleted by 1955 Pt. II Prot., par. 1, sec P. (i)	7 Oct. 1957	278 UNTS 200
Subpar. (h)	1955 Pt. II Prot., par. 1, sec. P(ii)	7 Oct. 1957	278 UNTS 200
Subpar. (j)	1955 Pt. II Prot., par. 1, sec. P(iii)	7 Oct. 1957	278 UNTS 200
Article XXI	GATT	1 Jan. 1948	55 UNTS 266
Article XXII	1955 Pt. II Prot., par. 1, sec. Q	7 Oct. 1957	278 UNTS 200
Article XXIII	GATT	1 Jan. 1948	55 UNTS 266
Par. 2	Last two sentences modified by 1955 Pt. II Prot. par. 1 sec. R	7 Oct. 1957	278 UNTS 200
Part III	GATT	1 Jan. 1948	55 UNTS 268

Contd.

GATT provision	Source	Effective	Citation
1	2	3	4
Par. 4	1955 Pt. II Prot., par. 1, sec. S(i)	7 Oct. 1957	278 UNTS 202
Par. 7			
Subpar (*b*)	First clause modified by 1955 Pt. II Prot., par. 1, sec. S(ii)	7 Oct. 1957	278 UNTS 202
Article XXV	GATT	1 Jan. 1948	55 UNTS 272
	1948 Mod. Prot., sec. 1	15 Apr. 1948	62 UNTS 30
Par. 5	Former subpars. (*b*) through (*d*) and subpar. designation following par. no. deleted by 1955 Pt. II Prot., par. 1, sec. T	7 Oct. 1957	278 UNTS 202
Article XXVI	1955 Pt. II Prot., par. 1, sec. U(i)	7 Oct. 1957	278 UNTS 202
Article XXVII	GATT	1 Jan. 1948	55 UNTS 276
	Final sentence modified by 1955 Pt. II Prot., par. 1, sec. V	7 Oct. 1957	278 UNTS 204
Article XXVIII	1955 Pt. II Prot., par. 1, sec. W	7 Oct. 1957	278 UNTS 204
Article XXVIII *bis*	1955 Pt. II Prot., par. 1, sec. X(i)	7 Oct. 1957	278 UNTS 208
Article XXIX	1948 Pt. I Prot., par. 1, sec. C	24 Sept. 1952	38 UNTS 336
Article XXX	GATT	1 Jan. 1948	55 UNTS 282
Article XXXI	GATT	1 Jan. 1948	55 UNTS 282
	Reference to Art. XVIII added by 1955 Pt. II Prot., par. 1, sec. Y(i)	7 Oct. 1957	278 UNTS 210
	Connecting words added to first clause by 1955 Rectif. P.-V., Art. I, sec. B, par 5	7 Oct. 1957	278 UNTS 248
	Former limiting date deleted from each sentence by 1955 Pt. II Prot., par 1, sec. Y(ii) and (iii)	7 Oct. 1957	278 UNTS 210
	Provisions in supplementary agreements providing for different termination		

Contd.

GATT provision	*Source*	*Effective*	*Citation*
1	2	3	4
Article XXXII	GATT	1 Jan. 1948	55 UNTS 282
Par. 1	1948 Mod. Prot., sec. II	15 Apr. 1948	62 UNTS 32
Par. 2	Cross references modified by 1955 Pt. II Prot., par. 1, sec. SS	7 Oct. 1957	278 UNTS 234
Article XXXIII	1948 Mod. Prot., sec. III	15 Apr. 1948.	62 UNTS 34
Article XXXIV	GATT	1 Jan. 1948	55 UNTS 284
Article XXXV	1955 Pt. II Prot., par. 1, sec. Z	7 Oct. 1957	278 UNTS 210
Part IV	1965 Pt. IV Prot., par. 1, sec. A	27 June 1966	GATT, Final Act 2nd Sp. Sess. 25
Article XXXVI	1965 Pt. IV Prot., par. 1, sec. A.	27 June 1966	GATT, Final Act 2nd Sp. Sess. 25
Article XXXVII	1965 Pt. IV Prot., par. 1, sec. A.	27 June 1966	GATT, Final Act 2nd Sp. Sess. 27
Article XXXVIII	1965 Pt. IV Prot., par. 1, sec. A.	27 June 1966	GATT, Final Act 2nd Sp. Sess. 30
Annex A	GATT	1 Jan. 1948	55 UNTS 284
Final par.	1948 Pt. I prot., par. 1, sec. D	24 Sept. 1952	138 UNTS 338
Annex B	1955 5th Rectif. and Modif. Prot., par. 1	23 Jan. 1959	324 UNTS 302
Annex C	1950 4th Rectif. Prot., par. 1 (*a*)	24 Sept. 1952	138 UNTS 399
	Last name in list modified by 1950 5th Rectif. Prot. par. 1(*a*)	30 June 1953	167 UNTS 266
Annex D	GATT	1 Jan. 1948	55 UNTS 290
Annex E	GATT	1 Jan. 1948	55 UNTS 290
Annex F	GATT	1 Jan. 1948	55 UNTS 290
Annex G	GATT	1 Jan. 1948	55 UNTS 290
Annex H	1955 Pt. II Prot., par. 1, sec. AA(i)	7 Oct. 1957	278 UNTS 212
Annex I	GATT	1 Jan. 1948	55 UNTS 292
Title	1955 Pt. II Prot., par. 1, sec BB(ii)	7 Oct. 1957	278 UNTS 214
Ad Article I	GATT	1 Jan. 1948	55 UNTS 292

Contd.

GATT provision	*Source*	*Effective*	*Citation*
1	2	3	4
Par. 1			
First par.	Cross reference to Art. III modified by 1948 Pt. I Prot., par. 1, sec. E(i)	24 Sept. 1948	138 UNTS 338
Second par.	1948 Pt. I Prot., par. 1, sec. E(ii)	24 Sept. 1952	138 UNTS 338
Par. 3	Par. No. modified by 1948 Pt. I Prot., par. 1, sec. E(iii)	24 Sept. 1952	138 UNTS 340
Ad Article II	GATT	1 Jan. 1948	55 UNTS 294
Par. 2 (*a*)	1948 Pt. I Prot., par. 1, sec. E(iv)	24 Sept. 1952	138 UNTS 340
Par. 4	1948 Pt. I Prot., par. 1, sec. E(v)	24 Sept. 1952	138 UNTS 340
Ad Article III	1948 Pt. II Prot., par. 1, sec. G(i)	14 Dec. 1948	62 UNTS 104
Ad Article V	GATT	1 Jan. 1948	55 UNTS 296
Ad Article VI	1948 Pt. II Prot., par. 1, sec. G(ii)	14 Dec. 1948	62 UNTS 106
Par. 1			
Note 1	Note No. added by 1955 Pt. II Prot., par. 1, sec. CC(i)	7 Oct. 1957	278 UNTS 214
Note 2	1955 Pt. II Prot., par. 1, sec. CC(ii)	7 Oct. 1957	278 UNTS 214
Par. 6 (*b*)	1955 Pt. II Prot., par. 1, sec. CC(iii)	7 Oct. 1957	278 UNTS 214
Ad Article VII	GATT	1 Jan. 1948	55 UNTS 296
Par. 1	1955 Pt. II Prot., par 1, sec. DD(i)	7 Oct. 1957	278 UNTS 214
Par. 2	1955 Pt. II Prot., par 1, sec. DD(ii)	7 Oct. 1957	278 UNTS 214
Ad Article VIII	1955 Pt. II Prot., par. 1, sec. EE	7 Oct. 1957	278 UNTS 216
Ad Article XI, XII, XIII, XIV and XVIII	1955 Rectif. P.-V., Art. I, sec. B, par. 7	7 Oct. 1957	278 UNTS 248
Ad Article XI	GATT	1 Jan. 1948	55 UNTS 298
Ad Article XII	1955 Pt. II Prot., par. 1, sec. GG	7 Oct. 1957	278 UNTS 216

Contd.

GATT provision	***Source***	***Effective***	***Citation***
1	2	3	4
Ad Article XIII	GATT	1 Jan. 1948	55 UNTS 300
Ad Article XIV			
Par. 1	1955 Pt. II Prot., par. 1, sec. HH	15 Feb. 1961	278 UNTS 218
Par. 2	1948 Art. XIV Prot., sec. II	1 Jan. 1949	62 UNTS 46
Ad Article XV	GATT	1 Jan. 1948	55 UNTS 302
Ad Article XVI	1955 Pt. II Prot., par. 1, sec. II	7 Oct. 1957	278 UNTS 218
Ad Article XVII	GATT	1 Jan. 1948	55 UNTS 302
Par. 3	1955 Pt. II Prot., par. 1, sec. JJ	7 Oct. 1957	278 UNTS 220
Par. 4(*b*)	1955 Pt. II Prot., par. 1, sec. JJ	7 Oct. 1957	278 UNTS 220
Ad Article XVIII	1955 Pt. II Prot., par. 1, sec. KK	7 Oct. 1957	278 UNTS 220
Ad Article XX	1955 Pt. II Prot., par. 1, sec. LL	7 Oct 1957	278 UNTS 226
Ad Article XXIV	1948 Art. XXIV Prot., sec. II	7 June 1948	62 UNTS 64
Par. 9	1949 3rd Rectif. Prot., par. 1	21 Oct. 1951	107 UNTS 314
Ad Article XXVIII	1955 Pt. II Prot., par. 1, sec. NN	7 Oct. 1957	278 UNTS 226
Ad Article XXVIII *bis*	1955 Pt. II Prot., par. 1, sec. OO(i)	7 Oct. 1957	278 UNTS 232
Ad Article XXIX	1948 Pt. I Prot., par. 1, sec. E (vi)	24 Sept. 1952	138 UNTS 340
Ad Part IV	1965 Pt. IV Prot., par. 1, sec. B	27 June 1966	GATT, Final Act 2nd Sp. Sess. 31
Ad Article XXXVI	1965 Pt. IV Prot., par. 1, sec. B	27 June 1966	GATT, Final Act 2nd Sp. Sess. 31
Ad Article XXXVII	1965 Pt. IV Prot., par. 1, sec. B	27 June 1966	GATT, Final Act 2nd Sp. Sess. 32

II. KEY TO ABBREVIATIONS USED IN THIS APPENDIX AND TO PROVISIONS IN SUPPLEMENTARY AGREEMENTS AFFECTING THE APPLICATION OF CERTAIN PORTIONS OF THE GENERAL AGREEMENT

Abbreviated agreement title used	*Agreement title*	*Citation*	*Qualification* re *application of pt. I*	*Qualification* re *application of pt. II*	*Different date* re *certain concessions*	*Different date* re *certain parties*	*Different termination period*
(1)	(2)	(3)	(4)	(5)	(6)	(7)	(8)
GATT	General Agreement on Tariffs and Trade	55 UNTS 194	–	–	–	–	–
	Protocol of Provisional Application of the General Agreement on Tariffs and Trade, 30 October 1947	55 UNTS 308	–	Par. 1 (*b*)	–	–	Par. 5
1948 Mod. Prot.	Protocol modifying certain provisions of the General Agreement on Tariffs and Trade, 24 March 1948	62 UNTS 30	–	–	–	–	–
1948 Art. XIV Prot.	Special Protocol modifying Article XIV of the General Agreement on Tariffs and Trade, 24 March 1948	62 UNTS 40	–	–	–	–	–
1948 Art, XXIV	Special Protocol relating to Article	62 UNTS 56	–	–	–	–	–

Contd.

Abbreviated agreement title used	Agreement title	Citation	Qualification re application of pt. I	Qualification re application of pt. II	Different date re certain concessions	Different date re certain parties	Different termination period
(1)	(2)	(3)	(4)	(5)	(6)	(7)	(8)
	Agreement on Tariffs and Trade, 10 October 1949						
Prot.	XXIV of the General Agreement on Tariffs and Trade, 24 March 1948						
1948 Pt. I Prot.	Protocol modifying Part I and Article XXIX of the General Agreement on Tariffs and Trade, 14 September 1948	138 UNTS 334	–	–	–	–	–
1948 Pt. II Prot.	Protocol modifying Part II and Article XXVI of the General Agreement on Tariffs and Trade 14 September 1948	62 UNTS 80	–	–	–	–	–
–	Protocol for the Accession of Signatories of the Final Act of 30 October 1947, 14 Sept. 1948	62 UNTS 68	–	Par. 1	–	–	Par. 1
1949 3rd Rectif.	Third Protocol of Rectifications to	107 UNTS 312	-	-	-	-	-

Contd.

Abbreviated agreement title used	*Agreement title*	*Citation*	*Qualification* re *application of pt. I*	*Qualification* re *application of pt. II*	*Different date* re *certain concessions*	*Different date* re *certain parties*	*Different termination period*
(1)	(2)	(3)	(4)	(5)	(6)	(7)	(8)
Prot.	the General Agreement on Tariffs and Trade, 13 August 1949						
-	Annecy Protocol of Terms of Accession to the General Agreement on Tariffs and Trade, 10 October 1949	62 UNTS 122	Par. 1 (*d*)	Par. 1 (*a*)(ii)	Par. 5 (*a*)	Par.5(*b*)121	Par. 7
1950 4th Rectif.	Fourth Protocol of Rectifications to the General Agreement on Tariffs and Trade, 3 April 1950	138 UNTS 398	-	-	-	-	-
1950 5th Rectif. Prot.	Fifth Protocol of Rectifications to the General Agreement on Tariffs and Trade, 16 December 1950	167 UNTS 265	-	-	-	-	-
-	Torquay Protocol to the General Agreement on Tariffs and Trade, 21 April 1951.	142 UNTS 34	-	Par. 1 (*a*)(iii)	Par. 5 (*a*)	Par. 5 (*b*)	Par. 8
-	First Protocol of Supplementary Concessions to the General Agreement on Tariffs and Trade (Union of South Africa and Germany), 27 October 1951	131 UNTS 316	-	-	Par. 3	-	-

Contd.

Abbreviated agreement title used	*Agreement title*	*Citation*	*Qualification re application of pt. I*	*Qualification re application of pt. II*	*Different date re certain concessions*	*Different date re certain parties*	*Different termination period*
(1)	(2)	(3)	(4)	(5)	(6)	(7)	(8)
	Second Protocol of Supplementary Concessions to the General Agreement on Tariffs and Trade (Austria and Germany), 22 November 1952	172 UNTS 340	-	-	Par. 3	-	-
1955 4th Rectif & Modif. Prot.	Fourth Protocol of Rectifications and Modifications to the Annexes and to the Texts of the Schedules to the General Agreement on Tariffs and Trade, 7 March 1955	324 UNTS 300	-	-	-	-	-
1955 Pt. II Prot.	Protocol amending the Preamble and Parts II and III of the General Agreement on Tariffs and Trade, 10 March 1955	278 UNTS 168	-	-	-	-	-
	Protocol of Terms of Accession of Japan to the General Agreement on Tariffs and Trade, 7 June 1955	220 UNTS 164	Par. 1 (*d*)	Par. 1 (*a*)(ii)	Par. 5 (*a*)	Par. 5 (*b*)	Par. 7

Contd.

Abbreviated agreement title used	Agreement title	Citation	Qualification re application of pt. I	Different Qualification re application of pt. II	Different date re certain concessions	date re certain parties	Different termination period
(1)	(2)	(3)	(4)	(5)	(6)	(7)	(8)
-	Third Protocol of Supplementary Concessions to the General Agreement on Tariffs and Trade (Denmark and Federal Republic of Germany), 15 July 1955	250 UNTS 292	-	-	Par. 2 (*a*)	-	-
-	Fourth Protocol of Supplementary Concessions to the General Agreement on Tariffs and Trade (Denmark and Federal Republic of Germany), 15 July 1955	250 UNTS 297	-	-	Par. 2 (*a*)	-	
-	Fifth Protocol of Supplementary Concessions to the General Agreement on Tariffs and Trade (Federal Republic of Germany and Sweden), 15 July 1955	250 UNTS 301	-	-	Par. 2 (*a*)	-	
1955 Rectif.P.-V.	Procs-Verbal of Rectification Concerning the Protocol Amending Part I and Articles XXIX and XXX	278 UNTS 246	-	-	-	-	-

Contd.

Abbreviated agreement title used	*Agreement title*	*Citation*	*Qualification re application of pt. I*	*Qualification re application of pt. II*	*Different date re certain concessions*	*Different date re certain parties*	*Different termination period*
(1)	(2)	(3)	(4)	(5)	(6)	(7)	(8)
	of the General Agreement on Tariffs and Trade, the Protocol Amending the Preamble and Parts II and III of the General Agreement on Tariffs and Trade and the Protocol of Organizational Amendments to the General Agreement on Tariffs and Trade, 3 December 1955						
-	Sixth Protocol of Supplementary Concessions to the General Agreement on Tariffs and Trade, 23 May 1956	244 UNTS 2	-	-	Par. 4	-	-
-	Seventh Protocol of Supplementary Concessions to the General Agreement on Tariffs and Trade (Austria and Federal Republic of Germany), 19 February 1957	309 UNTS 364	–	-	Par. 4	-	-
-	Eighth Protocol of Supplementary	274 UNTS 322	-	-	Par. 2	-	-

Contd.

Abbreviated agreement title used	*Agreement title*	*Citation*	*Qualification re application of pt. I*	*Qualification re application of pt. II*	*Different date re certain concessions*	*Different date re certain parties*	*Different termination period*
(1)	(2)	(3)	(4)	(5)	(6)	(7)	(8)
	Concessions to the General Agreement on Tariffs and Trade (Cuba and United States of America), 20 June 1957						
-	Protocol relating to Negotiations for the Establishment of New Schedule III - Brazil - to the General Agreement on Tariffs and Trade, 31 December 1958	398 UNTS 318	-	-	Par. 7	-	-
1960 Art. XVI:4 Prohib. Decl	Declaration giving effect to the Provisions of Article XVI:4 of the General Agreement on Tariffs and Trade, 19 November 1960	445 UNTS 294	-	-	-	-	-
-	Protocol for the Accession of Portugal to the General Agreement on Tariffs and Trade, 6 April 1962	431 UNTS 208	Par. 3	Par. 1 (*b*)	Par. 7	Par. 2 (*b*)	Par. 12
-	Protocol for the Accession of Israel to the General Agree-	431 UNTS 244	-	Par. 1 (*b*)	Par. 6	Par. 2 (*b*)	Par. 10

Contd.

Abbreviated agreement title used	*Agreement title*	*Citation*	*Qualification re application of pt. I*	*Qualification re application of pt. II*	*Different date re certain concessions*	*Different date re certain parties*	*Different termination period*
(1)	(2)	(3)	(4)	(5)	(6)	(7)	(8)
	ment on Tariffs and Trade, 6 April 1962						
-	Protocol to the General Agreement on Tariffs and Trade, Embodying Result of the 1960-61 Tariff Conference, 16 July 1962	440 UNTS 2	-	-	Par. 5	-	-
-	Tenth Protocol of Supplementary Concessions to the General Agreement on Tariffs and Trade (Japan and New Zealand), 28 January 1963	476 UNTS 254	-	-	Par. 4	-	-
-	Protocol Supplementary to the Protocol to the General Agreement on Tariffs and Trade embodying results of the 1960-61 Tariff Conference, 6 May 1963	501 UNTS 304	-	-	Par. 4	-	-
-	Protocol for the Accession of Spain to the General Agreement on Tariffs and Trade, 1 July 1963	476 UNTS 264	Par. 4	Par. 1 (*b*)	Par. 8	Par. 2 (*b*)	Par. 12

Contd.

Abbreviated agreement title used	*Agreement title*	*Citation*	*Qualification* re *application of pt. I*	*Qualification* re *application of pt. II*	*Different date* re *certain concessions*	*Different date* re *certain parties*	*Different termination period*
(1)	(2)	(3)	(4)	(5)	(6)	(7)	(8)
1965 Pt. IV Prot.	Protocol amending the General Agreement on Tariffs and Trade to introduce a Part IV on Trade and Development, 8 February 1965	GATT, Final Act 2nd Sp. Sess. 25	-	-	-	-	-
-	Protocol for the Accession of Switzerland to the General Agreement on Tariffs and Trade, 1 April 1966	GATT, Prot. Acc. Switz	-	Pars. 1 (*b*), 4 and 5	Par. 9	Par. 2 (*b*)	Par. 15
-	Protocol for the Accession of Yugoslavia to the General Agreement on Tariffs and Trade, 20 July 1966.	GATT, Prot. Acc. Yugo.	-	Par. 1 (*b*)	Par. 4	Par. 2 (*b*)	Par. 9
-	Protocol for the Accession of Korea to the General Agreement on Tariffs and Trade, 2 March 1967	GATT, Prot. Acc. Korea	-	Par. 1 (*b*)	Par. 4	Par. 2 (*b*)	Par. 9
-	Geneva (1967) Protocol to the	GATT, Instrs.	-	-	Par. 4	-	-

Contd.

Abbreviated agreement title used	*Agreement title*	*Citation*	*Qualification* re *application of pt. I*	*Qualification* re *application of pt. II*	*Different date* re *certain concessions*	*Different date* re *certain parties*	*Different termination period*
(1)	(2)	(3)	(4)	(5)	(6)	(7)	(8)
	General Agreement on Tariffs and Trade, 30 June 1967	1964-67 Conf., I, 21					
-	Protocol for the Accession of Argentina to the General Agreement on Tariffs and Trade, 30 June 1967	GATT, Instrs. 1964-67 Conf., V, 3719	-	Par. 1 (*b*)	Par. 4	Par. 2 (*b*)	Par. 9
-	Protocol for the Accession of Iceland to the General Agreement on Tariffs and Trade, 30 June 1967	GATT, Instrs. 1964-67 Conf., V, 3763	-	Par. 1 (*b*)	Par. 4	Par. 2 (*b*)	Par. 9
-	Protocol for the Accession of Ireland to the General Agreement on Tariffs and Trade, 30 June 1967	GATT, Instrs. 1964-67 Conf., V, 3789	Par. 2 (b)	Par. 1 (*b*)	Par. 4	Par. 2 (*c*)	Par. 9
-	Protocol for the Accession of Poland to the General Agreement on Tariffs and Trade, 30 June 1967	GATT, Instrs. 1964-67 Conf., V, 3959	Pars. 4 and 7	Par. 1 (*b*), 3,4,7 and 8	-	Par. 2 (*b*)	Par. 14

UNDERSTANDING ON THE INTERPRETATION OF ARTICLE II:1(B) OF THE GENERAL AGREEMENT ON TARIFFS AND TRADE 1994

Members hereby agree as follows:

1. In order to ensure transparency of the legal rights and obligations deriving from paragraph 1(b) of Article II, the nature and level of any "other duties or charges" levied on bound tariff items, as referred to in that provision, shall be recorded in the Schedules of concessions annexed to GATT 1994 against the tariff item to which they apply. It is understood that such recording does not change the legal character of "other duties or charges".

2. The date as of which "other duties or charges" are bound, for the purposes of Article II, shall be 15 April 1994. "Other duties or charges" shall therefore be recorded in the Schedules at the levels applying on this date. At each subsequent renegotiation of a concession or negotiation of a new concession the applicable date for the tariff item in question shall become the date of the incorporation of the new concession in the appropriate Schedule. However, the date of the instrument by which a concession on any particular tariff item was first incorporated into GATT 1947 or GATT 1994 shall also continue to be recorded in column 6 of the Loose-Leaf Schedules.

3. "Other duties or charges" shall be recorded in respect of all tariff bindings.

4. Where a tariff item has previously been the subject of a concession, the level of "other duties or charges" recorded in the appropriate Schedule shall not be higher than the level obtaining at the time of the first incorporation of the concession in that Schedule. It will be open to any Member to challenge the existence of an "other duty or charge", on the ground that no such "other duty or charge" existed at the time of the original binding of the item in question, as well as the consistency of the recorded level of any "other duty or charge" with the previously bound level, for a period of three years after the date of entry into force of the WTO Agreement or three years after the date of deposit with the Director-General of the WTO of the instrument incorporating the Schedule in question into GATT 1994, if that is a later date.

5. The recording of "other duties or charges" in the Schedules is without prejudice to their consistency with rights and obligations under GATT 1994 other than those affected by paragraph 4. All Members retain the right to challenge, at any time, the consistency of any "other duty or charge" with such obligations.

6. For the purposes of this Understanding, the provisions of Articles XXII and XXIII of GATT 1994 as elaborated and applied by the Dispute Settlement Understanding shall apply.

7. "Other duties or charges" omitted from a Schedule at the time of deposit of the instrument incorporating the Schedule in question into GATT 1994 with, until the date of entry into force of the WTO Agreement, the Director-General to the CONTRACTING PARTIES to GATT 1947 or, thereafter, with the Director-General of the WTO, shall not subsequently be added to it and any "other duty or charge" recorded at a level lower than that prevailing on the applicable date shall not be restored to that level unless such additions or changes are made within six months of the date of deposit of the instrument.

8. The decision in paragraph 2 regarding the date applicable to each concession for the purposes of paragraph 1(b) of Article II of GATT 1994 supersedes the decision regarding the applicable date taken on 26 March 1980 (BISD 27S/24).

UNDERSTANDING ON THE INTERPRETATION OF ARTICLE XVII OF THE GENERAL AGREEMENT ON TARIFFS AND TRADE 1994

Members,

Noting that Article XVII provides for obligations on Members in respect of the activities of the state trading enterprises referred to in paragraph 1 of Article XVII, which are required to be consistent with the general principles of non-discriminatory treatment prescribed in GATT 1994 for governmental measures affecting imports or exports by private traders;

Noting further that Members are subject to their GATT 1994 obligations in respect of those governmental measures affecting state trading enterprises;

Recognizing that this Understanding is without prejudice to the substantive disciplines prescribed in Article XVII;

Hereby *agree* as follows:

1. In order to ensure the transparency of the activities of state trading enterprises, Members shall notify such enterprises to the Council for Trade in Goods, for review by the working party to be set up under paragraph 5, in accordance with the following working definition:

> "Governmental and non-governmental enterprises, including marketing boards, which have been granted exclusive or special rights or privileges, including statutory or constitutional powers, in the exercise of which they influence through their purchases or sales the level or direction of imports or exports."

This notification requirement does not apply to imports of products for immediate or ultimate consumption in governmental use or in use by an enterprise as specified above and not otherwise for resale or use in the production of goods for sale.

2. Each Member shall conduct a review of its policy with regard to the submission of notifications on state trading enterprises to the Council for Trade in Goods, taking account of the provisions of this Understanding. In carrying out such a review, each Member should have regard to the need to ensure the maximum transparency possible in its notifications so as to permit a clear appreciation of the manner of operation of the enterprises notified and the effect of their operations on international trade.

3. Notifications shall be made in accordance with the questionnaire on state trading adopted on 24 May 1960 (BISD 9S/184-185), it being understood that Members shall notify the enterprises referred to in paragraph 1 whether or not imports or exports have in fact taken place.

4. Any Member which has reason to believe that another Member has not adequately met its notification obligation may raise the matter with the Member concerned. If the matter is not satisfactorily resolved it may make a counter-notification to the Council for Trade in Goods, for consideration by the working party set up under paragraph 5, simultaneously informing the Member concerned.

5. A working party shall be set up, on behalf of the Council for Trade in Goods, to review notifications and counter-notifications.

In the light of this review and without prejudice to paragraph 4(c) of Article XVII, the Council for Trade in Goods may make recommendations with regard to the adequacy of notifications and the need for further information. The working party shall also review, in the light of the notifications received, the adequacy of the above-mentioned questionnaire on state trading and the coverage of state trading enterprises notified under paragraph 1. It shall also develop an illustrative list showing the kinds of relationships between governments and enterprises, and the kinds of activities, engaged in by these enterprises, which may be relevant for the purposes of Article XVII. It is understood that the Secretariat will provide a general background paper for the working party on the operations of state trading enterprises as they relate to international trade. Membership of the working party shall be open to all Members indicating their wish to serve on it. It shall meet within a year of the date of entry into force of the WTO Agreement and thereafter at least once a year. It shall report annually to the Council for Trade in Goods.[1]

UNDERSTANDING ON THE BALANCE-OF PAYMENTS PROVISIONS OF THE GENERAL AGREEMENT ON TARIFFS AND TRADE 1994

Members,

Recognizing the provisions of Articles XII and XVIII:B of GATT 1994 and of the Declaration on Trade Measures Taken for Balance-of-Payments Purposes adopted on 28 November 1979 (BISD 26S/205-209, referred to in this Understanding as the "1979 Declaration") and in order to clarify such provisions[1];

Hereby *agree* as follows:

Application of Measures

1. Members confirm their commitment to announce publicly,

1. The activities of this working party shall be coordinated with those of the working group provided for in Section III of the Ministerial Decision on Notification Procedures adopted on 15 April 1994.

1. Nothing in this Understanding is intended to modify the rights and obligations of Members under Articles XII or XVIII:B of GATT 1994. The provisions of Articles XXII and XXIII of GATT 1994 as elaborated and applied by the Dispute Settlement Understanding may be invoked with respect to any matters arising from the application of restrictive import measures taken for balance-of-payments purposes.

as soon as possible, time-schedules for the removal of restrictive import measures taken for balance-of-payments purposes. It is understood that such time-schedules may be modified as appropriate to take into account changes in the balance-of-payments situation. Whenever a time-schedule is not publicly announced by a Member, that Member shall provide justification as to the reasons therefor.

2. Members confirm their commitment to give preference to those measures which have the least disruptive effect on trade. Such measures (referred to in this Understanding as "price-based measures") shall be understood to include import surcharges, import deposit requirements or other equivalent trade measures with an impact on the price of imported goods. It is understood that, notwithstanding the provisions of Article II, price-based measures taken for balance-of-payments purposes may be applied by a Member in excess of the duties inscribed in the Schedule of that Member. Furthermore, that Member shall indicate the amount by which the price-based measure exceeds the bound duty clearly and separately under the notification procedures of this Understanding.

3. Members shall seek to avoid the imposition of new quantitative restrictions for balance-of-payments purposes unless, because of a critical balance-of-payments situation, price-based measures cannot arrest a sharp deterioration in the external payments position. In those cases in which a Member applies .quantitative restrictions, it shall provide justification as to the reasons why price-based measures are not an adequate instrument to deal with the balance-of-payments situation. A Member maintaining quantitative restrictions shall indicate in successive consultations the progress made in significantly reducing the incidence and restrictive effect of such measures. It is understood that not more than one type of restrictive import measure taken for balance-of-payments purposes may be applied on the same product.

4. Members confirm that restrictive import measures taken for balance-of-payments purposes may only be applied to control the general level of imports and may not exceed what is necessary to address the balance-of-payments situation. In order to minimize any incidental protective effects, a Member shall administer restrictions in a transparent manner. The authorities of the importing Member shall provide adequate justification as to the criteria used to determine which products are subject to restriction. As provided in paragraph

3 of Article XII and paragraph 10 of Article XVIII, Members may, in the case of certain essential products, exclude or limit the application of surcharges applied across the board or other measures applied for balance-of-payments purposes. The term "essential products" shall be understood to mean products which meet basic consumption needs or which contribute to the Member's effort to improve its balance-of-payments situation, such as capital goods or inputs needed for production. In the administration of quantitative restrictions, a Member shall use discretionary licensing only when unavoidable and shall phase it out progressively. Appropriate justification shall be provided as to the criteria used to determine allowable import quantities or values.

Procedures for Balance-of-Payments Consultations

5. The Committee on Balance-of-Payments Restrictions (referred to in this Understanding as the "Committee") shall carry out consultations in order to review all restrictive import measures taken for balance-of-payments purposes. The membership of the Committee is open to all Members indicating their wish to serve on it. The Committee shall follow the procedures for consultations on balance-of-payments restrictions approved on 28 April 1970 (BISD 18S/48-53, referred to in this Understanding as "full consultation procedures"), subject to the provisions set out below.

6. A Member applying new restrictions or raising the general level of its existing restrictions by a substantial intensification of the measures shall enter into consultations with the Committee within four months of the adoption of such measures. The Member adopting such measures may request that a consultation be held under paragraph 4(a) of Article XII or paragraph 12(a) of Article XVIII as appropriate. If no such request has been made, the Chairman of the Committee shall invite the Member to hold such a consultation. Factors that may be examined in the consultation would include, *inter alia*, the introduction of new types of restrictive measures for balance-of-payments purposes, or an increase in the level or product coverage of restrictions.

7. All restrictions applied for balance-of-payments purposes shall be subject to periodic review in the Committee under paragraph 4(b) of Article XII or under paragraph 12(b) of Article XVIII, subject to the possibility of altering the periodicity of consultations in agreement

with the consulting Member or pursuant to any specific review procedure that may be recommended by the General Council.

8. Consultations may be held under the simplified procedures approved on 19 December 1972 (BISD 20S/47-49, referred to in this Understanding as "simplified consultation procedures") in the case of least-developed country Members or in the case of developing country Members which are pursuing liberalization efforts in conformity with the schedule presented to the Committee in previous consultations. Simplified consultation procedures may also be used when the Trade Policy Review of a developing country Member is scheduled for the same calendar year as the date fixed for the consultations. In such cases the decision as to whether full consultation procedures should be used will be made on the basis of the factors enumerated in paragraph 8 of the 1979 Declaration. Except in the case of least-developed country Members, no more than two successive consultations may be held under simplified consultation procedures.

Notification and Documentation

9. A Member shall notify to the General Council the introduction of or any changes in the application of restrictive import measures taken for balance-of-payments purposes, as well as any modifications in time-schedules for the removal of such measures as announced under paragraph 1. Significant changes shall be notified to the General Council prior to or not later than 30 days after their announcement. On a yearly basis, each Member shall make available to the Secretariat a consolidated notification, including all changes in laws, regulations, policy statements or public notices, for examination by Members. Notifications shall include full information, as far as possible, at the tariff-line level, on the type of measures applied, the criteria used for their administration, product coverage and trade flows affected.

10. At the request of any Member, notifications may be reviewed by the Committee. Such reviews would be limited to the clarification of specific issues raised by a notification or examination of whether a consultation under paragraph 4(a) of Article XII or paragraph 12(a) of Article XVIII is required. Members which have reasons to believe that a restrictive import measure applied by another Member was taken for balance-of-payments purposes may bring the matter to the attention of the Committee. The Chairman of the Committee shall request information on the measure and make it available to all

Members. Without prejudice to the right of any member of the Committee to seek appropriate clarifications in the course of consultations, questions may be submitted in advance for consideration by the consulting Member.

11. The consulting Member shall prepare a Basic Document for the consultations which, in addition to any other information considered to be relevant, should include: *(a)* an overview of the balance-of-payments situation and prospects, including a consideration of the internal and external factors having a bearing on the balance-of-payments situation and the domestic policy measures taken in order to restore equilibrium on a sound and lasting basis; *(b)* a full description of the restrictions applied for balance-of-payments purposes, their legal basis and steps taken to reduce incidental protective effects; *(c)* measures taken since the last consultation to liberalize import restrictions, in the light of the conclusions of the Committee; *(d)* a plan for the elimination and progressive relaxation of remaining restrictions. References may be made, when relevant, to the information provided in other notifications or reports made to the WTO. Under simplified consultation procedures, the consulting Member shall submit a written statement containing essential information on the elements covered by the Basic Document.

12. The Secretariat shall, with a view to facilitating the consultations in the Committee, prepare a factual background paper dealing with the different aspects of the plan for consultations. In the case of developing country Members, the Secretariat document shall include relevant background and analytical material on the incidence of the external trading environment on the balance-of-payments situation and prospects of the consulting Member. The technical assistance services of the Secretariat shall, at the request of a developing country Member, assist in preparing the documentation for the consultations.

Conclusions of Balance-of-Payments Consultations

13. The Committee shall report on its consultations to the General Council. When full consultation procedures have been used, the report should indicate the Committee's conclusions on the different elements of the plan for consultations, as well as the facts and reasons on which they are based. The Committee shall endeavour to include in its conclusions proposals for recommendations aimed at promoting the implementation of Articles XII and XVIII:B, the 1979

Declaration and this Understanding. In those cases in which a time-schedule has been presented for the removal of restrictive measures taken for balance-of-payments purposes, the General Council may recommend that, in adhering to such a time-schedule, a Member shall be deemed to be in compliance with its GATT 1994 obligations. Whenever the General Council has made specific recommendations, the rights and obligations of Members shall be assessed in the light of such recommendations. In the absence of specific proposals for recommendations by the General Council, the Committee's conclusions should record the different views expressed in the Committee. When simplified consultation procedures have been used, the report shall include a summary of the main elements discussed in the Committee and a decision on whether full consultation procedures are required.

UNDERSTANDING ON THE INTERPRETATION OF ARTICLE XXIV OF THE GENERAL AGREEMENT ON TARIFFS AND TRADE 1994

Members,

Having regard to the provisions of Article XXIV of GATT 1994;

Recognizing that customs unions and free trade areas have greatly increased in number and importance since the establishment of GATT 1947 and today cover a significant proportion of world trade;

Recognizing the contribution to the expansion of world trade that may be made by closer integration between the economies of the parties to such agreements;

Recognizing also that such contribution is increased if the elimination between the constituent territories of duties and other restrictive regulations of commerce extends to all trade, and diminished if any major sector of trade is excluded;

Reaffirming that the purpose of such agreements should be to facilitate trade between the constituent territories and not to raise barriers to the trade of other Members with such tèrritories; and that in their formation or enlargement the parties to them should to the greatest possible extent avoid creating adverse effects on the trade of other Members;

Convinced also of the need to reinforce the effectiveness of the role of the Council for Trade in Goods in reviewing agreements notified under Article XXIV, by clarifying the criteria and procedures for the assessment of new or enlarged agreements, and improving the transparency of all Article XXIV agreements;

Recognizing the need for a common understanding of the obligations of Members under paragraph 12 of Article XXIV;

Hereby *agree* as follows:

1. Customs unions, free-trade areas, and interim agreements leading to the formation of a customs union or free-trade area, to be consistent with Article XXIV, must satisfy, *inter alia*, the provisions of paragraphs 5, 6, 7 and 8 of that Article.

Article XXIV:5

2. The evaluation under paragraph 5(a) of Article XXIV of the general incidence of the duties and other regulations of commerce applicable before and after the formation of a customs union shall in respect of duties and charges be based upon an overall assessment of weighted average tariff rates and of customs duties collected. This assessment shall be based on import statistics for a previous representative period to be supplied by the customs union, on a tariff-line basis and in values and quantities, broken down by WTO country of origin. The Secretariat shall compute the weighted average tariff rates and customs duties collected in accordance with the methodology used in the assessment of tariff offers in the Uruguay Round of Multilateral Trade Negotiations. For this purpose, the duties and charges to be taken into consideration shall be the applied rates of duty. It is recognized that for the purpose of the overall assessment of the incidence of other regulations of commerce for which quantification and aggregation are difficult, the examination of individual measures, regulations, products covered and trade flows affected may be required.

3. The "reasonable length of time" referred to in paragraph 5(c) of Article XXIV should exceed 10 years only in exceptional cases. In cases where Members parties to an interim agreement believe that 10 years would be insufficient they shall provide a full explanation to the Council for Trade in Goods of the need for a longer period.

Article XXIV:6

4. Paragraph 6 of Article XXIV establishes the procedure to be followed when a Member forming a customs union proposes to increase a bound rate of duty. In this regard Members reaffirm that the procedure set forth in Article XXVIII, as elaborated in the

guidelines adopted on 10 November 1980 (BISD 27S/26-28) and in the Understanding on the Interpretation of Article XXVIII of GATT 1994, must be commenced before tariff concessions are modified or withdrawn upon the formation of a customs union or an interim agreement leading to the formation of a customs union.

5. These negotiations will be entered into in good faith with a view to achieving mutually satisfactory compensatory adjustment. In such negotiations, as required by paragraph 6 of Article XXIV, due account shall be taken of reductions of duties on the same tariff line made by other constituents of the customs union upon its formation. Should such reductions not be sufficient to provide the necessary compensatory adjustment, the customs union would offer compensation, which may take the form of reductions of duties on other tariff lines. Such an offer shall be taken into consideration by the Members having negotiating rights in the binding being modified or withdrawn. Should the compensatory adjustment remain unacceptable, negotiations should be continued. Where, despite such efforts, agreement in negotiations on compensatory adjustment under Article XXVIII as elaborated by the Understanding on the Interpretation of Article XXVIII of GATT 1994 cannot be reached within a reasonable period from the initiation of negotiations, the customs union shall, nevertheless, be free to modify or withdraw the concessions; affected Members shall then be free to withdraw substantially equivalent concessions in accordance with Article XXVIII.

6. GATT 1994 imposes no obligation on Members benefiting from a reduction of duties consequent upon the formation of a customs union, or an interim agreement leading to the formation of a customs union, to provide compensatory adjustment to its constituents.

Review of Customs Unions and Free-Trade Areas

7. All notifications made under paragraph 7(a) of Article XXIV shall be examined by a working party in the light of the relevant provisions of GATT 1994 and of paragraph 1 of this Understanding. The working party shall submit a report to the Council for Trade in Goods on its findings in this regard. The Council for Trade in Goods may make such recommendations to Members as it deems appropriate.

8. In regard to interim agreements, the working party may in its report make appropriate recommendations on the proposed time-

frame and on measures required to complete the formation of the customs union or free-trade area. It may if necessary provide for further review of the agreement.

9. Members parties to an interim agreement shall notify substantial changes in the plan and schedule included in that agreement to the Council for Trade in Goods and, if so requested, the Council shall examine the changes.

10. Should an interim agreement notified under paragraph 7(a) of Article XXIV not include a plan and schedule, contrary to paragraph 5(c) of Article XXIV, the working party shall in its report recommend such a plan and schedule. The parties shall not maintain or put into force, as the case may be, such agreement if they are not prepared to modify it in accordance with these recommendations. Provision shall be made for subsequent review of the implementation of the recommendations.

11. Customs unions and constituents of free-trade areas shall report periodically to the Council for Trade in Goods, as envisaged by the CONTRACTING PARTIES to GATT 1947 in their instruction to the GATT 1947 Council concerning reports on regional agreements (BISD 18S/38), on the operation of the relevant agreement. Any significant changes and/or developments in the agreements should be reported as they occur.

Dispute Settlement

12. The provisions of Articles XXII and XXIII of GATT 1994 as elaborated and applied by the Dispute Settlement Understanding may be invoked with respect to any matters arising from the application of those provisions of Article XXIV relating to customs unions, free-trade areas or interim agreements leading to the formation of a customs union or free-trade area.

Article XXIV:12

13. Each Member is fully responsible under GATT 1994 for the observance of all provisions of GATT 1994, and shall take such reasonable measures as may be available to it to ensure such observance by regional and local governments and authorities within its territory.

14. The provisions of Articles XXII and XXIII of GATT 1994 as elaborated and applied by the Dispute Settlement Understanding

may be invoked in respect of measures affecting its observance taken by regional or local governments or authorities within the territory of a Member. When the Dispute Settlement Body has ruled that a provision of GATT 1994 has not been observed, the responsible Member shall take such reasonable measures as may be available to it to ensure its observance. The provisions relating to compensation and suspension of concessions or other obligations apply in cases where it has not been possible to secure such observance.

15. Each Member undertakes to accord sympathetic consideration to and afford adequate opportunity for consultation regarding any representations made by another Member concerning measures affecting the operation of GATT 1994 taken within the territory of the former.

UNDERSTANDING IN RESPECT OF WAIVERS OF OBLIGATIONS UNDER THE GENERAL AGREEMENT ON TARIFFS AND TRADE 1994

Members hereby *agree* as follows:

1. A request for a waiver or for an extension of an existing waiver shall describe the measures which the Member proposes to take, the specific policy objectives which the Member seeks to pursue and the reasons which prevent the Member from achieving its policy objectives by measures consistent with its obligations under GATT 1994.

2. Any waiver in effect on the date of entry into force of the WTO Agreement shall terminate, unless extended in accordance with the procedures above and those of Article IX of the WTO Agreement, on the date of its expiry or two years from the date of entry into force of the WTO Agreement, whichever is earlier.

3. Any Member considering that a benefit accruing to it under GATT 1994 is being nullified or impaired as a result of:

(a) the failure of the Member to whom a waiver was granted to observe the terms or conditions of the waiver, or

(b) the application of a measure consistent with the terms and conditions of the waiver

may invoke the provisions of Article XXIII of GATT 1994 as elaborated and applied by the Dispute Settlement Understanding.

UNDERSTANDING ON THE INTERPRETATION OF ARTICLE XXVIII OF THE GENERAL AGREEMENT ON TARIFFS AND TRADE 1994

Members hereby *agree* as follows:

1. For the purposes of modification or withdrawal of a concession, the Member which has the highest ratio of exports affected by the concession (i.e. exports of the product to the market of the Member modifying or withdrawing the concession) to its total exports shall be deemed to have a principal supplying interest if it does not already have an initial negotiating right or a principal supplying interest as provided for in paragraph 1 of Article XXVIII. It is however agreed that this paragraph will be reviewed by the Council for Trade in Goods five years from the date of entry into force of the WTO Agreement with a view to deciding whether this criterion has worked satisfactorily in securing a redistribution of negotiating rights in favour of small and medium-sized exporting Members. If this is not the case, consideration will be given to possible improvements, including, in the light of the availability of adequate data, the adoption of a criterion based on the ratio of exports affected by the concession to exports to all markets of the product in question.

2. Where a Member considers that it has a principal supplying interest in terms of paragraph 1, it should communicate its claim in writing, with supporting evidence, to the Member proposing to modify or withdraw a concession, and at the same time inform the Secretariat. Paragraph 4 of the "Procedures for Negotiations under Article XXVIII" adopted on 10 November 1980 (BISD 27S/26-28) shall apply in these cases.

3. In the determination of which Members have a principal supplying interest (whether as provided for in paragraph 1 above or in paragraph 1 of Article XXVIII) or substantial interest, only trade in the affected product which has taken place on an MFN basis shall be taken into consideration. However, trade in the affected product which has taken place under non-contractual preferences shall also be taken into account if the trade in question has ceased to benefit from such preferential treatment, thus becoming MFN trade, at the time of the negotiation for the modification or withdrawal of the concession, or will do so by the conclusion of that negotiation.

4. When a tariff concession is modified or withdrawn on a new product (i.e. a product for which three years' trade statistics are not available) the Member possessing initial negotiating rights on the tariff line where the product is or was formerly classified shall be deemed to have an initial negotiating right in the concession in question. The determination of principal supplying and substantial interests and the calculation of compensation shall take into account, *inter alia,* production capacity and investment in the affected product in the exporting Member and estimates of export growth, as well as forecasts of demand for the product in the importing Member. For the purposes of this paragraph, "new product" is understood to include a tariff item created by means of a breakout from an existing tariff line.

5. Where a Member considers that it has a principal supplying or a substantial interest in terms of paragraph 4, it should communicate its claim in writing, with supporting evidence, to the Member proposing to modify or withdraw a concession, and at the same time inform the Secretariat. Paragraph 4 of the above-mentioned "Procedures for Negotiations under Article XXVIII" shall apply in these cases.

6. When an unlimited tariff concession is replaced by a tariff rate quota, the amount of compensation provided should exceed the amount of the trade actually affected by the modification of the concession. The basis for the calculation of compensation should be the amount by which future trade prospects exceed the level of the quota. It is understood that the calculation of future trade prospects should be based on the greater of:

(a) the average annual trade in the most recent representative three-year period, increased by the average annual growth rate of imports in that same period, or by 10 per cent, whichever is the greater; or

(b) trade in the most recent year increased by 10 per cent.

In no case shall a Member's liability for compensation exceed that which would be entailed by complete withdrawal of the concession.

7. Any Member having a principal supplying interest, whether as provided for in paragraph 1 above or in paragraph 1 of Article XXVIII, in a concession which is modified or withdrawn shall be accorded an initial negotiating right in the compensatory concessions,

unless another form of compensation is agreed by the Members concerned.

MARRAKESH PROTOCOL TO THE GENERAL AGREEMENT ON TARIFFS AND TRADE 1994

Members,

Having carried out negotiations within the framework of GATT 1947, pursuant to the Ministerial Declaration on the Uruguay Round,

Hereby *agree* as follows:

1. The schedule annexed to this Protocol relating to a Member shall become a Schedule to GATT 1994 relating to that Member on the day on which the WTO Agreement enters into force for that Member. Any schedule submitted in accordance with the Ministerial Decision on measures in favour of least-developed countries shall be deemed to be annexed to this Protocol.

2. The tariff reductions agreed upon by each Member shall be implemented in five equal rate reductions, except as may be otherwise specified in a Member's Schedule. The first such reduction shall be made effective on the date of entry into force of the WTO Agreement, each successive reduction shall be made effective on 1 January of each of the following years, and the final rate shall become effective no later than the date four years after the date of entry into force of the WTO Agreement, except as may be otherwise specified in that Member's Schedule. Unless otherwise specified in its Schedule, a Member that accepts the WTO Agreement after its entry into force shall, on the date that Agreement enters into force for it, make effective all rate reductions that have already taken place together with the reductions which it would under the preceding sentence have been obligated to make effective on 1 January of the year following, and shall make effective all remaining rate reductions on the schedule specified in the previous sentence. The reduced rate should in each stage be rounded off to the first decimal. For agricultural products, as defined in Article 2 of the Agreement on Agriculture, the staging of reductions shall be implemented as specified in the relevant parts of the schedules.

3. The implementation of the concessions and commitments contained in the schedules annexed to this Protocol shall, upon request, be subject to multilateral examination by the Members. This

would be without prejudice to the rights and obligations of Members under Agreements in Annex 1A of the WTO Agreement.

4. After the schedule annexed to this Protocol relating to a Member has become a Schedule to GATT 1994 pursuant to the provisions of paragraph 1, such Member shall be free at any time to withhold or to withdraw in whole or in part the concession in such Schedule with respect to any product for which the principal supplier is any other Uruguay Round participant the schedule of which has not yet become a Schedule to GATT 1994. Such action can, however, only be taken after written notice of any such withholding or withdrawal of a concession has been given to the Council for Trade in Goods and after consultations have been held, upon request, with any Member, the relevant schedule relating to which has become a Schedule to GATT 1994 and which has a substantial interest in the product involved. Any concessions so withheld or withdrawn shall be applied on and after the day on which the schedule of the Member which has the principal supplying interest becomes a Schedule to GATT 1994.

5. (a) Without prejudice to the provisions of paragraph 2 of Article 4 of the Agreement on Agriculture, for the purpose of the reference in paragraphs 1:(b) and 1(c) of Article II of GATT 1994 to the date of that Agreement, the applicable date in respect of each product which is the subject of a concession provided for in a schedule of concessions annexed to this Protocol shall be the date of this Protocol.

(b) For the purpose of the reference in paragraph 6(a) of Article II of GATT 1994 to the date of that Agreement, the applicable date in respect of a schedule of concessions annexed to this Protocol shall be the date of this Protocol.

6. In cases of modification or withdrawal of concessions relating to non-tariff measures as contained in Part III of the schedules, the provisions of Article XXVIII of GATT 1994 and the "Procedures for Negotiations under Article XXVIII" adopted on 10 November 1980 (BISD 27S/26-28) shall apply. This would be without prejudice to the rights and obligations of Members under GATT 1994.

7. In each case in which a schedule annexed to this Protocol

results for any product in treatment less favourable than was provided for such product in the Schedules of GATT 1947 prior to the entry into force of the WTO Agreement, the Member to whom the schedule relates shall be deemed to have taken appropriate action as would have been otherwise necessary under the relevant provisions of Article XXVIII of GATT 1947 or 1994. The provisions of this paragraph shall apply only to Egypt, Peru, South Africa and Uruguay.

8. The Schedules annexed hereto are authentic in the English, French or Spanish language as specified in each Schedule.

9. The date of this Protocol is 15 April 1994.

[The agreed schedules of participants will be annexed to the Marrakesh Protocol in the treaty copy of the WTO Agreement.]

AGREEMENT ON AGRICULTURE

Members,

Having decided to establish a basis for initiating a process of reform of trade in agriculture in line with the objectives of the negotiations as set out in the Punta del Este Declaration;

Recalling that their long-term objective as agreed at the Mid-Term Review of the Uruguay Round "is to establish a fair and market-oriented agricultural trading system and that a reform process should be initiated through the negotiation of commitments on support and protection and through the establishment of strengthened and more operationally effective GATT rules and disciplines";

Recalling further that "the above-mentioned long-term objective is to provide for substantial progressive reductions in agricultural support and protection sustained over an agreed period of time, resulting in correcting and preventing restrictions and distortions in world agricultural markets";

Committed to achieving specific binding commitments in each of the following areas: market access; domestic support; export competition; and to reaching an agreement on sanitary and phytosanitary issues;

Having agreed that in implementing their commitments on market access, developed country Members would take fully into account the particular needs and conditions of developing country Members by providing for a greater improvement of opportunities and terms of access for agricultural products of particular interest to these

Members, including the fullest liberalization of trade in tropical agricultural products as agreed at the Mid-Term Review, and for products of particular importance to the diversification of production from the growing of illicit narcotic crops;

Noting that commitments under the reform programme should be made in an equitable way among all Members, having regard to non-trade concerns, including food security and the need to protect the environment; having regard to the agreement that special and differential treatment for developing countries is an integral element of the negotiations, and taking into account the possible negative effects of the implementation of the reform programme on least-developed and net food-importing developing countries;

Hereby *agree* as follows:

PART I

ARTICLE 1

Definition of Terms

In this Agreement, unless the context otherwise requires:

(a) "Aggregate Measurement of Support" and "AMS" mean the annual level of support, expressed in monetary terms, provided for an agricultural product in favour of the producers of the basic agricultural product or non-product-specific support provided in favour of agricultural producers in general, other than support provided under programmes that qualify as exempt from reduction under Annex 2 to this Agreement, which is:

(i) with respect to support provided during the base period, specified in the relevant tables of supporting material incorporated by reference in Part IV of a Member's Schedule; and

(ii) with respect to support provided during any year of the implementation period and thereafter, calculated in accordance with the provisions of Annex 3 of this Agreement and taking into account the constituent data and methodology used in the tables of supporting material incorporated by reference in Part IV of the Member's Schedule;

(b) "basic agricultural product" in relation to domestic support commitments is defined as the product as close as practicable to the point of first sale as specified in a Member's Schedule and in the related supporting material;

(c) "budgetary outlays" or "outlays" includes revenue foregone;

(d) "Equivalent Measurement of Support" means the annual level of support, expressed in monetary terms, provided to producers of a basic agricultural product through the application of one or more measures, the calculation of which in accordance with the AMS methodology is impracticable, other than support provided under programmes that qualify as exempt from reduction under Annex 2 to this Agreement, and which is:

(i) with respect to support provided during the base period, specified in the relevant tables of supporting material incorporated by reference in Part IV of a Member's Schedule; and

(ii) with respect to support provided during any year of the implementation period and thereafter, calculated in accordance with the provisions of Annex 4 of this Agreement and taking into account the constituent data and methodology used in the tables of supporting material incorporated by reference in Part IV of the Member's Schedule;

(e) "export subsidies" refers to subsidies contingent upon export performance, including the export subsidies listed in Article 9 of this Agreement;

(f) "implementation period" means the six-year period commencing in the year 1995, except that, for the purposes of Article 13, it means the nine-year period commencing in 1995;

(g) "market access concessions" includes all market access commitments undertaken pursuant to this Agreement;

(h) "Total Aggregate Measurement of Support" and "Total AMS" mean the sum of all domestic support provided in favour of agricultural producers, calculated as the sum of all aggregate measurements of support for basic agricultural products, all non-product-specific aggregate measurements of support and all equivalent measurements of support for agricultural products, and which is:

(i) with respect to support provided during the base period (i.e. the "Base Total AMS") and the maximum support permitted to be provided during any year of the implementation period or thereafter (i.e. the "Annual and Final Bound Commitment Levels"), as specified in Part IV of a Member's Schedule; and

(ii) with respect to the level of support actually provided during any year of the implementation period and thereafter (i.e. the "Current Total AMS"), calculated in accordance with the provisions of this Agreement, including Article 6, and with the constituent data and methodology used in the tables of supporting material incorporated by reference in Part IV of the Member's Schedule;

(i) "year" in paragraph (f) above and in relation to the specific commitments of a Member refers to the calendar, financial or marketing year specified in the Schedule relating to that Member.

ARTICLE 2

Product Coverage

This Agreement applies to the products listed in Annex 1 to this Agreement, hereinafter referred to as agricultural products.

PART II

ARTICLE 3

Incorporation of Concessions and Commitments

1. The domestic support and export subsidy commitments in

Part IV of each Member's Schedule constitute commitments limiting subsidization and are hereby made an integral part of GATT 1994.

2. Subject to the provisions of Article 6, a Member shall not provide support in favour of domestic producers in excess of the commitment levels specified in Section I of Part IV of its Schedule.

3. Subject to the provisions of paragraphs 2(b) and 4 of Article 9, a Member shall not provide export subsidies listed in paragraph 1 of Article 9 in respect of the agricultural products or groups of products specified in Section II of Part IV of its Schedule in excess of the budgetary outlay and quantity commitment levels specified therein and shall not provide such subsidies in respect of any agricultural product not specified in that Section of its Schedule.

PART III

ARTICLE 4

Market Access

1. Market access concessions contained in Schedules relate to bindings and reductions of tariffs, and to other market access commitments as specified therein.

2. Members shall not maintain, resort to, or revert to any measures of the kind which have been required to be converted into ordinary customs duties[1], except as otherwise provided for in Article 5 and Annex 5.

ARTICLE 5

Special Safeguard Provisions

1. Notwithstanding the provisions of paragraph 1(b) of Article II of GATT 1994, any Member may take recourse to the provisions of paragraphs 4 and 5 below in connection with the importation of an agricultural product, in respect of which measures referred to in paragraph 2 of Article 4 of this Agreement have been converted into

---

1. These measures include quantitative import restrictions, variable import levies, minimum import prices, discretionary import licensing, non-tariff measures maintained through state-trading enterprises, voluntary export restraints, and similar border measures other than ordinary customs duties, whether or not the measures are maintained under country-specific derogations from the provisions of GATT 1947, but not measures maintained under balance-of-payments provisions or under other general, non-agriculture-specific provisions of GATT 1994 or of the other Multilateral Trade Agreements in Annex 1A to the WTO Agreement.

an ordinary customs duty and which is designated in its Schedule with the symbol "SSG" as being the subject of a concession in respect of which the provisions of this Article may be invoked, if:

(a) the volume of imports of that product entering the customs territory of the Member granting the concession during any year exceeds a trigger level which relates to the existing market access opportunity as set out in paragraph 4; or, but not concurrently:

(b) the price at which imports of that product may enter the customs territory of the Member granting the concession, as determined on the basis of the c.i.f. import price of the shipment concerned expressed in terms of its domestic currency, falls below a trigger price[2] equal to the average 1986 to 1988 reference price for the product concerned.

2. Imports under current and minimum access commitments established as part of a concession referred to in paragraph 1 above shall be counted for the purpose of determining the volume of imports required for invoking the provisions of subparagraph 1(a) and paragraph 4, but imports under such commitments shall not be affected by any additional duty imposed under either subparagraph 1(a) and paragraph 4 or subparagraph 1(b) and paragraph 5 below.

3. Any supplies of the product in question which were *en route* on the basis of a contract settled before the additional duty is imposed under subparagraph 1(a) and paragraph 4 shall be exempted from any such additional duty, provided that they may be counted in the volume of imports of the product in question during the following year for the purposes of triggering the provisions of subparagraph 1(a) in that year.

4. Any additional duty imposed under subparagraph 1(a) shall only be maintained until the end of the year in which it has been imposed, and may only be levied at a level which shall not exceed one third of the level of the ordinary customs duty in effect in the

2. The reference price used to invoke the provisions of this subparagraph shall, in general, be the average c.i.f. unit value of the product concerned, or otherwise shall be an appropriate price in terms of the quality of the product and its stage of processing. It shall, following its initial use, be publicly specified and available to the extent necessary to allow other Members to assess the additional duty that may be levied.

year in which the action is taken. The trigger level shall be set according to the following schedule based on market access opportunities defined as imports as a percentage of the corresponding domestic consumption[3] during the three preceding years for which data are available:

(a) where such market access opportunities for a product are less than or equal to 10 per cent, the base trigger level shall equal 125 per cent;

(b) where such market access opportunities for a product are greater than 10 per cent but less than or equal to 30 per cent, the base trigger level shall equal 110 per cent;

(c) where such market access opportunities for a product are greater than 30 per cent, the base trigger level shall equal 105 per cent.

In all cases the additional duty may be imposed in any year where the absolute volume of imports of the product concerned entering the customs territory of the Member granting the concession exceeds the sum of (*x*) the base trigger level set out above multiplied by the average quantity of imports during the three preceding years for which data are available and (*y*) the absolute volume change in domestic consumption of the product concerned in the most recent year for which data are available compared to the preceding year, provided that the trigger level shall not be less than 105 per cent of the average quantity of imports in (*x*) above.

5. The additional duty imposed under subparagraph 1(b) shall be set according to the following schedule:

(a) if the difference between the c.i.f. import price of the shipment expressed in terms of the domestic currency (hereinafter referred to as the "import price") and the trigger price as defined under that subparagraph is less than or equal to 10 per cent of the trigger price, no additional duty shall be imposed;

(b) if the difference between the import price and the trigger price (hereinafter referred to as the "difference") is greater than 10 per cent but less than or equal to

---

3. Where domestic consumption is not taken into account, the base trigger level under subparagraph 4(a) shall apply.

40 per cent of the trigger price, the additional duty shall equal 30 per cent of the amount by which the difference exceeds 10 per cent;

(c) if the difference is greater than 40 per cent but less than or equal to 60 per cent of the trigger price, the additional duty shall equal 50 per cent of the amount by which the difference exceeds 40 per cent, plus the additional duty allowed under (b);

(d) if the difference is greater than 60 per cent but less than or equal to 75 per cent, the additional duty shall equal 70 per cent of the amount by which the difference exceeds 60 per cent of the trigger price, plus the additional duties allowed under (b) and (c);

(e) if the difference is greater than 75 per cent of the trigger price, the additional duty shall equal 90 per cent of the amount by which the difference exceeds 75 per cent, plus the additional duties allowed under (b), (c) and (d).

6. For perishable and seasonal products, the conditions set out above shall be applied in such a manner as to take account of the specific characteristics of such products. In particular, shorter time periods under subparagraph 1(a) and paragraph 4 may be used in reference to the corresponding periods in the base period and different reference prices for different periods may be used under subparagraph 1(b).

7. The operation of the special safeguard shall be carried out in a transparent manner. Any Member taking action under subparagraph 1(a) above shall give notice in writing, including relevant data, to the Committee on Agriculture as far in advance as may be practicable and in any event within 10 days of the implementation of such action. In cases where changes in consumption volumes must be allocated to individual tariff lines subject to action under paragraph 4, relevant data shall include the information and methods used to allocate these changes. A Member taking action under paragraph 4 shall afford any interested Members the opportunity to consult with it in respect of the conditions of application of such action. Any Member taking action under subparagraph 1(b) above shall give notice in writing, including relevant data, to the Committee on Agriculture within 10 days of the implementation of the first such action or, for

perishable and seasonal products, the first action in any period. Members undertake, as far as practicable, not to take recourse to the provisions of subparagraph 1(b) where the volume of imports of the products concerned are declining. In either case a Member taking such action shall afford any interested Members the opportunity to consult with it in respect of the conditions of application of such action.

8. Where measures are taken in conformity with paragraphs 1 through 7 above, Members undertake not to have recourse, in respect of such measures, to the provisions of paragraphs 1(a) and 3 of Article XIX of GATT 1994 or paragraph 2 of Article 8 of the Agreement on Safeguards.

9. The provisions of this Article shall remain in force for the duration of the reform process as determined under Article 20.

PART IV

ARTICLE 6

Domestic Support Commitments

1. The domestic support reduction commitments of each Member contained in Part IV of its Schedule shall apply to all of its domestic support measures in favour of agricultural producers with the exception of domestic measures which are not subject to reduction in terms of the criteria set out in this Article and in Annex 2 to this Agreement. The commitments are expressed in terms of Total Aggregate Measurement of Support and "Annual and Final Bound Commitment Levels".

2. In accordance with the Mid-Term Review Agreement that government measures of assistance, whether direct or indirect, to encourage agricultural and rural development are an integral part of the development programmes of developing countries, investment subsidies which are generally available to agriculture in developing country Members and agricultural input subsidies generally available to low-income or resource-poor producers in developing country Members shall be exempt from domestic support reduction commitments that would otherwise be applicable to such measures, as shall domestic support to producers in developing country Members to encourage diversification from growing illicit narcotic crops. Domestic support meeting the criteria of this paragraph shall not be

required to be included in a Member's calculation of its Current Total AMS.

3. A Member shall be considered to be in compliance with its domestic support reduction commitments in any year in which its domestic support in favour of agricultural producers expressed in terms of Current Total AMS does not exceed the corresponding annual or final bound commitment level specified in Part IV of the Member's Schedule.

4. (a) A Member shall not be required to include in thecalculation of its Current Total AMS and shall not be required to reduce:

(i) product-specific domestic support which would otherwise be required to be included in a Member's calculation of its Current AMS where such support does not exceed 5 per cent of that Member's total value of production of a basic agricultural product during the relevant year; and

(ii) non-product-specific domestic support which would otherwise be required to be included in a Member's calculation of its Current AMS where such support does not exceed 5 per cent of the value of that Member's total agricultural production.

(b) For developing country Members, the *de minimis* percentage under this paragraph shall be 10 per cent.

5. (a) Direct payments under production-limiting programmes shall not be subject to the commitment to reduce domestic support if:

(i) such payments are based on fixed area and yields; or

(ii) such payments are made on 85 per cent or less of the base level of production; or

(iii) livestock payments are made on a fixed number of head.

(b) The exemption from the reduction commitment for direct payments meeting the above criteria shall be reflected by the exclusion of the value of those direct payments in a Member's calculation of its Current Total AMS.

ARTICLE 7

General Disciplines on Domestic Support

1. Each Member shall ensure that any domestic support measures in favour of agricultural producers which are not subject to reduction commitments because they qualify under the criteria set out in Annex 2 to this Agreement are maintained in conformity therewith.

2. (a) Any domestic support measure in favour of agricultural producers, including any modification to such measure, and any measure that is subsequently introduced that cannot be shown to satisfy the criteria in Annex 2 to this Agreement or to be exempt from reduction by reason of any other provision of this Agreement shall be included in the Member's calculation of its Current Total AMS.

(b) Where no Total AMS commitment exists in Part IV of a Member's Schedule, the Member shall not provide support to agricultural producers in excess of the relevant *de minimis* level set out in paragraph 4 of Article 6.

PART V

ARTICLE 8

Export Competition Commitments

Each Member undertakes not to provide export subsidies otherwise than in conformity with this Agreement and with the commitments as specified in that Member's Schedule.

ARTICLE 9

Export Subsidy Commitments

1. The following export subsidies are subject to reduction commitments under this Agreement:

(a) the provision by governments or their agencies of direct subsidies, including payments-in-kind, to a firm, to an industry, to producers of an agricultural product, to a cooperative or other association of such producers, or to a marketing board, contingent on export performance;

(b) the sale or disposal for export by governments or their agencies of non-commercial stocks of agricultural products at a price lower than the comparable price charged for the like product to buyers in the domestic market;

(c) payments on the export of an agricultural product that are financed by virtue of governmental action, whether or not a charge on the public account is involved, including payments that are financed from the proceeds of a levy imposed on the agricultural product concerned or on an agricultural product from which the exported product is derived;

(d) the provision of subsidies to reduce the costs of marketing exports of agricultural products (other than widely available export promotion and advisory services) including handling, upgrading and other processing costs, and the costs of international transport and freight;

(e) internal transport and freight charges on export shipments, provided or mandated by governments, on terms more favourable than for domestic shipments;

(f) subsidies on agricultural products contingent on their incorporation in exported products.

2. (a) Except as provided in subparagraph (b), the export subsidy commitment levels for each year of the implementation period, as specified in a Member's Schedule, represent with respect to the export subsidies listed in paragraph 1 of this Article:

(i) in the case of budgetary outlay reduction commitments, the maximum level of expenditure for such subsidies that may be allocated or incurred in that year in respect of the agricultural product, or group of products, concerned; and

(ii) in the case of export quantity reduction commitments, the maximum quantity of an agricultural product, or group of products, in respect of which such export subsidies may be granted in that year.

(b) In any of the second through fifth years of the implementation period, a Member may provide export subsidies listed in paragraph 1 above in a given year in excess of the corresponding annual commitment levels in respect of the products or groups of products specified in Part IV of the Member's Schedule, provided that:

(i) the cumulative amounts of budgetary outlays for such subsidies, from the beginning of the implementation period through the year in question, does not exceed the cumulative amounts that would have resulted from full compliance with the relevant annual outlay commitment levels specified in the Member's Schedule by more than 3 per cent of the base period level of such budgetary outlays;

(ii) the cumulative quantities exported with the benefit of such export subsidies, from the beginning of the implementation period through the year in question, does not exceed the cumulative quantities that would have resulted from full compliance with the relevant annual quantity commitment levels specified in the Member's Schedule by more than 1.75 per cent of the base period quantities;

(iii) the total cumulative amounts of budgetary outlays for such export subsidies and the quantities benefiting from such export subsidies over the entire implementation period are no greater than the totals that would have resulted from full compliance with the relevant annual commitment levels specified in the Member's Schedule; and

(iv) the Member's budgetary outlays for export subsidies and the quantities benefiting from such subsidies, at the conclusion of the implementation period, are no greater than 64 per cent and 79 per cent of the 1986-1990 base period levels, respectively. For developing country Members these percentages shall be 76 and 86 per cent, respectively.

3. Commitments relating to limitations on the extension of the scope of export subsidization are as specified in Schedules.

4. During the implementation period, developing country Members shall not be required to undertake commitments in respect of the export subsidies listed in subparagraphs (d) and (e) of paragraph 1 above, provided that these are not applied in a manner that would circumvent reduction commitments.

ARTICLE 10

Prevention of Circumvention of Export Subsidy Commitments

1. Export subsidies not listed in paragraph 1 of Article 9 shall not be applied in a manner which results in, or which threatens to lead to, circumvention of export subsidy commitments; nor shall non-commercial transactions be used to circumvent such commitments.

2. Members undertake to work toward the development of internationally agreed disciplines to govern the provision of export credits, export credit guarantees or insurance programmes and, after agreement on such disciplines, to provide export credits, export credit guarantees or insurance programmes only in conformity therewith.

3. Any Member which claims that any quantity exported in excess of a reduction commitment level is not subsidized must establish that no export subsidy, whether listed in Article 9 or not, has been granted in respect of the quantity of exports in question.

4. Members donors of international food aid shall ensure:

(a) that the provision of international food aid is not tied directly or indirectly to commercial exports of agricultural products to recipient countries;

(b) that international food aid transactions, including bilateral food aid which is monetized, shall be carried out in accordance with the FAO "Principles of Surplus Disposal and Consultative Obligations", including, where appropriate, the system of Usual Marketing Requirements (UMRs); and

(c) that such aid shall be provided to the extent possible in fully grant form or on terms no less concessional than those provided for in Article IV of the Food Aid Convention 1986.

ARTICLE 11

Incorporated Products

In no case may the per-unit subsidy paid on an incorporated agricultural primary product exceed the per-unit export subsidy that would be payable on exports of the primary product as such.

PART VI

Article 12

Disciplines on Export Prohibitions and Restrictions

1. Where any Member institutes any new export prohibition or restriction on foodstuffs in accordance with paragraph 2(a) of Article XI of GATT 1994, the Member shall observe the following provisions:

(a) the Member instituting the export prohibition or restriction shall give due consideration to the effects of such prohibition or restriction on importing Members' food security;

(b) before any Member institutes an export prohibition or restriction, it shall give notice in writing, as far in advance as practicable, to the Committee on Agriculture comprising such information as the nature and the duration of such measure, and shall consult, upon request, with any other Member having a substantial interest as an importer with respect to any matter related to the measure in question. The Member instituting such export prohibition or restriction shall provide, upon request, such a Member with necessary information.

2. The provisions of this Article shall not apply to any developing country Member, unless the measure is taken by a developing country Member which is a net-food exporter of the specific foodstuff concerned.

PART VII

ARTICLE 13

Due Restraint

During the implementation period, notwithstanding the provisions of GATT 1994 and the Agreement on Subsidies and Countervailing Measures (referred to in this Article as the "Subsidies Agreement"):

(a) domestic support measures that conform fully to the provisions of Annex 2 to this Agreement shall be:

(i) non-actionable subsidies for purposes of countervailing duties[4];

(ii) exempt from actions based on Article XVI of GATT 1994 and Part III of the Subsidies Agreement; and

(iii) exempt from actions based on non-violation nullification or impairment of the benefits of tariff concessions accruing to another Member under Article II of GATT 1994, in the sense of paragraph 1(b) of Article XXIII of GATT 1994;

(b) domestic support measures that conform fully to the provisions of Article 6 of this Agreement including direct payments that conform to the requirements of paragraph 5 thereof, as reflected in each Member's Schedule, as well as domestic support within *de minimis* levels and in conformity with paragraph 2 of Article 6, shall be:

(i) exempt from the imposition of countervailing duties unless a determination of injury or threat thereof is made in accordance with Article VI of GATT 1994 and Part V of the Subsidies Agreement, and due restraint shall be shown in initiating any countervailing duty investigations;

(ii) exempt from actions based on paragraph 1 of Article XVI of GATT 1994 or Articles 5 and 6 of the Subsidies Agreement, provided that such measures do not grant support to a specific commodity in excess of that decided during the 1992 marketing year; and

(iii) exempt from actions based on non-violation nullification or impairment of the benefits of tariff

---

4. "Countervailing duties" where referred to in this Article are those covered by Article VI of GATT 1994 and Part V of the Agreement on Subsidies and Countervailing Measures.

concessions accruing to another Member under Article II of GATT 1994, in the sense of paragraph 1(b) of Article XXIII of GATT 1994, provided that such measures do not grant support to a specific commodity in excess of that decided during the 1992 marketing year;

(c) export subsidies that conform fully to the provisions of Part V of this Agreement, as reflected in each Member's Schedule, shall be:

(i) subject to countervailing duties only upon a determination of injury or threat thereof based on volume, effect on prices, or consequent impact in accordance with Article VI of GATT 1994 and Part V of the Subsidies Agreement, and due restraint shall be shown in initiating any countervailing duty investigations; and

(ii) exempt from actions based on Article XVI of GATT 1994 or Articles 3, 5 and 6 of the Subsidies Agreement.

PART VIII

ARTICLE 14

Sanitary and Phytosanitary Measures

Members agree to give effect to the Agreement on the Application of Sanitary and Phytosanitary Measures.

PART IX

ARTICLE 15

Special and Differential Treatment

1. In keeping with the recognition that differential and more favourable treatment for developing country Members is an integral part of the negotiation, special and differential treatment in respect of commitments shall be provided as set out in the relevant provisions of this Agreement and embodied in the Schedules of concessions and commitments.

2. Developing country Members shall have the flexibility to implement reduction commitments over a period of up to 10 years.

Least-developed country Members shall not be required to undertake reduction commitments.

PART X
ARTICLE 16
Least-Developed and Net Food-Importing Developing Countries

1. Developed country Members shall take such action as is provided for within the framework of the Decision on Measures Concerning the Possible Negative Effects of the Reform Programme on Least-Developed and Net Food-Importing Developing Countries.

2. The Committee on Agriculture shall monitor, as appropriate, the follow-up to this Decision.

PART XI
ARTICLE 17
Committee on Agriculture

A Committee on Agriculture is hereby established.

ARTICLE 18
Review of the Implementation of Commitments

1. Progress in the implementation of commitments negotiated under the Uruguay Round reform programme shall be reviewed by the Committee on Agriculture.

2. The review process shall be undertaken on the basis of notifications submitted by Members in relation to such matters and at such intervals as shall be determined, as well as on the basis of such documentation as the Secretariat may be requested to prepare in order to facilitate the review process.

3. In addition to the notifications to be submitted under paragraph 2, any new domestic support measure, or modification of an existing measure, for which exemption from reduction is claimed shall be notified promptly. This notification shall contain details of the new or modified measure and its conformity with the agreed criteria as set out either in Article 6 or in Annex 2.

4. In the review process Members shall give due consideration to the influence of excessive rates of inflation on the ability of any Member to abide by its domestic support commitments.

5. Members agree to consult annually in the Committee on Agriculture with respect to their participation in the normal growth of world trade in agricultural products within the framework of the commitments on export subsidies under this Agreement.

6. The review process shall provide an opportunity for Members to raise any matter relevant to the implementation of commitments under the reform programme as set out in this Agreement.

7. Any Member may bring to the attention of the Committee on Agriculture any measure which it considers ought to have been notified by another Member.

ARTICLE 19

Consultation and Dispute Settlement

The provisions of Articles XXII and XXIII of GATT 1994, as elaborated and applied by the Dispute Settlement Understanding, shall apply to consultations and the settlement of disputes under this Agreement.

PART XII

ARTICLE 20

Continuation of the Reform Process

Recognizing that the long-term objective of substantial progressive reductions in support and protection resulting in fundamental reform is an ongoing process, Members agree that negotiations for continuing the process will be initiated one year before the end of the implementation period, taking into account:

(a) the experience to that date from implementing the reduction commitments;

(b) the effects of the reduction commitments on world trade in agriculture;

(c) non-trade concerns, special and differential treatment to developing country Members, and the objective to establish a fair and market-oriented agricultural trading system, and the other objectives and concerns mentioned in the preamble to this Agreement; and

(d) what further commitments are necessary to achieve the above mentioned long-term objectives.

PART XIII

ARTICLE 21

Final Provisions

1. The provisions of GATT 1994 and of other Multilateral Trade Agreements in Annex 1A to the WTO Agreement shall apply subject to the provisions of this Agreement.

2. The Annexes to this Agreement are hereby made an integral part of this Agreement.

ANNEX 1

PRODUCT COVERAGE

1. This Agreement shall cover the following products:

(i) HS Chapters 1 to 24 less fish and fish products, plus*

(ii)	HS Code	2905.43	(mannitol)
	HS Code	2905.44	(sorbitol)
	HS Heading	33.01	(essential oils)
	HS Headings	35.01 to 35.05	(albuminoidal substances, modified starches, glues)
	HS Code	3809.10	(finishing agents)
	HS Code	3823.60	(sorbitol n.e.p.)
	HS Headings	41.01 to 41.03	(hides and skins)
	HS Heading	43.01	(raw furskins)
	HS Headings	50.01 to 50.03	(raw silk and silk waste)
	HS Headings	51.01 to 51.03	(wool and animal hair)
	HS Headings	52.01 to 52.03	(raw cotton, waste and cotton carded or combed)
	HS Heading	53.01	(raw flax)
	HS Heading	53.02	(raw hemp)

2. The foregoing shall not limit the product coverage of the Agreement on the Application of Sanitary and Phytosanitary Measures.

* The product descriptions in round brackets are not necessarily exhaustive.

ANNEX 2

DOMESTIC SUPPORT: THE BASIS FOR EXEMPTION FROM THE REDUCTION COMMITMENTS

1. Domestic support measures for which exemption from the

reduction commitments is claimed shall meet the fundamental requirement that they have no, or at most minimal, trade-distorting effects or effects on production. Accordingly, all measures for which exemption is claimed shall conform to the following basic criteria:

(a) the support in question shall be provided through a publicly-funded government programme (including government revenue foregone) not involving transfers from consumers; and,

(b) the support in question shall not have the effect of providing price support to producers;

plus policy-specific criteria and conditions as set out below.

Government Service Programmes

2. General services

Policies in this category involve expenditures (or revenue foregone) in relation to programmes which provide services or benefits to agriculture or the rural community. They shall not involve direct payments to producers or processors. Such programmes, which include but are not restricted to the following list, shall meet the general criteria in paragraph 1 above and policy-specific conditions where set out below:

(a) research, including general research, research in connection with environmental programmes, and research programmes relating to particular products;

(b) pest and disease control, including general and product-specific pest and disease control measures, such as early-warning systems, quarantine and eradication;

(c) training services, including both general and specialist training facilities;

(d) extension and advisory services, including the provision of means to facilitate the transfer of information and the results of research to producers and consumers;

(e) inspection services, including general inspection services and the inspection of particular products for health, safety, grading or standardization purposes;

(f) marketing and promotion services, including market information, advice and promotion relating to particular products but excluding expenditure for unspecified purposes that could be used by sellers to reduce their selling price or confer a direct economic benefit to purchasers; and

(g) infrastructural services, including: electricity reticulation, roads and other means of transport, market and port facilities, water supply facilities, dams and drainage schemes, and infrastructural works associated with environmental programmes. In all cases the expenditure shall be directed to the provision or construction of capital works only, and shall exclude the subsidized provision of on-farm facilities other than for the reticulation of generally available public utilities. It shall not include subsidies to inputs or operating costs, or preferential user charges.

3. Public stockholding for food security purposes[5]

Expenditures (or revenue foregone) in relation to the accumulation and holding of stocks of products which form an integral part of a food security programme identified in national legislation. This may include government aid to private storage of products as part of such a programme.

The volume and accumulation of such stocks shall correspond to predetermined targets related solely to food security. The process of stock accumulation and disposal shall be financially transparent. Food purchases by the government shall be made at current market prices and sales from food security stocks shall be made at no less than the current domestic market price for the product and quality in question.

4. Domestic food aid[6]

5. For the purposes of paragraph 3 of this Annex, governmental stockholding programmes for food security purposes in developing countries whose operation is transparent and conducted in accordance with officially published objective criteria or guidelines shall be considered to be in conformity with the provisions of this paragraph, including programmes under which stocks of foodstuffs for food security purposes are acquired and released at administered prices, provided that the difference between the acquisition price and the external reference price is accounted for in the AMS.

5&6. For the purposes of paragraphs 3 and 4 of this Annex, the provision of foodstuffs at subsidized prices with the objective of meeting food requirements of urban and rural poor in developing countries on a regular basis at reasonable prices shall be considered to be in conformity with the provisions of this paragraph.

Expenditures (or revenue foregone) in relation to the provision of domestic food aid to sections of the population in need.

Eligibility to receive the food aid shall be subject to clearly-defined criteria related to nutritional objectives. Such aid shall be in the form of direct provision of food to those concerned or the provision of means to allow eligible recipients to buy food either at market or at subsidized prices. Food purchases by the government shall be made at current market prices and the financing and administration of the aid shall be transparent.

5. Direct payments to producers

Support provided through direct payments (or revenue foregone, including payments in kind) to producers for which exemption from reduction commitments is claimed shall meet the basic criteria set out in paragraph 1 above, plus specific criteria applying to individual types of direct payment as set out in paragraphs 6 through 13 below. Where exemption from reduction is claimed for any existing or new type of direct payment other than those specified in paragraphs 6 through 13, it shall conform to criteria (b) through (e) in paragraph 6, in addition to the general criteria set out in paragraph 1.

6. Decoupled income support

(a) Eligibility for such payments shall be determined by clearly-defined criteria such as income, status as a producer or landowner, factor use or production level in a defined and fixed base period.

(b) The amount of such payments in any given year shall not be related to, or based on, the type or volume of production (including livestock units) undertaken by the producer in any year after the base period.

(c) The amount of such payments in any given year shall not be related to, or based on, the prices, domestic or international, applying to any production undertaken in any year after the base period.

(d) The amount of such payments in any given year shall not be related to, or based on, the factors of production employed in any year after the base period.

(e) No production shall be required in order to receive such payments.

7. Government financial participation in income insurance and income safety-net programmes

(a) Eligibility for such payments shall be determined by an income loss, taking into account only income derived from agriculture, which exceeds 30 per cent of average gross income or the equivalent in net income terms (excluding any payments from the same or similar schemes) in the preceding three-year period or a three-year average based on the preceding five-year period, excluding the highest and the lowest entry. Any producer meeting this condition shall be eligible to receive the payments.

(b) The amount of such payments shall compensate for less than 70 per cent of the producer's income loss in the year the producer becomes eligible to receive this assistance.

(c) The amount of any such payments shall relate solely to income; it shall not relate to the type or volume of production (including livestock units) undertaken by the producer; or to the prices, domestic or international, applying to such production; or to the factors of production employed.

(d) Where a producer receives in the same year payments under this paragraph and under paragraph 8 (relief from natural disasters), the total of such payments shall be less than 100 per cent of the producer's total loss.

8. Payments (made either directly or by way of government financial participation in crop insurance schemes) for relief from natural disasters

(a) Eligibility for such payments shall arise only following a formal recognition by government authorities that a natural or like disaster (including disease outbreaks, pest infestations, nuclear accidents, and war on the territory of the Member concerned) has occurred or is occurring; and shall be determined by a production loss which exceeds 30 per cent of the average of production in the preceding three-year period or a three-year average based on the preceding five-year period, excluding the highest and the lowest entry.

(b) Payments made following a disaster shall be applied only in respect of losses of income, livestock (including payments in connection with the veterinary treatment of animals), land or other production factors due to the natural disaster in question.

(c) Payments shall compensate for not more than the total cost of replacing such losses and shall not require or specify the type or quantity of future production.

(d) Payments made during a disaster shall not exceed the level required to prevent or alleviate further loss as defined in criterion (b) above.

(e) Where a producer receives in the same year payments under this paragraph and under paragraph 7 (income insurance and income safety-net programmes), the total of such payments shall be less than 100 per cent of the producer's total loss.

9. Structural adjustment assistance provided through producer retirement programmes

(a) Eligibility for such payments shall be determined by reference to clearly defined criteria in programmes designed to facilitate the retirement of persons engaged in marketable agricultural production, or their movement to non-agricultural activities.

(b) Payments shall be conditional upon the total and permanent retirement of the recipients from marketable agricultural production.

10. Structural adjustment assistance provided through resource retirement programmes

(a) Eligibility for such payments shall be determined by reference to clearly defined criteria in programmes designed to remove land or other resources, including livestock, from marketable agricultural production.

(b) Payments shall be conditional upon the retirement of land from marketable agricultural production for a minimum of three years, and in the case of livestock on its slaughter or definitive permanent disposal.

(c) Payments shall not require or specify any alternative use for such land or other resources which involves the production of marketable agricultural products.

(d) Payments shall not be related to either the type or quantity of production or to the prices, domestic or international, applying to production undertaken using the land or other resources remaining in production.

11. Structural adjustment assistance provided through investment aids

(a) Eligibility for such payments shall be determined by reference to clearly-defined criteria in government programmes designed to assist the financial or physical restructuring of a producer's operations in response to objectively demonstrated structural disadvantages. Eligibility for such programmes may also be based on a clearly-defined government programme for the reprivatization of agricultural land.

(b) The amount of such payments in any given year shall not be related to, or based on, the type or volume of production (including livestock units) undertaken by the producer in any year after the base period other than as provided for under criterion (e) below.

(c) The amount of such payments in any given year shall not be related to, or based on, the prices, domestic or international, applying to any production undertaken in any year after the base period.

(d) The payments shall be given only for the period of time necessary for the realization of the investment in respect of which they are provided.

(e) The payments shall not mandate or in any way designate the agricultural products to be produced by the recipients except to require them not to produce a particular product.

(f) The payments shall be limited to the amount required to compensate for the structural disadvantage.

12. Payments under environmental programmes

(a) Eligibility for such payments shall be determined as part of a clearly-defined government environmental or conservation programme and be dependent on the fulfilment of specific conditions under the government programme, including conditions related to production methods or inputs.

(b) The amount of payment shall be limited to the extra costs or loss of income involved in complying with the government programme.

13. Payments under regional assistance programmes

(a) Eligibility for such payments shall be limited to producers in disadvantaged regions. Each such region must be a clearly designated contiguous geographical area with a definable economic and administrative identity, considered as disadvantaged on the basis of neutral and objective criteria clearly spelt out in law or regulation and indicating that the region's difficulties arise out of more than temporary circumstances.

(b) The amount of such payments in any given year shall not be related to, or based on, the type or volume of production (including livestock units) undertaken by the producer in any year after the base period other than to reduce that production.

(c) The amount of such payments in any given year shall not be related to, or based on, the prices, domestic or international, applying to any production undertaken in any year after the base period.

(d) Payments shall be available only to producers in eligible regions, but generally available to all producers within such regions.

(e) Where related to production factors, payments shall be made at a degressive rate above a threshold level of the factor concerned.

(f) The payments shall be limited to the extra costs or loss of income involved in undertaking agricultural production in the prescribed area.

ANNEX 3

DOMESTIC SUPPORT: CALCULATION OF AGGREGATE MEASUREMENT OF SUPPORT

1. Subject to the provisions of Article 6, an Aggregate Measurement of Support (AMS) shall be calculated on a product-specific basis for each basic agricultural product receiving market price support, non-exempt direct payments, or any other subsidy not exempted from the reduction commitment ("other non-exempt policies"). Support which is non-product specific shall be totalled into one non-product-specific AMS in total monetary terms.

2. Subsidies under paragraph 1 shall include both budgetary outlays and revenue foregone by governments or their agents.

3. Support at both the national and sub-national level shall be included.

4. Specific agricultural levies or fees paid by producers shall be deducted from the AMS.

5. The AMS calculated as outlined below for the base period shall constitute the base level for the implementation of the reduction commitment on domestic support.

6. For each basic agricultural product, a specific AMS shall be established, expressed in total monetary value terms.

7. The AMS shall be calculated as close as practicable to the point of first sale of the basic agricultural product concerned. Measures directed at agricultural processors shall be included to the extent that such measures benefit the producers of the basic agricultural products.

8. Market price support: market price support shall be calculated using the gap between a fixed external reference price and the applied administered price multiplied by the quantity of production eligible to receive the applied administered price. Budgetary payments made to maintain this gap, such as buying-in or storage costs, shall not be included in the AMS.

9. The fixed external reference price shall be based on the years 1986 to 1988 and shall generally be the average f.o.b. unit value for the basic agricultural product concerned in a net exporting country and the average c.i.f. unit value for the basic agricultural product

concerned in a net importing country in the base period. The fixed reference price may be adjusted for quality differences as necessary.

10. Non-exempt direct payments: non-exempt direct payments which are dependent on a price gap shall be calculated either using the gap between the fixed reference price and the applied administered price multiplied by the quantity of production eligible to receive the administered price, or using budgetary outlays.

11. The fixed reference price shall be based on the years 1986 to 1988 and shall generally be the actual price used for determining payment rates.

12. Non-exempt direct payments which are based on factors other than price shall be measured using budgetary outlays.

13. Other non-exempt measures, including input subsidies and other measures such as marketing-cost reduction measures: the value of such measures shall be measured using government budgetary outlays or, where the use of budgetary outlays does not reflect the full extent of the subsidy concerned, the basis for calculating the subsidy shall be the gap between the price of the subsidized good or service and a representative market price for a similar good or service multiplied by the quantity of the good or service.

ANNEX 4

DOMESTIC SUPPORT: CALCULATION OF EQUIVALENT MEASUREMENT OF SUPPORT

1. Subject to the provisions of Article 6, equivalent measurements of support shall be calculated in respect of all basic agricultural products where market price support as defined in Annex 3 exists but for which calculation of this component of the AMS is not practicable. For such products the base level for implementation of the domestic support reduction commitments shall consist of a market price support component expressed in terms of equivalent measurements of support under paragraph 2 below, as well as any non-exempt direct payments and other non-exempt support, which shall be evaluated as provided for under paragraph 3 below. Support at both national and sub-national level shall be included.

2. The equivalent measurements of support provided for in paragraph 1 shall be calculated on a product-specific basis for all basic agricultural products as close as practicable to the point of

first sale receiving market price support and for which the calculation of the market price support component of the AMS is not practicable. For those basic agricultural products, equivalent measurements of market price support shall be made using the applied administered price and the quantity of production eligible to receive that price or, where this is not practicable, on budgetary outlays used to maintain the producer price.

3. Where basic agricultural products falling under paragraph 1 are the subject of non-exempt direct payments or any other product-specific subsidy not exempted from the reduction commitment, the basis for equivalent measurements of support concerning these measures shall be calculations as for the corresponding AMS components (specified in paragraphs 10 through 13 of Annex 3).

4. Equivalent measurements of support shall be calculated on the amount of subsidy as close as practicable to the point of first sale of the basic agricultural product concerned. Measures directed at agricultural processors shall be included to the extent that such measures benefit the producers of the basic agricultural products. Specific agricultural levies or fees paid by producers shall reduce the equivalent measurements of support by a corresponding amount.

ANNEX 5

SPECIAL TREATMENT WITH RESPECT TO PARAGRAPH 2 OF ARTICLE 4

SECTION A

1. The provisions of paragraph 2 of Article 4 shall not apply with effect from the entry into force of the WTO Agreement to any primary agricultural product and its worked and/or prepared products ("designated products") in respect of which the following conditions are complied with (hereinafter referred to as "special treatment"):

(a) imports of the designated products comprised less than 3 per cent of corresponding domestic consumption in the base period 1986-1988 ("the base period");

(b) no export subsidies have been provided since the beginning of the base period for the designated products;

(c) effective production-restricting measures are applied to the primary agricultural product;

(d) such products are designated with the symbol "ST-Annex 5" in Section I-B of Part I of a Member's Schedule annexed to the Marrakesh Protocol, as being subject to special treatment reflecting factors of non-trade concerns, such as food security and environmental protection; and

(e) minimum access opportunities in respect of the designated products correspond, as specified in Section I-B of Part I of the Schedule of the Member concerned, to 4 per cent of base period domestic consumption of the designated products from the beginning of the first year of the implementation period and, thereafter, are increased by 0.8 per cent of corresponding domestic consumption in the base period per year for the remainder of the implementation period.

2. At the beginning of any year of the implementation period a Member may cease to apply special treatment in respect of the designated products by complying with the provisions of paragraph 6. In such a case, the Member concerned shall maintain the minimum access opportunities already in effect at such time and increase the minimum access opportunities by 0.4 per cent of corresponding domestic consumption in the base period per year for the remainder of the implementation period. Thereafter, the level of minimum access opportunities resulting from this formula in the final year of the implementation period shall be maintained in the Schedule of the Member concerned.

3. Any negotiation on the question of whether there can be a continuation of the special treatment as set out in paragraph 1 after the end of the implementation period shall be completed within the time-frame of the implementation period itself as a part of the negotiations set out in Article 20 of this Agreement, taking into account the factors of non-trade concerns.

4. If it is agreed as a result of the negotiation referred to in paragraph 3 that a Member may continue to apply the special treatment, such Member shall confer additional and acceptable concessions as determined in that negotiation.

5. Where the special treatment is not to be continued at the end of the implementation period, the Member concerned shall

implement the provisions of paragraph 6. In such a case, after the end of the implementation period the minimum access opportunities for the designated products shall be maintained at the level of 8 per cent of corresponding domestic consumption in the base period in the Schedule of the Member concerned.

6. Border measures other than ordinary customs duties maintained in respect of the designated products shall become subject to the provisions of paragraph 2 of Article 4 with effect from the beginning of the year in which the special treatment ceases to apply. Such products shall be subject to ordinary customs duties, which shall be bound in the Schedule of the Member concerned and applied, from the beginning of the year in which special treatment ceases and thereafter, at such rates as would have been applicable had a reduction of at least 15 per cent been implemented over the implementation period in equal annual instalments. These duties shall be established on the basis of tariff equivalents to be calculated in accordance with the guidelines prescribed in the attachment hereto.

SECTION B

7. The provisions of paragraph 2 of Article 4 shall also not apply with effect from the entry into force of the WTO Agreement to a primary agricultural product that is the predominant staple in the traditional diet of a developing country Member and in respect of which the following conditions, in addition to those specified in paragraph 1(a) through 1(d), as they apply to the products concerned, are complied with:

(a) minimum access opportunities in respect of the products concerned, as specified in Section I-B of Part I of the Schedule of the developing country Member concerned, correspond to 1 per cent of base period domestic consumption of the products concerned from the beginning of the first year of the implementation period and are increased in equal annual instalments to 2 per cent of corresponding domestic consumption in the base period at the beginning of the fifth year of the implementation period. From the beginning of the sixth year of the implementation period, minimum access opportunities in respect of the products concerned correspond to 2 per cent of corresponding domestic consumption in the base period and are increased in equal annual instalments to 4 per cent of corresponding domestic consumption in the base period until the beginning of the 10th year. Thereafter, the level of minimum access opportunities resulting from this formula in the 10th year shall be maintained in the Schedule of the developing country Member concerned;

(b) appropriate market access opportunities have been provided for in other products under this Agreement.

8. Any negotiation on the question of whether there can be a continuation of the special treatment as set out in paragraph 7 after the end of the 10th year following the beginning of the implementation period shall be initiated and completed within the time-frame of the 10th year itself following the beginning of the implementation period.

9. If it is agreed as a result of the negotiation referred to in paragraph 8 that a Member may continue to apply the special treatment, such Member shall confer additional and acceptable concessions as determined in that negotiation.

10. In the event that special treatment under paragraph 7 is not to be continued beyond the 10th year following the beginning of the implementation period, the products concerned shall be subject to ordinary customs duties, established on the basis of a tariff equivalent to be calculated in accordance with the guidelines prescribed in the attachment hereto, which shall be bound in the Schedule of the Member concerned. In other respects, the provisions of paragraph 6 shall apply as modified by the relevant special and differential treatment accorded to developing country Members under this Agreement.

ATTACHMENT TO ANNEX 5

Guidelines for the Calculation of Tariff Equivalents for the Specific Purpose Specified in Paragraphs 6 and 10 of this Annex

1. The calculation of the tariff equivalents, whether expressed as *ad valorem* or specific rates, shall be made using the actual difference between internal and external prices in a transparent manner. Data used shall be for the years 1986 to 1988. Tariff equivalents:

(a) shall primarily be established at the four-digit level of the HS;

(b) shall be established at the six-digit or a more detailed level of the HS wherever appropriate;

(c) shall generally be established for worked and/or prepared products by multiplying the specific tariff equivalent(s) for the primary agricultural product(s) by the proportion(s) in value terms or in physical terms as appropriate of the primary agricultural product(s) in the worked and/or prepared products, and take account, where necessary, of any additional elements currently providing protection to industry.

2. External prices shall be, in general, actual average c.i.f. unit values for the importing country. Where average c.i.f. unit values are not available or appropriate, external prices shall be either:

(a) appropriate average c.i.f. unit values of a near country; or

(b) estimated from average f.o.b. unit values of (an) appropriate major exporter(s) adjusted by adding an estimate of insurance, freight and other relevant costs to the importing country.

3. The external prices shall generally be converted to domestic currencies using the annual average market exchange rate for the same period as the price data.

4. The internal price shall generally be a representative wholesale price ruling in the domestic market or an estimate of that price where adequate data is not available.

5. The initial tariff equivalents may be adjusted, where necessary, to take account of differences in quality or variety using an appropriate coefficient.

6. Where a tariff equivalent resulting from these guidelines is negative or lower than the current bound rate, the initial tariff equivalent may be established at the current bound rate or on the basis of national offers for that product.

7. Where an adjustment is made to the level of a tariff equivalent which would have resulted from the above guidelines, the Member

concerned shall afford, on request, full opportunities for consultation with a view to negotiating appropriate solutions.

AGREEMENT ON THE APPLICATION OF SANITARY AND PHYTOSANITARY MEASURES

Members,

Reaffirming that no Member should be prevented from adopting or enforcing measures necessary to protect human, animal or plant life or health, subject to the requirement that these measures are not applied in a manner which would constitute a means of arbitrary or unjustifiable discrimination between Members where the same conditions prevail or a disguised restriction on international trade;

Desiring to improve the human health, animal health and phytosanitary situation in all Members;

Noting that sanitary and phytosanitary measures are often applied on the basis of bilateral agreements or protocols;

Desiring the establishment of a multilateral framework of rules and disciplines to guide the development, adoption and enforcement of sanitary and phytosanitary measures in order to minimize their negative effects on trade;

Recognizing the important contribution that international standards, guidelines and recommendations can make in this regard;

Desiring to further the use of harmonized sanitary and phytosanitary measures between Members, on the basis of international standards, guidelines and recommendations developed by the relevant international organizations, including the Codex Alimentarius Commission, the International Office of Epizootics, and the relevant international and regional organizations operating within the framework of the International Plant Protection Convention, without requiring Members to change their appropriate level of protection of human, animal or plant life or health;

Recognizing that developing country Members may encounter special difficulties in complying with the sanitary or phytosanitary measures of importing Members, and as a consequence in access to markets, and also in the formulation and application of sanitary or phytosanitary measures in their own territories, and desiring to assist them in their endeavours in this regard;

Desiring therefore to elaborate rules for the application of the provisions of GATT 1994 which relate to the use of sanitary or phytosanitary measures, in particular the provisions of Article XX(b);[1]

Hereby agree as follows:

ARTICLE 1

General Provisions

1. This Agreement applies to all sanitary and phytosanitary measures which may, directly or indirectly, affect international trade. Such measures shall be developed and applied in accordance with the provisions of this Agreement.

2. For the purposes of this Agreement, the definitions provided in Annex A shall apply.

3. The annexes are an integral part of this Agreement.

4. Nothing in this Agreement shall affect the rights of Members under the Agreement on Technical Barriers to Trade with respect to measures not within the scope of this Agreement.

ARTICLE 2

Basic Rights and Obligations

1. Members have the right to take sanitary and phytosanitary measures necessary for the protection of human, animal or plant life or health, provided that such measures are not inconsistent with the provisions of this Agreement.

2. Members shall ensure that any sanitary or phytosanitary measure is applied only to the extent necessary to protect human, animal or plant life or health, is based on scientific principles and is not maintained without sufficient scientific evidence, except as provided for in paragraph 7 of Article 5.

3. Members shall ensure that their sanitary and phytosanitary measures do not arbitrarily or unjustifiably discriminate between Members where identical or similar conditions prevail, including between their own territory and that of other Members. Sanitary and phytosanitary measures shall not be applied in a manner which would constitute a disguised restriction on international trade.

---

1. In this Agreement, reference to Article XX(b) includes also the chapeau of that Article.

4. Sanitary or phytosanitary measures which conform to the relevant provisions of this Agreement shall be presumed to be in accordance with the obligations of the Members under the provisions of GATT 1994 which relate to the use of sanitary or phytosanitary measures, in particular the provisions of Article XX(b).

ARTICLE 3

Harmonization

1. To harmonize sanitary and phytosanitary measures on as wide a basis as possible, Members shall base their sanitary or phytosanitary measures on international standards, guidelines or recommendations, where they exist, except as otherwise provided for in this Agreement, and in particular in paragraph 3.

2. Sanitary or phytosanitary measures which conform to international standards, guidelines or recommendations shall be deemed to be necessary to protect human, animal or plant life or health, and presumed to be consistent with the relevant provisions of this Agreement and of GATT 1994.

3. Members may introduce or maintain sanitary or phytosanitary measures which result in a higher level of sanitary or phytosanitary protection than would be achieved by measures based on the relevant international standards, guidelines or recommendations, if there is a scientific justification, or as a consequence of the level of sanitary or phytosanitary protection a Member determines to be appropriate in accordance with the relevant provisions of paragraphs 1 through 8 of Article 5.[2] Notwithstanding the above, all measures which result in a level of sanitary or phytosanitary protection different from that which would be achieved by measures based on international standards, guidelines or recommendations shall not be inconsistent with any other provision of this Agreement.

4. Members shall play a full part, within the limits of their resources, in the relevant international organizations and their subsidiary bodies, in particular the Codex Alimentarius Commission, the

---

2. For the purposes of paragraph 3 of Article 3, there is a scientific justification if, on the basis of an examination and evaluation of available scientific information in conformity with the relevant provisions of this Agreement, a Member determines that the relevant international standards, guidelines or recommendations are not sufficient to achieve its appropriate level of sanitary or phytosanitary protection.

International Office of Epizootics, and the international and regional organizations operating within the framework of the International Plant Protection Convention, to promote within these organizations the development and periodic review of standards, guidelines and recommendations with respect to all aspects of sanitary and phytosanitary measures.

5. The Committee on Sanitary and Phytosanitary Measures provided for in paragraphs 1 and 4 of Article 12 (referred to in this Agreement as the "Committee") shall develop a procedure to monitor the process of international harmonization and coordinate efforts in this regard with the relevant international organizations.

ARTICLE 4
Equivalence

1. Members shall accept the sanitary or phytosanitary measures of other Members as equivalent, even if these measures differ from their own or from those used by other Members trading in the same product, if the exporting Member objectively demonstrates to the importing Member that its measures achieve the importing Member's appropriate level of sanitary or phytosanitary protection. For this purpose, reasonable access shall be given, upon request, to the importing Member for inspection, testing and other relevant procedures.

2. Members shall, upon request, enter into consultations with the aim of achieving bilateral and multilateral agreements on recognition of the equivalence of specified sanitary or phytosanitary measures.

ARTICLE 5
Assessment of Risk and Determination of the Appropriate Level of Sanitary or Phytosanitary Protection

1. Members shall ensure that their sanitary or phytosanitary measures are based on an assessment, as appropriate to the circumstances, of the risks to human, animal or plant life or health, taking into account risk assessment techniques developed by the relevant international organizations.

2. In the assessment of risks, Members shall take into account available scientific evidence; relevant processes and production methods; relevant inspection, sampling and testing methods; prevalence of specific diseases or pests; existence of pest- or disease-

free areas; relevant ecological and environmental conditions; and quarantine or other treatment.

3. In assessing the risk to animal or plant life or health and determining the measure to be applied for achieving the appropriate level of sanitary or phytosanitary protection from such risk, Members shall take into account as relevant economic factors: the potential damage in terms of loss of production or sales in the event of the entry, establishment or spread of a pest or disease; the costs of control or eradication in the territory of the importing Member; and the relative cost-effectiveness of alternative approaches to limiting risks.

4. Members should, when determining the appropriate level of sanitary or phytosanitary protection, take into account the objective of minimizing negative trade effects.

5. With the objective of achieving consistency in the application of the concept of appropriate level of sanitary or phytosanitary protection against risks to human life or health, or to animal and plant life or health, each Member shall avoid arbitrary or unjustifiable distinctions in the levels it considers to be appropriate in different situations, if such distinctions result in discrimination or a disguised restriction on international trade. Members shall cooperate in the Committee, in accordance with paragraphs 1, 2 and 3 of Article 12, to develop guidelines to further the practical implementation of this provision. In developing the guidelines, the Committee shall take into account all relevant factors, including the exceptional character of human health risks to which people voluntarily expose themselves.

6. Without prejudice to paragraph 2 of Article 3, when establishing or maintaining sanitary or phytosanitary measures to achieve the appropriate level of sanitary or phytosanitary protection, Members shall ensure that such measures are not more trade-restrictive than required to achieve their appropriate level of sanitary or phytosanitary protection, taking into account technical and economic feasibility.[3]

7. In cases where relevant scientific evidence is insufficient, a

3. For purposes of paragraph 6 of Article 5, a measure is not more trade-restrictive than required unless there is another measure, reasonably available taking into account technical and economic feasibility, that achieves the appropriate level of sanitary or phytosanitary protection and is significantly less restrictive to trade.

Member may provisionally adopt sanitary or phytosanitary measures on the basis of available pertinent information, including that from the relevant international organizations as well as from sanitary or phytosanitary measures applied by other Members. In such circumstances, Members shall seek to obtain the additional information necessary for a more objective assessment of risk and review the sanitary or phytosanitary measure accordingly within a reasonable period of time.

8. When a Member has reason to believe that a specific sanitary or phytosanitary measure introduced or maintained by another Member is constraining, or has the potential to constrain, its exports and the measure is not based on the relevant international standards, guidelines or recommendations, or such standards, guidelines or recommendations do not exist, an explanation of the reasons for such sanitary or phytosanitary measure may be requested and shall be provided by the Member maintaining the measure.

ARTICLE 6

Adaptation to Regional Conditions, Including Pest- or Disease-Free Areas and Areas of Low Pest or Disease Prevalence

1. Members shall ensure that their sanitary or phytosanitary measures are adapted to the sanitary or phytosanitary characteristics of the area - whether all of a country, part of a country, or all or parts of several countries - from which the product originated and to which the product is destined. In assessing the sanitary or phytosanitary characteristics of a region, Members shall take into account, *inter alia*, the level of prevalence of specific diseases or pests, the existence of eradication or control programmes, and appropriate criteria or guidelines which may be developed by the relevant international organizations.

2. Members shall, in particular, recognize the concepts of pest- or disease-free areas and areas of low pest or disease prevalence. Determination of such areas shall be based on factors such as geography, ecosystems, epidemiological surveillance, and the effectiveness of sanitary or phytosanitary controls.

3. Exporting Members claiming that areas within their territories are pest- or disease-free areas or areas of low pest or disease prevalence shall provide the necessary evidence thereof in order to objectively demonstrate to the importing Member that such areas are,

and are likely to remain, pest- or disease-free areas or areas of low pest or disease prevalence, respectively. For this purpose, reasonable access shall be given, upon request, to the importing Member for inspection, testing and other relevant procedures.

ARTICLE 7

Transparency

Members shall notify changes in their sanitary or phytosanitary measures and shall provide information on their sanitary or phytosanitary measures in accordance with the provisions of Annex B.

ARTICLE 8

Control, Inspection and Approval Procedures

Members shall observe the provisions of Annex C in the operation of control, inspection and approval procedures, including national systems for approving the use of additives or for establishing tolerances for contaminants in foods, beverages or feedstuffs, and otherwise ensure that their procedures are not inconsistent with the provisions of this Agreement.

ARTICLE 9

Technical Assistance

1. Members agree to facilitate the provision of technical assistance to other Members, especially developing country Members, either bilaterally or through the appropriate international organizations. Such assistance may be, *inter alia*, in the areas of processing technologies, research and infrastructure, including in the establishment of national regulatory bodies, and may take the form of advice, credits, donations and grants, including for the purpose of seeking technical expertise, training and equipment to allow such countries to adjust to, and comply with, sanitary or phytosanitary measures necessary to achieve the appropriate level of sanitary or phytosanitary protection in their export markets.

2. Where substantial investments are required in order for an exporting developing country Member to fulfil the sanitary or phytosanitary requirements of an importing Member, the latter shall consider providing such technical assistance as will permit the developing country Member to maintain and expand its market access opportunities for the product involved.

ARTICLE 10

Special and Differential Treatment

1. In the preparation and application of sanitary or phytosanitary measures, Members shall take account of the special needs of developing country Members, and in particular of the least-developed country Members.

2. Where the appropriate level of sanitary or phytosanitary protection allows scope for the phased introduction of new sanitary or phytosanitary measures, longer time-frames for compliance should be accorded on products of interest to developing country Members so as to maintain opportunities for their exports.

3. With a view to ensuring that developing country Members are able to comply with the provisions of this Agreement, the Committee is enabled to grant to such countries, upon request, specified, time-limited exceptions in whole or in part from obligations under this Agreement, taking into account their financial, trade and development needs.

4. Members should encourage and facilitate the active participation of developing country Members in the relevant international organizations.

ARTICLE 11

Consultations and Dispute Settlement

1. The provisions of Articles XXII and XXIII of GATT 1994 as elaborated and applied by the Dispute Settlement Understanding shall apply to consultations and the settlement of disputes under this Agreement, except as otherwise specifically provided herein.

2. In a dispute under this Agreement involving scientific or technical issues, a panel should seek advice from experts chosen by the panel in consultation with the parties to the dispute. To this end, the panel may, when it deems it appropriate, establish an advisory technical experts group, or consult the relevant international organizations, at the request of either party to the dispute or on its own initiative.

3. Nothing in this Agreement shall impair the rights of Members under other international agreements, including the right to resort to the good offices or dispute settlement mechanisms of other

international organizations or established under any international agreement.

ARTICLE 12

Administration

1. A Committee on Sanitary and Phytosanitary Measures is hereby established to provide a regular forum for consultations. It shall carry out the functions necessary to implement the provisions of this Agreement and the furtherance of its objectives, in particular with respect to harmonization. The Committee shall reach its decisions by consensus.

2. The Committee shall encourage and facilitate ad hoc consultations or negotiations among Members on specific sanitary or phytosanitary issues. The Committee shall encourage the use of international standards, guidelines or recommendations by all Members and, in this regard, shall sponsor technical consultation and study with the objective of increasing coordination and integration between international and national systems and approaches for approving the use of food additives or for establishing tolerances for contaminants in foods, beverages or feedstuffs.

3. The Committee shall maintain close contact with the relevant international organizations in the field of sanitary and phytosanitary protection, especially with the Codex Alimentarius Commission, the International Office of Epizootics, and the Secretariat of the International Plant Protection Convention, with the objective of securing the best available scientific and technical advice for the administration of this Agreement and in order to ensure that unnecessary duplication of effort is avoided.

4. The Committee shall develop a procedure to monitor the process of international harmonization and the use of international standards, guidelines or recommendations. For this purpose, the Committee should, in conjunction with the relevant international organizations, establish a list of international standards, guidelines or recommendations relating to sanitary or phytosanitary measures which the Committee determines to have a major trade impact. The list should include an indication by Members of those international standards, guidelines or recommendations which they apply as conditions for import or on the basis of which imported products

conforming to these standards can enjoy access to their markets. For those cases in which a Member does not apply an international standard, guideline or recommendation as a condition for import, the Member should provide an indication of the reason therefor, and, in particular, whether it considers that the standard is not stringent enough to provide the appropriate level of sanitary or phytosanitary protection. If a Member revises its position, following its indication of the use of a standard, guideline or recommendation as a condition for import, it should provide an explanation for its change and so inform the Secretariat as well as the relevant international organizations, unless such notification and explanation is given according to the procedures of Annex B.

5. In order to avoid unnecessary duplication, the Committee may decide, as appropriate, to use the information generated by the procedures, particularly for notification, which are in operation in the relevant international organizations.

6. The Committee may, on the basis of an initiative from one of the Members, through appropriate channels invite the relevant international organizations or their subsidiary bodies to examine specific matters with respect to a particular standard, guideline or recommendation, including the basis of explanations for non-use given according to paragraph 4.

7. The Committee shall review the operation and implementation of this Agreement three years after the date of entry into force of the WTO Agreement, and thereafter as the need arises. Where appropriate, the Committee may submit to the Council for Trade in Goods proposals to amend the text of this Agreement having regard, *inter alia*, to the experience gained in its implementation.

ARTICLE 13

Implementation

Members are fully responsible under this Agreement for the observance of all obligations set forth herein. Members shall formulate and implement positive measures and mechanisms in support of the observance of the provisions of this Agreement by other than central government bodies. Members shall take such reasonable measures as may be available to them to ensure that non-governmental entities within their territories, as well as regional bodies in which relevant entities within their territories are members, comply with the relevant provisions of this Agreement. In addition, Members shall not take measures which have the effect of, directly or indirectly, requiring or encouraging such regional or non-governmental entities, or local governmental bodies, to act in a manner inconsistent with the provisions of this Agreement. Members shall ensure that they rely on the services of non-governmental entities for implementing sanitary or phytosanitary measures only if these entities comply with the provisions of this Agreement.

ARTICLE 14

Final Provisions

The least-developed country Members may delay application of the provisions of this Agreement for a period of five years following the date of entry into force of the WTO Agreement with respect to their sanitary or phytosanitary measures affecting importation or imported products. Other developing country Members may delay application of the provisions of this Agreement, other than paragraph 8 of Article 5 and Article 7, for two years following the date of entry into force of the WTO Agreement with respect to their existing sanitary or phytosanitary measures affecting importation or imported products, where such application is prevented by a lack of technical expertise, technical infrastructure or resources.

ANNEX A

DEFINITIONS[4]

1. *Sanitary or phytosanitary measure* - Any measure applied:

(a) to protect animal or plant life or health within the territory of the Member from risks arising from the entry, establishment or spread of pests, diseases, disease-carrying organisms or disease-causing organisms;

(b) to protect human or animal life or health within the territory of the Member from risks arising from additives, contaminants, toxins or disease-causing organisms in foods, beverages or feedstuffs;

(c) to protect human life or health within the territory of the Member from risks arising from diseases carried

4. For the purpose of these definitions, "animal" includes fish and wild fauna; "plant" includes forests and wild flora; "pests" include weeds; and "contaminants" include pesticide and veterinary drug residues and extraneous matter.

by animals, plants or products thereof, or from the entry, establishment or spread of pests; or

(d) to prevent or limit other damage within the territory of the Member from the entry, establishment or spread of pests.

Sanitary or phytosanitary measures include all relevant laws, decrees, regulations, requirements and procedures including, *inter alia*, end product criteria; processes and production methods; testing, inspection, certification and approval procedures; quarantine treatments including relevant requirements associated with the transport of animals or plants, or with the materials necessary for their survival during transport; provisions on relevant statistical methods, sampling procedures and methods of risk assessment; and packaging and labelling requirements directly related to food safety.

2. *Harmonization* - The establishment, recognition and application of common sanitary and phytosanitary measures by different Members.

3. *International standards, guidelines and recommendations*

(a) for food safety, the standards, guidelines and recommendations established by the Codex Alimentarius Commission relating to food additives, veterinary drug and pesticide residues, contaminants, methods of analysis and sampling, and codes and guidelines of hygienic practice;

(b) for animal health and zoonoses, the standards, guidelines and recommendations developed under the auspices of the International Office of Epizootics;

(c) for plant health, the international standards, guidelines and recommendations developed under the auspices of the Secretariat of the International Plant Protection Convention in cooperation with regional organizations operating within the framework of the International Plant Protection Convention; and

(d) for matters not covered by the above organizations, appropriate standards, guidelines and recommendations promulgated by other relevant international organizations open for membership to all Members, as identified by the Committee.

4. *Risk assessment* - The evaluation of the likelihood of entry,

establishment or spread of a pest or disease within the territory of an importing Member according to the sanitary or phytosanitary measures which might be applied, and of the associated potential biological and economic consequences; or the evaluation of the potential for adverse effects on human or animal health arising from the presence of additives, contaminants, toxins or disease-causing organisms in food, beverages or feedstuffs.

5. *Appropriate level of sanitary or phytosanitary protection* - The level of protection deemed appropriate by the Member establishing a sanitary or phytosanitary measure to protect human, animal or plant life or health within its territory.

NOTE: Many Members otherwise refer to this concept as the "acceptable level of risk".

6. *Pest- or disease-free area* - An area, whether all of a country, part of a country, or all or parts of several countries, as identified by the competent authorities, in which a specific pest or disease does not occur.

NOTE: A pest- or disease-free area may surround, be surrounded by, or be adjacent to an area - whether within part of a country or in a geographic region which includes parts of or all of several countries -in which a specific pest or disease is known to occur but is subject to regional control measures such as the establishment of protection, surveillance and buffer zones which will confine or eradicate the pest or disease in question.

7. *Area of low pest or disease prevalence* - An area, whether all of a country, part of a country, or all or parts of several countries, as identified by the competent authorities, in which a specific pest or disease occurs at low levels and which is subject to effective surveillance, control or eradication measures.

ANNEX B

TRANSPARENCY OF SANITARY AND PHYTOSANITARY REGULATIONS

Publication of regulations

1. Members shall ensure that all sanitary and phytosanitary regulations[5] which have been adopted are published promptly in such

5. Sanitary and phytosanitary measures such as laws, decrees or ordinances which are applicable generally.

a manner as to enable interested Members to become acquainted with them.

2. Except in urgent circumstances, Members shall allow a reasonable interval between the publication of a sanitary or phytosanitary regulation and its entry into force in order to allow time for producers in exporting Members, and particularly in developing country Members, to adapt their products and methods of production to the requirements of the importing Member.

Enquiry points

3. Each Member shall ensure that one enquiry point exists which is responsible for the provision of answers to all reasonable questions from interested Members as well as for the provision of relevant documents regarding:

(a) any sanitary or phytosanitary regulations adopted or proposed within its territory;

(b) any control and inspection procedures, production and quarantine treatment, pesticide tolerance and food additive approval procedures, which are operated within its territory;

(c) risk assessment procedures, factors taken into consideration, as well as the determination of the appropriate level of sanitary or phytosanitary protection;

(d) the membership and participation of the Member, or of relevant bodies within its territory, in international and regional sanitary and phytosanitary organizations and systems, as well as in bilateral and multilateral agreements and arrangements within the scope of this Agreement, and the texts of such agreements and arrangements.

4. Members shall ensure that where copies of documents are requested by interested Members, they are supplied at the same price (if any), apart from the cost of delivery, as to the nationals[6] of the Member concerned.

6. When "nationals" are referred to in this Agreement, the term shall be deemed, in the case of a separate customs territory Member of the WTO, to mean persons, natural or legal, who are domiciled or who have a real and effective industrial or commercial establishment in that customs territory.

Notification procedures

5. Whenever an international standard, guideline or recommendation does not exist or the content of a proposed sanitary or phytosanitary regulation is not substantially the same as the content of an international standard, guideline or recommendation, and if the regulation may have a significant effect on trade of other Members, Members shall:

(a) publish a notice at an early stage in such a manner as to enable interested Members to become acquainted with the proposal to introduce a particular regulation;

(b) notify other Members, through the Secretariat, of the products to be covered by the regulation together with a brief indication of the objective and rationale of the proposed regulation. Such notifications shall take place at an early stage, when amendments can still be introduced and comments taken into account;

(c) provide upon request to other Members copies of the proposed regulation and, whenever possible, identify the parts which in substance deviate from international standards, guidelines or recommendations;

(d) without discrimination, allow reasonable time for other Members to make comments in writing, discuss these comments upon request, and take the comments and the results of the discussions into account.

6. However, where urgent problems of health protection arise or threaten to arise for a Member, that Member may omit such of the steps enumerated in paragraph 5 of this Annex as it finds necessary, provided that the Member:

(a) immediately notifies other Members, through the Secretariat, of the particular regulation and the products covered, with a brief indication of the objective and the rationale of the regulation, including the nature of the urgent problem(s);

(b) provides, upon request, copies of the regulation to other Members;

(c) allows other Members to make comments in writing, discusses these comments upon request, and takes the comments and the results of the discussions into account.

7. Notifications to the Secretariat shall be in English, French or Spanish.

8. Developed country Members shall, if requested by other Members, provide copies of the documents or, in case of voluminous documents, summaries of the documents covered by a specific notification in English, French or Spanish.

9. The Secretariat shall promptly circulate copies of the notification to all Members and interested international organizations and draw the attention of developing country Members to any notifications relating to products of particular interest to them.

10. Members shall designate a single central government authority as responsible for the implementation, on the national level, of the provisions concerning notification procedures according to paragraphs 5, 6, 7 and 8 of this Annex.

General reservations

11. Nothing in this Agreement shall be construed as requiring:

(a) the provision of particulars or copies of drafts or the publication of texts other than in the language of the Member except as stated in paragraph 8 of this Annex; or

(b) Members to disclose confidential information which would impede enforcement of sanitary or phytosanitary legislation or which would prejudice the legitimate commercial interests of particular enterprises.

ANNEX C

CONTROL, INSPECTION AND APPROVAL PROCEDURES[7]

1. Members shall ensure, with respect to any procedure to check and ensure the fulfilment of sanitary or phytosanitary measures, that:

(a) such procedures are undertaken and completed without undue delay and in no less favourable manner for imported products than for like domestic products;

7. Control, inspection and approval procedures include, *inter alia*, procedures for sampling, testing and certification.

(b) the standard processing period of each procedure is published or that the anticipated processing period is communicated to the applicant upon request; when receiving an application, the competent body promptly examines the completeness of the documentation and informs the applicant in a precise and complete manner of all deficiencies; the competent body transmits as soon as possible the results of the procedure in a precise and complete manner to the applicant so that corrective action may be taken if necessary; even when the application has deficiencies, the competent body proceeds as far as practicable with the procedure if the applicant so requests; and that upon request, the applicant is informed of the stage of the procedure, with any delay being explained;

(c) information requirements are limited to what is necessary for appropriate control, inspection and approval procedures, including for approval of the use of additives or for the establishment of tolerances for contaminants in food, beverages or feedstuffs;

(d) the confidentiality of information about imported products arising from or supplied in connection with control, inspection and approval is respected in a way no less favourable than for domestic products and in such a manner that legitimate commercial interests are protected;

(e) any requirements for control, inspection and approval of individual specimens of a product are limited to what is reasonable and necessary;

(f) any fees imposed for the procedures on imported products are equitable in relation to any fees charged on like domestic products or products originating in any other Member and should be no higher than the actual cost of the service;

(g) the same criteria should be used in the siting of facilities used in the procedures and the selection of samples of imported products as for domestic products so as to minimize the inconvenience to applicants, importers, exporters or their agents;

(h) whenever specifications of a product are changed subsequent to its control and inspection in light of the applicable regulations, the procedure for the modified product is limited to what is necessary to determine whether adequate confidence exists that the product still meets the regulations concerned; and

(i) a procedure exists to review complaints concerning the operation of such procedures and to take corrective action when a complaint is justified.

Where an importing Member operates a system for the approval of the use of food additives or for the establishment of tolerances for contaminants in food, beverages or feedstuffs which prohibits or restricts access to its domestic markets for products based on the absence of an approval, the importing Member shall consider the use of a relevant international standard as the basis for access until a final determination is made.

2. Where a sanitary or phytosanitary measure specifies control at the level of production, the Member in whose territory the production takes place shall provide the necessary assistance to facilitate such control and the work of the controlling authorities.

3. Nothing in this Agreement shall prevent Members from carrying out reasonable inspection within their own territories.

AGREEMENT ON TEXTILES AND CLOTHING

Members,

Recalling that Ministers agreed at Punta del Este that "negotiations in the area of textiles and clothing shall aim to formulate modalities that would permit the eventual integration of this sector into GATT on the basis of strengthened GATT rules and disciplines, thereby also contributing to the objective of further liberalization of trade";

Recalling also that in the April 1989 Decision of the Trade Negotiations Committee it was agreed that the process of integration should commence following the conclusion of the Uruguay Round of Multilateral Trade Negotiations and should be progressive in character;

Recalling further that it was agreed that special treatment should be accorded to the least-developed country Members;

Hereby *agree* as follows:

ARTICLE 1

1. This Agreement sets out provisions to be applied by Members during a transition period for the integration of the textiles and clothing sector into GATT 1994.

2. Members agree to use the provisions of paragraph 18 of Article 2 and paragraph 6(b) of Article 6 in such a way as to permit meaningful increases in access possibilities for small suppliers and the development of commercially significant trading opportunities for new entrants in the field of textiles and clothing trade.[1]

3. Members shall have due regard to the situation of those Members which have not accepted the Protocols extending the Arrangement Regarding International Trade in Textiles (referred to in this Agreement as the "MFA") since 1986 and, to the extent possible, shall afford them special treatment in applying the provisions of this Agreement.

4. Members agree that the particular interests of the cotton-producing exporting Members should, in consultation with them, be reflected in the implementation of the provisions of this Agreement.

5. In order to facilitate the integration of the textiles and clothing sector into GATT 1994, Members should allow for continuous autonomous industrial adjustment and increased competition in their markets.

6. Unless otherwise provided in this Agreement, its provisions shall not affect the rights and obligations of Members under the provisions of the WTO Agreement and the Multilateral Trade Agreements.

7. The textile and clothing products to which this Agreement applies are set out in the Annex.

ARTICLE 2

1. All quantitative restrictions within bilateral agreements maintained under Article 4 or notified under Article 7 or 8 of the MFA in force on the day before the entry into force of the WTO Agreement shall, within 60 days following such entry into force, be notified in detail, including the restraint levels, growth rates and

---

1. To the extent possible, exports from a least-developed country Member may also benefit from this provision.

flexibility provisions, by the Members maintaining such restrictions to the Textiles Monitoring Body provided for in Article 8 (referred to in this Agreement as the "TMB"). Members agree that as of the date of entry into force of the WTO Agreement, all such restrictions maintained between GATT 1947 contracting parties, and in place on the day before such entry into force, shall be governed by the provisions of this Agreement.

2. The TMB shall circulate these notifications to all Members for their information. It is open to any Member to bring to the attention of the TMB, within 60 days of the circulation of the notifications, any observations it deems appropriate with regard to such notifications. Such observations shall be circulated to the other Members for their information. The TMB may make recommendations, as appropriate, to the Members concerned.

3. When the 12-month period of restrictions to be notified under paragraph 1 does not coincide with the 12-month period immediately preceding the date of entry into force of the WTO Agreement, the Members concerned should mutually agree on arrangements to bring the period of restrictions into line with the agreement year[2], and to establish notional base levels of such restrictions in order to implement the provisions of this Article. Concerned Members agree to enter into consultations promptly upon request with a view to reaching such mutual agreement. Any such arrangements shall take into account, *inter alia*, seasonal patterns of shipments in recent years. The results of these consultations shall be notified to the TMB, which shall make such recommendations as it deems appropriate to the Members concerned.

4. The restrictions notified under paragraph 1 shall be deemed to constitute the totality of such restrictions applied by the respective Members on the day before the entry into force of the WTO Agreement. No new restrictions in terms of products or Members shall be introduced except under the provisions of this Agreement or relevant GATT 1994 provisions.[3] Restrictions not notified within

2. The "agreement year" is defined to mean a 12-month period beginning from the date of entry into force of the WTO Agreement and at the subsequent 12-month intervals.

3. The relevant GATT 1994 provisions shall not include Article XIX in respect of products not yet integrated into GATT 1994, except as specifically provided in paragraph 3 of the Annex.

60 days of the date of entry into force of the WTO Agreement shall be terminated forthwith.

5. Any unilateral measure taken under Article 3 of the MFA prior to the date of entry into force of the WTO Agreement may remain in effect for the duration specified therein, but not exceeding 12 months, if it has been reviewed by the Textiles Surveillance Body (referred to in this Agreement as the "TSB") established under the MFA. Should the TSB not have had the opportunity to review any such unilateral measure, it shall be reviewed by the TMB in accordance with the rules and procedures governing Article 3 measures under the MFA. Any measure applied under an MFA Article 4 agreement prior to the date of entry into force of the WTO Agreement that is the subject of a dispute which the TSB has not had the opportunity to review shall also be reviewed by the TMB in accordance with the MFA rules and procedures applicable for such a review.

6. On the date of entry into force of the WTO Agreement, each Member shall integrate into GATT 1994 products which accounted for not less than 16 per cent of the total volume of the Member's 1990 imports of the products in the Annex, in terms of HS lines or categories. The products to be integrated shall encompass products from each of the following four groups: tops and yarns, fabrics, made-up textile products, and clothing.

7. Full details of the actions to be taken pursuant to paragraph 6 shall be notified by the Members concerned according to the following:

(a) Members maintaining restrictions falling under paragraph 1 undertake, notwithstanding the date of entry into force of the WTO Agreement, to notify such details to the GATT Secretariat not later than the date determined by the Ministerial Decision of 15 April 1994. The GATT Secretariat shall promptly circulate these notifications to the other participants for information. These notifications will be made available to the TMB, when established, for the purposes of paragraph 21;

(b) Members which have, pursuant to paragraph 1 of Article 6, retained the right to use the provisions of Article 6, shall notify such details to the TMB not later than 60 days following the date of entry into force of the WTO Agreement, or, in the case of those Members covered by paragraph 3 of Article 1, not later than at the end of the 12th month that the WTO Agreement is in effect. The TMB shall circulate these notifications to the other Members for information and review them as provided in paragraph 21.

8. The remaining products, i.e. the products not integrated into GATT 1994 under paragraph 6, shall be integrated, in terms of HS lines or categories, in three stages, as follows:

(a) on the first day of the 37th month that the WTO Agreement is in effect, products which accounted for not less than 17 per cent of the total volume of the Member's 1990 imports of the products in the Annex. The products to be integrated by the Members shall encompass products from each of the following four groups: tops and yarns, fabrics, made-up textile products, and clothing;

(b) on the first day of the 85th month that the WTO Agreement is in effect, products which accounted for not less than 18 per cent of the total volume of the Member's 1990 imports of the products in the Annex. The products to be integrated by the Members shall encompass products from each of the following four groups: tops and yarns, fabrics, made-up textile products, and clothing;

(c) on the first day of the 121st month that the WTO Agreement is in effect, the textiles and clothing sector shall stand integrated into GATT 1994, all restrictions under this Agreement having been eliminated.

9. Members which have notified, pursuant to paragraph 1 of Article 6, their intention not to retain the right to use the provisions of Article 6 shall, for the purposes of this Agreement, be deemed to have integrated their textiles and clothing products into GATT 1994. Such Members shall, therefore, be exempted from complying with the provisions of paragraphs 6 to 8 and 11.

10. Nothing in this Agreement shall prevent a Member which has submitted an integration programme pursuant to paragraph 6 or

8 from integrating products into GATT 1994 earlier than provided for in such a programme. However, any such integration of products shall take effect at the beginning of an agreement year, and details shall be notified to the TMB at least three months prior thereto for circulation to all Members.

11. The respective programmes of integration, in pursuance of paragraph 8, shall be notified in detail to the TMB at least 12 months before their coming into effect, and circulated by the TMB to all Members.

12. The base levels of the restrictions on the remaining products, mentioned in paragraph 8, shall be the restraint levels referred to in paragraph 1.

13. During Stage 1 of this Agreement (from the date of entry into force of the WTO Agreement to the 36th month that it is in effect, inclusive) the level of each restriction under MFA bilateral agreements in force for the 12-month period prior to the date of entry into force of the WTO Agreement shall be increased annually by not less than the growth rate established for the respective restrictions, increased by 16 per cent.

14. Except where the Council for Trade in Goods or the Dispute Settlement Body decides otherwise under paragraph 12 of Article 8, the level of each remaining restriction shall be increased annually during subsequent stages of this Agreement by not less than the following:

(a) for Stage 2 (from the 37th to the 84th month that the WTO Agreement is in effect, inclusive), the growth rate for the respective restrictions during Stage 1, increased by 25 per cent;

(b) for Stage 3 (from the 85th to the 120th month that the WTO Agreement is in effect, inclusive), the growth rate for the respective restrictions during Stage 2, increased by 27 per cent.

15. Nothing in this Agreement shall prevent a Member from eliminating any restriction maintained pursuant to this Article, effective at the beginning of any agreement year during the transition period, provided the exporting Member concerned and the TMB are notified at least three months prior to the elimination coming into effect. The period for prior notification may be shortened to 30 days with

the agreement of the restrained Member. The TMB shall circulate such notifications to all Members. In considering the elimination of restrictions as envisaged in this paragraph, the Members concerned shall take into account the treatment of similar exports from other Members.

16. Flexibility provisions, i.e. swing, carryover and carry forward, applicable to all restrictions maintained pursuant to this Article, shall be the same as those provided for in MFA bilateral agreements for the 12-month period prior to the entry into force of the WTO Agreement. No quantitative limits shall be placed or maintained on the combined use of swing, carryover and carry forward.

17. Administrative arrangements, as deemed necessary in relation to the implementation of any provision of this Article, shall be a matter for agreement between the Members concerned. Any such arrangements shall be notified to the TMB.

18. As regards those Members whose exports are subject to restrictions on the day before the entry into force of the WTO Agreement and whose restrictions represent 1.2 per cent or less of the total volume of the restrictions applied by an importing Member as of 31 December 1991 and notified under this Article, meaningful improvement in access for their exports shall be provided, at the entry into force of the WTO Agreement and for the duration of this Agreement, through advancement by one stage of the growth rates set out in paragraphs 13 and 14, or through at least equivalent changes as may be mutually agreed with respect to a different mix of base levels, growth and flexibility provisions. Such improvements shall be notified to the TMB.

19. In any case, during the duration of this Agreement, in which a safeguard measure is initiated by a Member under Article XIX of GATT 1994 in respect of a particular product during a period of one year immediately following the integration of that product into GATT 1994 in accordance with the provisions of this Article, the provisions of Article XIX, as interpreted by the Agreement on Safeguards, will apply, save as set out in paragraph 20.

20. Where such a measure is applied using non-tariff means, the importing Member concerned shall apply the measure in a manner as set forth in paragraph 2(d) of Article XIII of GATT 1994 at the request of any exporting Member whose exports of such products were subject to restrictions under this Agreement at any time in the

one-year period immediately prior to the initiation of the safeguard measure. The exporting Member concerned shall administer such a measure. The applicable level shall not reduce the relevant exports below the level of a recent representative period, which shall normally be the average of exports from the Member concerned in the last three representative years for which statistics are available. Furthermore, when the safeguard measure is applied for more than one year, the applicable level shall be progressively liberalized at regular intervals during the period of application. In such cases the exporting Member concerned shall not exercise the right of suspending substantially equivalent concessions or other obligations under paragraph 3(a) of Article XIX of GATT 1994.

21. The TMB shall keep under review the implementation of this Article. It shall, at the request of any Member, review any particular matter with reference to the implementation of the provisions of this Article. It shall make appropriate recommendations or findings within 30 days to the Member or Members concerned, after inviting the participation of such Members.

ARTICLE 3

1. Within 60 days following the date of entry into force of the WTO Agreement, Members maintaining restrictions[4] on textile and clothing products (other than restrictions maintained under the MFA and covered by the provisions of Article 2), whether consistent with GATT 1994 or not, shall (*a*) notify them in detail to the TMB, or (*b*) provide to the TMB notifications with respect to them which have been submitted to any other WTO body. The notifications should, wherever applicable, provide information with respect to any GATT 1994 justification for the restrictions. including GATT 1994 provisions on which they are based.

2. Members maintaining restrictions falling under paragraph 1, except those justified under a GATT 1994 provision, shall either:

(a) bring them into conformity with GATT 1994 within one year following the entry into force of the WTO Agreement, and notify this action to the TMB for its information; or

(b) phase them out progressively according to a programme

4. Restrictions denote all unilateral quantitative restrictions, bilateral arrangements and other measures having a similar effect.

to be presented to the TMB by the Member maintaining the restrictions not later than six months after the date of entry into force of the WTO Agreement. This programme shall provide for all restrictions to be phased out within a period not exceeding the duration of this Agreement. The TMB may make recommendations to the Member concerned with respect to such a programme.

3. During the duration of this Agreement, Members shall provide to the TMB, for its information, notifications submitted to any other WTO bodies with respect to any new restrictions or changes in existing restrictions on textile and clothing products, taken under any GATT 1994 provision, within 60 days of their coming into effect.

4. It shall be open to any Member to make reverse notifications to the TMB, for its information, in regard to the GATT 1994 justification, or in regard to any restrictions that may not have been notified under the provisions of this Article. Actions with respect to such notifications may be pursued by any Member under relevant GATT 1994 provisions or procedures in the appropriate WTO body.

5. The TMB shall circulate the notifications made pursuant to this Article to all Members for their information.

ARTICLE 4

1. Restrictions referred to in Article 2, and those applied under Article 6, shall be administered by the exporting Members. Importing Members shall not be obliged to accept shipments in excess of the restrictions notified under Article 2, or of restrictions applied pursuant to Article 6.

2. Members agree that the introduction of changes, such as changes in practices, rules, procedures and categorization of textile and clothing products, including those changes relating to the Harmonized System, in the implementation or administration of those restrictions notified or applied under this Agreement should not: upset the balance of rights and obligations between the Members concerned under this Agreement; adversely affect the access available to a Member; impede the full utilization of such access; or disrupt trade under this Agreement.

3. If a product which constitutes only part of a restriction is notified for integration pursuant to the provisions of Article 2, Members

agree that any change in the level of that restriction shall not upset the balance of rights and obligations between the Members concerned under this Agreement.

4. When changes mentioned in paragraphs 2 and 3 are necessary, however, Members agree that the Member initiating such changes shall inform and, wherever possible, initiate consultations with the affected Member or Members prior to the implementation of such changes, with a view to reaching a mutually acceptable solution regarding appropriate and equitable adjustment. Members further agree that where consultation prior to implementation is not feasible, the Member initiating such changes will, at the request of the affected Member, consult, within 60 days if possible, with the Members concerned with a view to reaching a mutually satisfactory solution regarding appropriate and equitable adjustments. If a mutually satisfactory solution is not reached, any Member involved may refer the matter to the TMB for recommendations as provided in Article 8. Should the TSB not have had the opportunity to review a dispute concerning such changes introduced prior to the entry into force of the WTO Agreement, it shall be reviewed by the TMB in accordance with the rules and procedures of the MFA applicable for such a review.

ARTICLE 5

1. Members agree that circumvention by transshipment, re-routing, false declaration concerning country or place of origin, and falsification of official documents, frustrates the implementation of this Agreement to integrate the textiles and clothing sector into GATT 1994. Accordingly, Members should establish the necessary legal provisions and/or administrative procedures to address and take action against such circumvention. Members further agree that, consistent with their domestic laws and procedures, they will cooperate fully to address problems arising from circumvention.

2. Should any Member believe that this Agreement is being circumvented by transshipment, re-routing, false declaration concerning country or place of origin, or falsification of official documents, and that no, or inadequate, measures are being applied to address and/or to take action against such circumvention, that Member should consult with the Member or Members concerned with a view to seeking a mutually satisfactory solution. Such consultations should be held promptly, and within 30 days when possible. If a mutually

satisfactory solution is not reached, the matter may be referred by any Member involved to the TMB for recommendations.

3. Members agree to take necessary action, consistent with their domestic laws and procedures, to prevent, to investigate and, where appropriate, to take legal and/or administrative action against circumvention practices within their territory. Members agree to cooperate fully, consistent with their domestic laws and procedures, in instances of circumvention or alleged circumvention of this Agreement, to establish the relevant facts in the places of import, export and, where applicable, transshipment. It is agreed that such cooperation, consistent with domestic laws and procedures, will include: investigation of circumvention practices which increase restrained exports to the Member maintaining such restraints; exchange of documents, correspondence, reports and other relevant information to the extent available; and facilitation of plant visits and contacts, upon request and on a case-by-case basis. Members should endeavour to clarify the circumstances of any such instances of circumvention or alleged circumvention, including the respective roles of the exporters or importers involved.

4. Where, as a result of investigation, there is sufficient evidence that circumvention has occurred (e.g. where evidence is available concerning the country or place of true origin, and the circumstances of such circumvention), Members agree that appropriate action, to the extent necessary to address the problem, should be taken. Such action may include the denial of entry of goods or, where goods have entered, having due regard to the actual circumstances and the involvement of the country or place of true origin, the adjustment of charges to restraint levels to reflect the true country or place of origin. Also, where there is evidence of the involvement of the territories of the Members through which the goods have been transshipped, such action may include the introduction of restraints with respect to such Members. Any such actions, together with their timing and scope, may be taken after consultations held with a view to arriving at a mutually satisfactory solution between the concerned Members and shall be notified to the TMB with full justification. The Members concerned may agree on other remedies in consultation. Any such agreement shall also be notified to the TMB, and the TMB may make such recommendations to the Members concerned as it deems appropriate. If a mutually satisfactory solution

is not reached, any Member concerned may refer the matter to the TMB for prompt review and recommendations.

5. Members note that some cases of circumvention may involve shipments transiting through countries or places with no changes or alterations made to the goods contained in such shipments in the places of transit. They note that it may not be generally practicable for such places of transit to exercise control over such shipments.

6. Members agree that false declaration concerning fibre content, quantities, description or classification of merchandise also frustrates the objective of this Agreement. Where there is evidence that any such false declaration has been made for purposes of circumvention, Members agree that appropriate measures, consistent with domestic laws and procedures, should be taken against the exporters or importers involved. Should any Member believe that this Agreement is being circumvented by such false declaration and that no, or inadequate, administrative measures are being applied to address and/or to take action against such circumvention, that Member should consult promptly with the Member involved with a view to seeking a mutually satisfactory solution. If such a solution is not reached, the matter may be referred by any Member involved to the TMB for recommendations. This provision is not intended to prevent Members from making technical adjustments when inadvertent errors in declarations have been made.

ARTICLE 6

1. Members recognize that during the transition period it may be necessary to apply a specific transitional safeguard mechanism (referred to in this Agreement as "transitional safeguard"). The transitional safeguard may be applied by any Member to products covered by the Annex, except those integrated into GATT 1994 under the provisions of Article 2. Members not maintaining restrictions falling under Article 2 shall notify the TMB within 60 days following the date of entry into force of the WTO Agreement, as to whether or not they wish to retain the right to use the provisions of this Article. Members which have not accepted the Protocols extending the MFA since 1986 shall make such notification within 6 months following the entry into force of the WTO Agreement. The transitional safeguard should be applied as sparingly as possible, consistently with the provisions of this Article and the effective implementation of the integration process under this Agreement.

2. Safeguard action may be taken under this Article when, on the basis of a determination by a Member[5], it is demonstrated that a particular product is being imported into its territory in such increased quantities as to cause serious damage, or actual threat thereof, to the domestic industry producing like and/or directly competitive products. Serious damage or actual threat thereof must demonstrably be caused by such increased quantities in total imports of that product and not by such other factors as technological changes or changes in consumer preference.

3. In making a determination of serious damage, or actual threat thereof, as referred to in paragraph 2, the Member shall examine the effect of those imports on the state of the particular industry, as reflected in changes in such relevant economic variables as output, productivity, utilization of capacity, inventories, market share, exports, wages, employment, domestic prices, profits and investment; none of which, either alone or combined with other factors, can necessarily give decisive guidance.

4. Any measure invoked pursuant to the provisions of this Article shall be applied on a Member-by-Member basis. The Member or Members to whom serious damage, or actual threat thereof, referred to in paragraphs 2 and 3, is attributed, shall be determined on the basis of a sharp and substantial increase in imports, actual or imminent[6], from such a Member or Members individually, and on the basis of the level of imports as compared with imports from other sources, market share, and import and domestic prices at a comparable stage of commercial transaction; none of these factors, either alone or combined with other factors, can necessarily give decisive guidance. Such safeguard measure shall not be applied to the exports of any Member whose exports of the particular product are already under restraint under this Agreement.

---

5. A customs union may apply a safeguard measure as a single unit or on behalf of a member State. When a customs union applies a safeguard measure as a single unit, all the requirements for the determination of serious damage or actual threat thereof under this Agreement shall be based on the conditions existing in the customs union as a whole. When a safeguard measure is applied on behalf of a member State, all the requirements for the determination of serious damage, or actual threat thereof, shall be based on the conditions existing in that member State and the measure shall be limited to that member State.

6. Such an imminent increase shall be a measurable one and shall not be determined to exist on the basis of allegation, conjecture or mere possibility arising, for example, from the existence of production capacity in the exporting Members.

5. The period of validity of a determination of serious damage or actual threat thereof for the purpose of invoking safeguard action shall not exceed 90 days from the date of initial notification as set forth in paragraph 7.

6. In the application of the transitional safeguard, particular account shall be taken of the interests of exporting Members as set out below:

(a) least-developed country Members shall be accorded treatment significantly more favourable than that provided to the other groups of Members referred to in this paragraph, preferably in all its elements but, at least, on overall terms;

(b) Members whose total volume of textile and clothing exports is small in comparison with the total volume of exports of other Members and who account for only a small percentage of total imports of that product into the importing Member shall be accorded differential and more favourable treatment in the fixing of the economic terms provided in paragraphs 8, 13 and 14. For those suppliers, due account will be taken, pursuant to paragraphs 2 and 3 of Article 1, of the future possibilities for the development of their trade and the need to allow commercial quantities of imports from them;

(c) with respect to wool products from wool-producing developing country Members whose economy and textiles and clothing trade are dependent on the wool sector, whose total textile and clothing exports consist almost exclusively of wool products, and whose volume of textiles and clothing trade is comparatively small in the markets of the importing Members, special consideration shall be given to the export needs of such Members when considering quota levels, growth rates and flexibility;

(d) more favourable treatment shall be accorded to re-imports by a Member of textile and clothing products which that Member has exported to another Member for processing and subsequent reimportation, as defined by the laws and practices of the importing Member, and subject to satisfactory control and certification procedures, when these products are imported from a Member for which this type of trade represents a significant proportion of its total exports of textiles and clothing.

7. The Member proposing to take safeguard action shall seek consultations with the Member or Members which would be affected by such action. The request for consultations shall be accompanied by specific and relevant factual information, as up-to-date as possible, particularly in regard to: (*a*) the factors, referred to in paragraph 3, on which the Member invoking the action has based its determination of the existence of serious damage or actual threat thereof; and (*b*) the factors, referred to in paragraph 4, on the basis of which it proposes to invoke the safeguard action with respect to the Member or Members concerned. In respect of requests made under this paragraph, the information shall be related, as closely as possible, to identifiable segments of production and to the reference period set out in paragraph 8. The Member invoking the action shall also indicate the specific level at which imports of the product in question from the Member or Members concerned are proposed to be restrained; such level shall not be lower than the level referred to in paragraph 8. The Member seeking consultations shall, at the same time, communicate to the Chairman of the TMB the request for consultations, including all the relevant factual data outlined in paragraphs 3 and 4, together with the proposed restraint level. The Chairman shall inform the members of the TMB of the request for consultations, indicating the requesting Member, the product in question and the Member having received the request. The Member or Members concerned shall respond to this request promptly and the consultations shall be held without delay and normally be completed within 60 days of the date on which the request was received.

8. If, in the consultations, there is mutual understanding that the situation calls for restraint on the exports of the particular product from the Member or Members concerned, the level of such restraint shall be fixed at a level not lower than the actual level of exports or imports from the Member concerned during the 12-month period terminating two months preceding the month in which the request for consultation was made.

9. Details of the agreed restraint measure shall be communicated

to the TMB within 60 days from the date of conclusion of the agreement. The TMB shall determine whether the agreement is justified in accordance with the provisions of this Article. In order to make its determination, the TMB shall have available to it the factual data provided to the Chairman of the TMB, referred to in paragraph 7, as well as any other relevant information provided by the Members concerned. The TMB may make such recommendations as it deems appropriate to the Members concerned.

10. If, however, after the expiry of the period of 60 days from the date on which the request for consultations was received, there has been no agreement between the Members, the Member which proposed to take safeguard action may apply the restraint by date of import or date of export, in accordance with the provisions of this Article, within 30 days following the 60-day period for consultations, and at the same time refer the matter to the TMB. It shall be open to either Member to refer the matter to the TMB before the expiry of the period of 60 days. In either case, the TMB shall promptly conduct an examination of the matter, including the determination of serious damage, or actual threat thereof, and its causes, and make appropriate recommendations to the Members concerned within 30 days. In order to conduct such examination, the TMB shall have available to it the factual data provided to the Chairman of the TMB, referred to in paragraph 7, as well as any other relevant information provided by the Members concerned.

11. In highly unusual and critical circumstances, where delay would cause damage which would be difficult to repair, action under paragraph 10 may be taken provisionally on the condition that the request for consultations and notification to the TMB shall be effected within no more than five working days after taking the action. In the case that consultations do not produce agreement, the TMB shall be notified at the conclusion of consultations, but in any case no later than 60 days from the date of the implementation of the action. The TMB shall promptly conduct an examination of the matter, and make appropriate recommendations to the Members concerned within 30 days. In the case that consultations do produce agreement, Members shall notify the TMB upon conclusion but, in any case, no later than 90 days from the date of the implementation of the action. The TMB may make such recommendations as it deems appropriate to the Members concerned.

12. A Member may maintain measures invoked pursuant to the provisions of this Article: (*a*) for up to three years without extension, or (*b*) until the product is integrated into GATT 1994, whichever comes first.

13. Should the restraint measure remain in force for a period exceeding one year, the level for subsequent years shall be the level specified for the first year increased by a growth rate of not less than 6 per cent per annum, unless otherwise justified to the TMB. The restraint level for the product concerned may be exceeded in either year of any two subsequent years by carry forward and/or carryover of 10 per cent of which carry forward shall not represent more than 5 per cent. No quantitative limits shall be placed on the combined use of carryover, carry forward and the provision of paragraph 14.

14. When more than one product from another Member is placed under restraint under this Article by a Member, the level of restraint agreed, pursuant to the provisions of this Article, for each of these products may be exceeded by 7 per cent, provided that the total exports subject to restraint do not exceed the total of the levels for all products so restrained under this Article, on the basis of agreed common units. Where the periods of application of restraints of these products do not coincide with each other, this provision shall be applied to any overlapping period on a *pro rata* basis.

15. If a safeguard action is applied under this Article to a product for which a restraint was previously in place under the MFA during the 12-month period prior to the entry into force of the WTO Agreement, or pursuant to the provisions of Article 2 or 6, the level of the new restraint shall be the level provided for in paragraph 8 unless the new restraint comes into force within one year of:

(a) the date of notification referred to in paragraph 15 of Article 2 for the elimination of the previous restraint; or

(b) the date of removal of the previous restraint put in place pursuant to the provisions of this Article or of the MFA

in which case the level shall not be less than the higher of (*i*) the level of restraint for the last 12-month period during which the product was under restraint, or (*ii*) the level of restraint provided for in paragraph 8.

16. When a Member which is not maintaining a restraint under Article 2 decides to apply a restraint pursuant to the provisions of this Article, it shall establish appropriate arrangements which: (*a*) take full account of such factors as established tariff classification and quantitative units based on normal commercial practices in export and import transactions, both as regards fibre composition and in terms of competing for the same segment of its domestic market, and (*b*) avoid over-categorization. The request for consultations referred to in paragraphs 7 or 11 shall include full information on such arrangements.

ARTICLE 7

1. As part of the integration process and with reference to the specific commitments undertaken by the Members as a result of the Uruguay Round, all Members shall take such actions as may be necessary to abide by GATT 1994 rules and disciplines so as to:

(a) achieve improved access to markets for textile and clothing products through such measures as tariff reductions and bindings, reduction or elimination of non-tariff barriers, and facilitation of customs, administrative and licensing formalities;

(b) ensure the application of policies relating to fair and equitable trading conditions as regards textiles and clothing in such areas as dumping and anti-dumping rules and procedures, subsidies and countervailing measures, and protection of intellectual property rights; and

(c) avoid discrimination against imports in the textiles and clothing sector when taking measures for general trade policy reasons.

Such actions shall be without prejudice to the rights and obligations of Members under GATT 1994.

2. Members shall notify to the TMB the actions referred to in paragraph 1 which have a bearing on the implementation of this Agreement. To the extent that these have been notified to other WTO bodies, a summary, with reference to the original notification, shall be sufficient to fulfil the requirements under this paragraph. It shall be open to any Member to make reverse notifications to the TMB.

3. Where any Member considers that another Member has not taken the actions referred to in paragraph 1, and that the balance of rights and obligations under this Agreement has been upset, that Member may bring the matter before the relevant WTO bodies and inform the TMB. Any subsequent findings or conclusions by the WTO bodies concerned shall form a part of the TMB's comprehensive report.

ARTICLE 8

1. In order to supervise the implementation of this Agreement, to examine all measures taken under this Agreement and their conformity therewith, and to take the actions specifically required of it by this Agreement, the Textiles Monitoring Body ("TMB") is hereby established. The TMB shall consist of a Chairman and 10 members. Its membership shall be balanced and broadly representative of the Members and shall provide for rotation of its members at appropriate intervals. The members shall be appointed by Members designated by the Council for Trade in Goods to serve on the TMB, discharging their function on an *ad personam* basis.

2. The TMB shall develop its own working procedures. It is understood, however, that consensus within the TMB does not require the assent or concurrence of members appointed by Members involved in an unresolved issue under review by the TMB.

3. The TMB shall be considered as a standing body and shall meet as necessary to carry out the functions required of it under this Agreement. It shall rely on notifications and information supplied by the Members under the relevant Articles of this Agreement, supplemented by any additional information or necessary details they may submit or it may decide to seek from them. It may also rely on notifications to and reports from other WTO bodies and from such other sources as it may deem appropriate.

4. Members shall afford to each other adequate opportunity for consultations with respect to any matters affecting the operation of this Agreement.

5. In the absence of any mutually agreed solution in the bilateral consultations provided for in this Agreement, the TMB shall, at the request of either Member, and following a thorough and prompt consideration of the matter, make recommendations to the Members concerned.

6. At the request of any Member, the TMB shall review promptly any particular matter which that Member considers to be detrimental to its interests under this Agreement and where consultations between it and the Member or Members concerned have failed to produce a mutually satisfactory solution. On such matters, the TMB may make such observations as it deems appropriate to the Members concerned and for the purposes of the review provided for in paragraph 11.

7. Before formulating its recommendations or observations, the TMB shall invite participation of such Members as may be directly affected by the matter in question.

8. Whenever the TMB is called upon to make recommendations or findings, it shall do so, preferably within a period of 30 days, unless a different time period is specified in this Agreement. All such recommendations or findings shall be communicated to the Members directly concerned. All such recommendations or findings shall also be communicated to the Council for Trade in Goods for its information.

9. The Members shall endeavour to accept in full the recommendations of the TMB, which shall exercise proper surveillance of the implementation of such recommendations.

10. If a Member considers itself unable to conform with the recommendations of the TMB, it shall provide the TMB with the reasons therefor not later than one month after receipt of such recommendations. Following thorough consideration of the reasons given, the TMB shall issue any further recommendations it considers appropriate forthwith. If, after such further recommendations, the matter remains unresolved, either Member may bring the matter before the Dispute Settlement Body and invoke paragraph 2 of Article XXIII of GATT 1994 and the relevant provisions of the Dispute Settlement Understanding.

11. In order to oversee the implementation of this Agreement, the Council for Trade in Goods shall conduct a major review before the end of each stage of the integration process. To assist in this review, the TMB shall, at least five months before the end of each stage, transmit to the Council for Trade in Goods a comprehensive report on the implementation of this Agreement during the stage under review, in particular in matters with regard to the integration process,

the application of the transitional safeguard mechanism, and relating to the application of GATT 1994 rules and disciplines as defined in Articles 2, 3, 6 and 7 respectively. The TMB's comprehensive report may include any recommendation as deemed appropriate by the TMB to the Council for Trade in Goods.

12. In the light of its review the Council for Trade in Goods shall by consensus take such decisions as it deems appropriate to ensure that the balance of rights and obligations embodied in this Agreement is not being impaired. For the resolution of any disputes that may arise with respect to matters referred to in Article 7, the Dispute Settlement Body may authorize, without prejudice to the final date set out under Article 9, an adjustment to paragraph 14 of Article 2, for the stage subsequent to the review, with respect to any Member found not to be complying with its obligations under this Agreement.

ARTICLE 9

This Agreement and all restrictions thereunder shall stand terminated on the first day of the 121st month that the WTO Agreement is in effect, on which date the textiles and clothing sector shall be fully integrated into GATT 1994. There shall be no extension of this Agreement.

ANNEX

LIST OF PRODUCTS COVERED BY THIS AGREEMENT

1. This Annex lists textile and clothing products defined by Harmonized Commodity Description and Coding System (HS) codes at the six-digit level.

2. Actions under the safeguard provisions in Article 6 will be taken with respect to particular textile and clothing products and not on the basis of the HS lines *per se*.

3. Actions under the safeguard provisions in Article 6 of this Agreement shall not apply to:

(a) developing country Members' exports of handloom fabrics of the cottage industry, or hand-made cottage industry products made of such handloom fabrics, or traditional folklore handicraft textile and clothing products, provided that such products are properly certified under arrangements established between the Members concerned;

(b) historically traded textile products which were internationally traded in commercially significant quantities prior to 1982, such as bags, sacks, carpetbacking, cordage, luggage, mats, mattings and carpets typically made from fibres such as jute, coir, sisal, abaca, maguey and henequen;

(c) products made of pure silk.

For such products, the provisions of Article XIX of the GATT 1994, as interpreted by the Agreement on Safeguards, shall be applicable.

Products within Section XI (Textiles and Textile Articles) of the Harmonized Commodity Description and Coding System (HS) Nomenclature

HS No.	Product Description
Ch. 50	**Silk**
5004.00	Silk yarn (other than yarn spun from silk wate) not put up for retail sale
5005.00	Yarn spun from silk waste, not put up for retail sale
5006.00	Silk yarn & yarn spun from silk waste, put up for retail sale; silk-worm gut
5007.10	Woven fabrics of noil silk
5007.20	Woven fabrics of silk/silk waste, other than noil silk, 85%/ more of such fibres
5007.90	Woven fabrics of silk, nes
Ch. 51	**Wool, fine/coarse animal hair, horsehair yarn & fabric**
5105.10	Carded wool
5105.21	Combed wool in fragments
5105.29	Wool tops and other combed wool, other than combed wool in fragments
5105.30	Fine animal hair, carded or combed
5106.10	Yarn of carded wool,>/=85% by weight of wool, not put up for retail sale
5106.20	Yarn of carded wool,<85% by weight of wool, not put up for retail sale
5107.10	Yarn of combed wool,>/=85% by weight of wool, not put up for retail sale

HS No.	Product Description
5107.20	Yarn of combed wool,<85% by weight of wool, not put up for retail sale
5108.10	Yarn of carded fine animal hair, not put up for retail sale
5108.20	Yarn of combed fine animal hair, not put up for retail sale
5109.10	Yarn of wool/of fine animal hair,>/=85% by weight of such fibres, put up
5109.90	Yarn of wool/of fine animal hair,<85% by weight of such fibres, put up
5110.00	Yarn of coarse animal hair or of horsehair
5111.11	Woven fabrics of carded wool/fine animal hair,>/=85% by weight,</=300 g/m2
5111.19	Woven fabrics of carded wool/fine animal hair,>/=85% by weight,>300 g/m2
5111.20	Woven fabric of carded wool/fine animal hair,>/=85% by weight, mixd with m-m fibres
5111.30	Woven fabric of carded wool/fine animal hair,>/=85% by weight, mixed with m-m fibres
5111.90	Woven fabrics of carded wool/fine animal hair,>/= 85% by weight, nes
5112.11	Woven fabric of combed wool/fine animal hair,>/=85% by weight,</=200 g/m2
5112.19	Woven fabrics of combed wool/fine animal hair,>/=85% by weight,>200 g/m2
5112.20	Woven fabrics of combed wool/fine animal hair,<85% by weight, mixed with m-m fibres
5112.30	Woven fabrics of combed wool/fine animal hair,<85% by weight, mixed with m-m fibres
5112.90	Woven fabrics of combed wool/fine animal hair, <85% by weight, nes
5113.00	Woven fabrics of coarse animal hair or of horsehair
Ch. 52	**Cotton**
5204.11	Cotton sewing thread >/=85% by weight of cotton, not put up for retail sale

HS No.	Product Description
5204.19	Cotton sewing thread,<85% by weight of cotton, not put up for retail sale
5204.20	Cotton sewing thread, put up for retail sale
5205.11	Cotton yarn,>/=85%, single, uncombed,>/=714.29 dtex, not put up
5205.12	Cotton yarn,>/=85%, single, uncombed, 714.29 >dtex>/=232.56, not put up
5205.13	Cotton yarn,>/=85%,single, uncombed, 232.56>dtex>/=192.31, not put up
5205.14	Cotton yarn,>/=85%,single, uncombed, 192.31 >dtex>/=125, not put up
5205.15	Cotton yarn,>/=85%,single, uncombed,<125 dtex, not put up for retail sale
5205.21	Cotton yarn,>/=85%, single, combed,>/=714.29, not put up
5205.22	Cotton yarn,>/=85%, single, combed, 714.29 >dtex>/=232.56, not put up
5205.23	Cotton yarn,>/=85%, single, combed, 232.56 >dtex>/=192.31, not put up
5205.24	Cotton yarn,>/=85%, single, combed, 192.31 >dtex>/=125, not put up
5205.25	Cotton yarn,>/=85%,single, combed,<125 dtex, not put up for retail sale
5205.31	Cotton yarn,>/=85%, multiple, uncombed,>/=714.29 dtex, not put up, nes
5205.32	Cotton yarn,>/=85%,multiple, uncombed, 714.29 >dtex>/=232.56, not put up, nes
5205.33	Cotton yarn,>/=85%,multiple, uncombed, 232.56 >dtex>/=192.31, not put up, nes
5205.34	Cotton yarn,>/=85%, multiple, uncombed, 192.31 >dtex>/=125, not put up, nes
5205.35	Cotton yarn,>/=85%, multiple, uncombed, <125 dtex, not put up, nes

HS No.	Product Description
5205.41	Cotton yarn,>/=85%, multiple, combed,>/=714.29 dtex, not put up, nes
5205.42	Cotton yarn,>/=85%, multiple, combed, 714.29 >dtex>/=232.56, not put up, nes
5205.43	Cotton yarn,>/=85%, multiple, combed, 232.56 >dtex>/=192.31, not put up, nes
5205.44	Cotton yarn,>/=85%, multiple, combed, 192.31 >dtex>/=125, not put up, nes
5205.45	Cotton yarn,>/=85%, multiple, combed, <125 dtex, not put up, nes
5206.11	Cotton yarn, <85%, single, uncombed,>/=714.29, not put up
5206.12	Cotton yarn, <85%, single, uncombed, 714.29 >dtex>/=232.56, not put up
5206.13	Cotton yarn, <85%, single, uncombed, 232.56 >dtex>/=192.31, not put up
5206.14	Cotton yarn, <85%, single, uncombed, 192.31 >dtex>/=125, not put up
5206.15	Cotton yarn,<85%,single, uncombed,<125 dtex, not put up for retail sale
5206.21	Cotton yarn, <85%, single, combed,>/=714.29 dtex, not put up
5206.22	Cotton yarn, <85%, single, combed, 714.29 >dtex>/=232.56, not put up
5206.23	Cotton yarn, <85%, single, combed, 232.56 >dtex>/=192.31, not put up
5206.24	Cotton yarn, <85%, single, combed, 192.31 >dtex>/=125, not put up
5206.25	Cotton yarn,<85%,single, combed,<125 dtex, not put up for retail sale
5206.31	Cotton yarn, <85%, multiple, uncombed,>/=714.29, not put up, nes
5206.32	Cotton yarn,<85%,multiple, uncombed, 714.29 >dtex>/=232.56, not put up, nes

HS No.	Product Description
5206.33	Cotton yarn,<85%, multiple, uncombed, 232.56 >dex>/=192.31, not put up, nes
5206.34	Cotton yarn,<85%, multiple, uncombed, 192.31 >dtex>/=125, not put up, nes
5206.35	Cotton yarn, <85%, multiple, uncombed, <125 dtex, not put up, nes
5206.41	Cotton yarn, <85%, multiple, combed,>/=714.29, not put up, nes
5206.42	Cotton yarn,<85%, multiple, combed, 714.29 >dtex>/=232.56, not put up, nes
5206.43	Cotton yarn,<85%, multiple, combed, 232.56 >dtex>/=192.31, not put up, nes
5206.44	Cotton yarn,<85%, multiple, combed, 192.31 >dtex>/=125, not put up, nes
5206.45	Cotton yarn, <85%, multiple, combed, <125 dtex, not put up, nes
5207.10	Cotton yarn (other than sewing thread)>/=85% by weight of cotton, put up
5207.90	Cotton yarn (other than sewing thread) <85% by weight of cotton, put up for retail sale
5208.11	Plain weave cotton fabric,>/=85%, not more than 100 g/m2, unbleached
5208.12	Plain weave cotton fabric,>/=85%, >100 g/m2 to 200 g/m2, unbleached
5208.13	Twill weave cotton fabric,>/=85%, not more than 200 g/m2, unbleached
5208.19	Woven fabrics of cotton,>/=85%, not more than 200 g/m2, unbleached, nes
5208.21	Plain weave cotton fabric,>/=85%, not more than 100 g/m2, bleached
5208.22	Plain weave cotton fabric,>/=85%, >100 g/m2 to 200 g/m2, bleached
5208.23	Twill weave cotton fabric,>/=85%, not more than 200 g/m2, bleached

HS No.	Product Description
5208.29	Woven fabrics of cotton,>/=85%, not more than 200 g/m2, bleached, nes
5208.31	Plain weave cotton fabric,>/=85%, not more than 100 g/m2, dyed
5208.32	Plain weave cotton fabric,>/=85%,>100g/m= to 200g/m=, dyed
5208.33	Twill weave cotton fabrics,>/=85%, not more than 200 g/m2, dyed
5208.39	Woven fabrics of cotton,>/=85%, not more than 200 g/m2, dyed, nes
5208.41	Plain weave cotton fabric,>/=85%, not more than 100 g/m2, yarn dyed
5208.42	Plain weave cotton fabrics,>/=85%, >100 g/m2 to 200 g/m2, yarn dyed
5208.43	Twill weave cotton fabric,>/=85%, not more than 200 g/m2, yarn dyed
5208.49	Woven fabrics of cotton,>/=85%,not more than 200 g/m2, yarn dyed, nes
5208.51	Plain weave cotton fabrics,>/=85%, not more than 100 g/m2, printed
5208.52	Plain weave cotton fabric,>/=85%, >100 g/m2 to 200 g/m2, printed
5208.53	Twill weave cotton fabric,>/=85%, not more than 200 g/m2, printed
5208.59	Woven fabrics of cotton,>/=85%, not more than 200 g/m2, printed, nes
5209.11	Plain weave cotton fabric,>/=85%, more than 200 g/m2, unbleached
5209.12	Twill weave cotton fabric,>/=85%, more than 200 g/m2, unbleached
5209.19	Woven fabrics of cotton,>/=85%,more than 200 g/m2, unbleached, nes
5209.21	Plain weave cotton fabric,>/=85%, more than 200 g/m2, bleached

HS No.	Product Description
5209.22	Twill weave cotton fabrics,>/=85%, more than 200 g/m2, bleached
5209.29	Woven fabrics of cotton,>/=85%, more than 200 g/m2, bleached, nes
5209.31	Plain weave cotton fabrics,>/=85%, more than 200 g/m2, dyed
5209.32	Twill weave cotton fabrics,>/=85%, more than 200 g/m2, dyed
5209.39	Woven fabrics of cotton,>/=85%, more than 200 g/m2, dyed, nes
5209.41	Plain weave cotton fabrics,>/=85%, more than 200 g/m2, yarn dyed
5209.42	Denim fabrics of cotton,>/=85%, more than 200 g/m2
5209.43	Twill weave cotton fabrics, other than denim,>/=85%,more than 200 g/m2, yarn dyed
5209.49	Woven fabrics of cotton,>/=85%, more than 200 g/m2, yarn dyed, nes
5209.51	Plain weave cotton fabrics,>/=85%, more than 200 g/m2, printed
5209.52	Twill weave cotton fabrics,>/=85%, more than 200 g/m2, printed
5209.59	Woven fabrics of cotton,>/=85%, more than 200 g/m2, printed, nes
5210.11	Plain weave cotton fabrics,<85% mixed with m-m fibers, not more than 200 g/m2, unbleached
5210.12	Twill weave cotton fabrics,<85% mixed with m-m fibers, not more than 200 g/m2, unbleached
5210.19	Woven fabrics of cotton,<85% mixed with m-m fibers,</=200 g/m2, unbleached, nes
5210.21	Plain weave cotton fabrics,<85% mixed with m-m fibres, not more than 200 g/m2, bleached
5210.22	Twill weave cotton fabrics,<85% mixed with m-m fibres, not more than 200 g/m2, bleached

HS No.	Product Description
5210.29	Woven fabrics of cotton,<85% mixed with m-m fibres,</=200 g/m2, bleached, nes
5210.31	Plain weave cotton fabrics,<85% mixed with m-m fibres, not more than 200 g/m2, dyed
5210.32	Twill weave cotton fabrics,<85% mixed with m-m fibres, not more than 200 g/m2, dyed
5210.39	Woven fabrics of cotton,<85% mixed with m-m fibres,</=200 g/m2, dyed, nes
5210.41	Plain weave cotton fabrics,<85% mixed with m-m fibres, not more than 200g/m2, yarn dyed
5210.42	Twill weave cotton fabrics,<85% mixed with m-m fibres, not more than 200g/m2, yarn dyed
5210.49	Woven fabrics of cotton,<85% mixed with m-m fibres,</=200g/m2, yarn dyed, nes
5210.51	Plain weave cotton fab,<85% mixed with m-m fibres, not more than 200 g/m2, printed
5210.52	Twill weave cotton fabrics,<85% mixed with m-m fibres, not more than 200g/m2, printed
5210.59	Woven fabrics of cotton,<85% mixed with m-m fibres,</=200g/m2, printed, nes
5211.11	Plain weave cotton fabrics,<85% mixed with m-m fibres, more than 200 g/m2, unbleachd
5211.12	Twill weave cotton fabrics,<85% mixed with m-m fibres, more than 200 g/m2, unbleached
5211.19	Woven fabrics of cotton,<85% mixed with m-m fibres, more than 200g/m2, unbleached, nes
5211.21	Plain weave cotton fabrics,<85% mixed with m-m fibres, more than 200 g/m2, bleachd
5211.22	Twill weave cotton fabrics,<85% mixed with m-m fibres, more than 200 g/m2, bleachd
5211.29	Woven fabrics of cotton,<85% mixed with m-m fibres, more than 200 g/m2, bleached, nes
5211.31	Plain weave cotton fabrics,<85% mixed with m-m fibres, more than 200 g/m2, dyed

HS No.	Product Description
5211.32	Twill weave cotton fabrics,<85% mixed with m-m fibres, more than 200 g/m2, dyed
5211.39	Woven fabrics of cotton,<85% mixed with m-m fibres, more than 200 g/m2, dyed, nes
5211.41	Plain weave cotton fabrics,<85% mixed with m-m fibres, more than 200 g/m2, yarn dyed
5211.42	Denim fabrics of cotton, <85% mixed with m-m fibres, more than 200 g/m2
5211.43	Twill weave cotton fabrics, other than denim,<85% mixed with m-m fibres,>200g/m2, yarn dyed
5211.49	Woven fabrics of cotton,<85% mixed with m-m fibres,>200 g/m2, yarn dyed, nes
5211.51	Plain weave cotton fabrics,<85% mixed with m-m fibres, more than 200 g/m2, printed
5211.52	Twill weave cotton fabrics,<85% mixed with m-m fibres, more than 200 g/m2, printed
5211.59	Woven fabrics of cotton,<85% mixed with m-m fibres, more than 200g/m2, printed, nes
5212.11	Woven fabrics of cotton, weighing not more than 200 g/m2, unbleached, nes
5212.12	Woven fabrics of cotton, weighing not more than 200 g/m2, bleached, nes
5212.13	Woven fabrics of cotton, weighing not more than 200 g/m2, dyed, nes
5212.14	Woven fabrics of cotton,</=200g/m2, of yarns of different colours, nes
5212.15	Woven fabrics of cotton, weighing not more than 200 g/m2, printed, nes
5212.21	Woven fabrics of cotton, weighing more than 200 g/m2, unbleached, nes
5212.22	Woven fabrics of cotton, weighing more than 200 g/m2, bleached, nes
5212.23	Woven fabrics of cotton, weighing more than 200 g/m2, dyed, nes

HS No.	Product Description
5212.24	Woven fabrics of cotton, >200 g/m2, of yarns of different colours, nes
5212.25	Woven fabrics of cotton, weighing more than 200 g/m2, printed, nes
Ch. 53	**Other vegetable textile fibres; paper yarn & woven fabrics**
5306.10	Flax yarn, single
5306.20	Flax yarn, multile (folded) or cabled
5307.10	Yarn of jute or of other textile bast fibres, single
5307.20	Yarn of jute or of other textile bast fibres, multiple (folded) or cabled
5308.20	True hemp yarn
5308.90	Yarn of other vegetable textile fibres
5309.11	Woven fabrics, containg 85% or more by weight of flax, unbleached or bleached
5309.19	Woven fabrics, containing 85% or more by weight of flax, other than unbleached or bleached
5309.21	Woven fabrics of flax, containg <85% by weight of flax, unbleached or bleached
5309.29	Woven fabrics of flax, containing <85% by weight of flax, other than unbleached or bleached
5310.10	Woven fabrics of jute or of other textile bast fibres, unbleached
5310.90	Woven fabrics of jute or of other textile bast fibres, other than unbleached
5311.00	Woven fabrics of both vegetable textile fibres; woven fabrics of paper yarn
Ch. 54	**Man-made filaments**
5401.10	Sewing thread of synthetic filaments
5401.20	Sewing thread of artificial filaments
5402.10	High tenacity yarn (other than sewing thread),nylon/other polyamides filaments, not put up
5402.20	High tenacity yarn (other than sewing thread),of polyester filaments, not put up

HS No.	**Product Description**
5402.31	Textured yarn nes, of nylon/other polyamides filaments,</=50tex/synthetic yarn, not put up
5402.32	Textured yarn nes, of nylon/other polyamides filaments,>50 textile/synthetic yarn, not put up
5402.33	Textured yarn nes, of polyester filaments, not put up for retail sale
5402.39	Textured yarn of synthetic filaments, nes, not put up
5402.41	Yarn of nylon or other polyamides filaments, single, untwisted, nes, not put up
5402.42	Yarn of polyester filaments, partially oriented, single, nes, not put up
5402.43	Yarn of polyester filaments, single, untwisted, nes, not put up
5402.49	Yarn of synthetic filaments, single, untwisted, nes, not put up
5402.51	Yarn of nylon or other polyamides filaments, single, >50 turns/metre, not put up
5402.52	Yarn of polyester filaments, single, >50 turns per metre, not put up
5402.59	Yarn of synthetic filaments, single,>50 turns per metre, nes, not put up
5402.61	Yarn of nylon or other polyamides filaments, multiple, nes, not put up
5402.62	Yarn of polyester filaments, multiple, nes, not put up
5402.69	Yarn of synthetic filaments, multiple, nes, not put up
5403.10	High tenacity yarn (other than sewing thread),of viscose rayon filaments, not put up
5403.20	Textured yarn nes, of artificial filaments, not put up for retail sale
5403.31	Yarn of viscose rayon filaments, single, untwisted, nes, not put up
5403.32	Yarn of viscose rayon filaments, single,>120 turns per metre, nes, not put up

HS No.	Product Description
5403.33	Yarn of cellulose acetate filaments, single, nes, not put up
5403.39	Yarn of artificial filaments, single, nes, not put up
5403.41	Yarn of viscose rayon filaments, multiple, nes, not put up
5403.42	Yarn of cellulose acetate filaments, multiple, nes, not put up
5403.49	Yarn of artificial filaments, multiple, nes, not put up
5404.10	Synthetic mono,>/=67dtex, no cross sectional dimension exceeds 1 mm
5404.90	Strip & the like of synthetic textile material of an apparent width not exceedg 5mm
5405.00	Artificial mono, 67 dtex, cross-sectional >1mm; strip of artificial textile material with </=5mm
5406.10	Yarn of synthetic filament (other than sewing thread), put up for retail sale
5406.20	Yarn of artificial filament (other than sewing thread),put up for retail sale
5407.10	Woven fabrics of high tenacity filaments yarns of nylon other polyamides/polyesters
5407.20	Woven fabrics obtaind from strip/the like of synthetic textile materials
5407.30	Fabrics specified in Note 9 Section XI (layers of parallel synthetic textile yarn)
5407.41	Woven fabrics,>/=85% of nylon/other polyamides filaments, unbleached or bleached, nes
5407.42	Woven fabrics,>/=85% of nylon/other polyamides filaments, dyed, nes
5407.43	Woven fabrics,>/=85% of nylon/other polyamides filaments, yarn dyed, nes
5407.44	Woven fabrics,>/=85% of nylon/other polyamides filaments, printed, nes
5407.51	Woven fabrics,>/=85% of textured polyester filaments, unbleached or bleached, nes

HS No.	Product Description
5407.52	Woven fabrics,>/=85% of textured polyester filaments, dyed, nes
5407.53	Woven fabrics,>/=85% of textured polyester filaments, yarn dyed, nes
5407.54	Woven fabrics,>/=85% of textured polyester filaments, printed, nes
5407.60	Woven fabrics,>/=85% of non-textured polyester filaments, nes
5407.71	Woven fabrics,>/=85% of synthetic filaments, unbleached or bleached, nes
5407.72	Woven fabrics,>/=85% of synthetic filaments, dyed, nes
5407.73	Woven fabrics,>/=85% of synthetic filaments, yarn dyed, nes
5407.74	Woven fabrics,>/=85% of synthetic filaments, printed, nes
5407.81	Woven fabrics of synthetic filaments,<85% mixed with cotton, unbleached or bleached, nes
5407.82	Woven fabrics of synthetic filaments,<85% mixed with cotton, dyed, nes
5407.83	Woven fabrics of synthetic filaments,<85% mixed with cotton, yarn dyed, nes
5407.84	Woven fabrics of synthetic filaments,<85% mixed with cotton, printed, nes
5407.91	Woven fabrics of synthetic filaments, unbleached or bleached, nes
5407.92	Woven fabrics of synthetic filaments, dyed, nes
5407.93	Woven fabrics of synthetic filaments, yarn dyed, nes
5407.94	Woven fabrics of synthetic filaments, printed, nes
5408.10	Woven fabrics of high tenacity filament yarns of viscose rayon
5408.21	Woven fabrics,>/=85% of artificial filaments or strip of artificial textile material, unbleached/bleached, nes
5408.22	Woven fabrics,>/=85% of artificial filaments or strip of artificial textile material, dyed, nes

HS No.	Product Description
5408.23	Woven fabrics,>/=85% of artificial filaments or strip of artificial textile material, yarn dyed, nes
5408.24	Woven fabrics,>/=85% of artificial filaments or strip of artificial textile material, printed, nes
5408.31	Woven fabrics of artificial filaments, unbleached or bleached, nes
5408.32	Woven fabrics of artificial filaments, dyed, nes
5408.33	Woven fabrics of artificial filaments, yarn dyed, nes
5408.34	Woven fabrics of artificial filaments, printed, nes
Ch. 55	**Man-made staple fibres**
5501.10	Filament tow of nylon or other polyamides
5501.20	Filament tow of polyesters
5501.30	Filament tow of acrylic or modacrylic
5501.90	Synthetic filament tow, nes
5502.00	Artificial filament tow
5503.10	Staple fibres of nylon or other polyamides, not carded or combed
5503.20	Staple fibres of polyesters, not carded or combed
5503.30	Staple fibres of acrylic or modacrylic, not carded or combed
5503.40	Staple fibres of polypropylene, not carded or combed
5503.90	Synthetic staple fibres, not carded or combed, nes
5504.10	Staple fibres of viscose, not carded or combed
5504.90	Artificial staple fibres, other than viscose, not carded or combed
5505.10	Waste of synthetic fibres
5505.20	Waste of artificial fibres
5506.10	Staple fibres of nylon or other polyamides, carded or combed
5506.20	Staple fibres of polyesters, carded or combed
5506.30	Staple fibres of acrylic or modacrylic, carded or combed
5506.90	Synthetic staple fibres, carded or combed, nes

HS No.	Product Description
5507.00	Artificial staple fibres, carded or combed
5508.10	Sewing thread of synthetic staple fibres
5508.20	Sewing thread of artificial staple fibres
5509.11	Yarn,>/=85% nylon or other polyamides staple fibres, single, not put up
5509.12	Yarn,>/=85% nylon or other polyamides staple fibres, multiple, not put up, nes
5509.21	Yarn,>/=85% of polyester staple fibres, single, not put up
5509.22	Yarn,>/=85% of polyester staple fibres, multiple, not put up, nes
5509.31	Yarn,>/=85% of acrylic or modacrylic staple fibres, single, not put up
5509.32	Yarn,>/=85% acrylic/modacrylic staple fibres, multiple, not put up, nes
5509.41	Yarn,>/=85% of other synthetic staple fibres, single, not put up
5509.42	Yarn,>/=85% of other synthetic staple fibres, multiple, not put up, nes
5509.51	Yarn of polyester staple fibres mixed with artificial staple fib, not put up, nes
5509.52	Yarn of polyester staple fibres mixed with wool/fine animal hair, not put up, nes
5509.53	Yarn of polyester staple fibres mixed with cotton, not put up, nes
5509.59	Yarn of polyester staple fibres, not put up, nes
5509.61	Yarn of acrylic staple fibres mixed with wool/fine animal hair, not put up, nes
5509.62	Yarn of acrylic staple fibres mixed with cotton, not put up, nes
5509.69	Yarn of acrylic staple fibres, not put up, nes
5509.91	Yarn of other synthetic staple fibres mixed with/wool/fine animal hair, nes
5509.92	Yarn of other synthetic staple fibres mixed with cotton, not put up, nes

HS No.	Product Description
5509.99	Yarn of other synthetic staple fibres, not put up, nes
5510.11	Yarn,>/=85% of artificial staple fibres, single, not put up
5510.12	Yarn,>/=85% of artificial staple fibres, multiple, not put up, nes
5510.20	Yarn of artificl staple fibres mixed with wool/fine animal hair, not put up, nes
5510.30	Yarn of artificial staple fibres mixed with cotton, not put up, nes
5510.90	Yarn of artificial staple fibres, not put up, nes
5511.10	Yarn,>/=85% of synthetic staple fibres, other than sewing thread, put up
5511.20	Yarn, <85% of synthetic staple fibres, put up for retail sale, nes
5511.30	Yarn of artificial fibres (other than sewing thread), put up for retail sale
5512.11	Woven fabrics, containing>/=85% of polyester staple fibres, unbleached or bleached
5512.19	Woven fabrics, containg>/=85% of polyester staple fibres, other than unbleached or bleached
5512.21	Woven fabrics, containg>/=85% of acrylic staple fibres, unbleached or bleached
5512.29	Woven fabrics, containing>/=85% of acrylic staple fibres, other than unbleached or bleached
5512.91	Woven fabrics, containing>/=85% of other synthetic staple fibres, unbleached/bleached
5512.99	Woven fabrics, containg>/=85% of other synthetic staple fibres, other than unbleached/bleached
5513.11	Plain weave polyester staple fibres fabrics,<85%,mixed with/cotton,</=170g/m2, unbleached/bleached
5513.12	Twill weave polyester staple fibres fabrics,<85%,mixed with/cottn,</=170g/m2, unbleached/bleached
5513.13	Woven fabrics of polyest staple fibres,<85%, mixed with/ cotton,</=170g/m2, unbleached/bleached, nes

HS No.	Product Description
5513.19	Woven fabrics of other synthetic staple fibres,<85%,mixed with/cotton,</=170g/m2, unbleached/bleached
5513.21	Plain weave polyester staple fibres fabrics,<85%,mixed with/cotton,</=170g/m2, dyed
5513.22	Twill weave polyester staple fibres fabrics,<85%,mixed with/cotton,</=170g/m2, dyed
5513.23	Woven fabrics of polyester staple fibres,<85%,mixed with/ cotton,</=170 g/m2, dyed, nes
5513.29	Woven fabrics of other synthetic staple fibres,<85% mixed with/cotton,</=170g/m2, dyed
5513.31	Plain weave polyester stapl fibres fabrics,<85% mixed with/cotton,</=170g/m2, yarn dyed
5513.32	Twill weave polyester staple fibres fabrics,<85% mixed with/cotton,</=170g/m2, yarn dyed
5513.33	Woven fabrics of polyester staple fibres,<85% mixed with/ cotton,</=170 g/m2, dyed nes
5513.39	Woven fabrics of other synthetic staple fibres,<85% mixed with/cotton,</=170g/m2, yarn dyed
5513.41	Plain weave polyester stapl fibres fabrics,<85%,mixed with/ cotton,</=170g/m2, printed
5513.42	Twill weave polyester staple fibres fabrics,<85%,mixed with/cotton,<=/170g/m2, printed
5513.43	Woven fabrics of polyester staple fibres,<85%,mixed with/ cotton,</=170g/m2, printed, nes
5513.49	Woven fabrics of other synthetic staple fibres,<85%,mixed with/cotton,</=170g/m2, printed
5514.11	Plain weave polyester staple fibres fabrics,<85%,mixed with/cotton,>170g/m2, unbleached/bleached
5514.12	Twill weave polyester staple fibres fabrics,<85%,mixed with/cotton,>170g/m2, unbleached/bleached
5514.13	Woven fabrics of polyester staple fibres,<85% mixed with/ cotton,>170g/m2, unbleached/bleached, nes
5514.19	Woven fabrics of other synthetic staple fibres,<85%,mixed with/cotton,>170 g/m2, unbleached/bleached

HS No.	Product Description
5514.21	Plain weave polyester staple fibres fabrics,<85%,mixed with/cotton,>170g/m2, dyed
5514.22	Twill weave polyester staple fibres fabrics,<85%,mixed with/cotton,>170g/m2, dyed
5514.23	Woven fabrics of polyester staple fibres,<85%,mixed with/ cotton,>170 g/m2, dyed
5514.29	Woven fabrics of other synthetic staple fibres,<85%,mixed with/cotton,>170g/m2, dyed
5514.31	Plain weave polyester staple fibres fabrics,<85% mixed with/cotton,>170g/m2, yarn dyed
5514.32	Twill weave polyester staple fibres fabrics,<85% mixed with/cotton,>170g/m2, yarn dyed
5514.33	Woven fabrics of polyester staple fibres,<85% mixed with/ cotton,>170g/m2, yarn dyed nes
5514.39	Woven fabrics of other synthetic staple fibres,<85% mixed with/cotton,>170 g/m2, yarn dyed
5514.41	Plain weave polyester staple fibres fabrics,<85%, mixed with/cotton,>170g/m2, printed
5514.42	Twill weave polyester staple fibre fabrics,<85%,mixed with/ cotton,>170g/m2, printed
5514.43	Woven fabrics of polyester staple fibres <85%, mixed with/ cotton,>170g/m2, printed, nes
5514.49	Woven fabrics of other synthetic staple fibres,<85%,mixed with/cotton,>170 g/m2, printed
5515.11	Woven fabrics of polyester staple fibres mixed with viscose rayon staple fibres, nes
5515.12	Woven fabrics of polyester staple fibres mixed with man-made filaments, nes
5515.13	Woven fabrics of polyester staple fibres mixed with/wool/ fine animal hair, nes
5515.19	Woven fabrics of polyester staple fibres, nes
5515.21	Woven fabrics of acrylic staple fibres, mixed with man-made filaments, nes

HS No.	Product Description
5515.22	Woven fabrics of acrylic staple fibres, mixed with/wool/ fine animal hair, nes
5515.29	Woven fabrics of acrylic or modacrylic staple fibres, nes
5515.91	Woven fabrics of other synthetic staple fiber, mixed with man-made filaments, nes
5515.92	Woven fabrics of other synthetic staple fiber, mixed with/ wool of fine animal hair, nes
5515.99	Woven fabrics of synthetic staple fibres, nes
5516.11	Woven fabrics, containg>/=85% of artificial staple fibres, unbleached/bleached
5516.12	Woven fabrics, containing>/=85% of artificial staple fibres, dyed
5516.13	Woven fabrics, containing>/=85% of artificial staple fibres, yarn dyed
5516.14	Woven fabrics, containing>/=85% of artificial staple fibres, printed
5516.21	Woven fabrics of artificial staple fibres,<85%,mixed with man-made filament, unbleached/bleached
5516.22	Woven fabrics of artificial staple fibres,<85%,mixed with man-made filament, dyed
5516.23	Woven fabrics of artificial staple fibres,<85%,mixed with m-m filament, yarn dyed
5516.24	Woven fabrics of artificial staple fibres,<85%,mixed with man-made filament, printed
5516.31	Woven fabrics of artificial staple fibres,<85% mixed with/ wool/fine animal hair, unbleached/bleached
5516.32	Woven fabrics of artificial staple fibres,<85% mixed with/ wool/fine animal hair, dyed
5516.33	Woven fabrics of artificial staple fibres,<85% mixed with/ wool/fine animal hair, yarn dyed
5516.34	Woven fabrics of artificial staple fibres,<85% mixed with/ wool/fine animal hair, printed
5516.41	Woven fabrics of artificial staple fibres,<85% mixed with cotton, unbleached or bleached

HS No.	Product Description
5516.42	Woven fabrics of artificial staple fibres, <85% mixed with cotton, dyed
5516.43	Woven fabrics of artificial staple fibres,<85% mixd with cotton, yarn dyed
5516.44	Woven fabrics of artificial staple fibres,<85% mixed with cotton, printed
5516.91	Woven fabrics of artificial staple fibres, unbleached or bleached, nes
5516.92	Woven fabrics of artificial staple fibres, dyed, nes
5516.93	Woven fabrics of artificial staple fibres, yarn dyed, nes
5516.94	Woven fabrics of artificial staple fibres, printed, nes
Ch. 56	**Wadding, felt & nonwoven; yarns; twine, cordage, etc.**
5601.10	Sanitary articles of wadding of textile materials *i.e.*, sanitary towels, tampons
5601.21	Wadding of cotton and articles thereof, other than sanitary articles
5601.22	Wadding of man-made fibres and articles thereof, other than sanitary articles
5601.29	Waddingg of other textile materials & articles thereof, other than sanitary articles
5601.30	Textile flock and dust and mill neps
5602.10	Needleloom felt and stitch-bonded fibre fabrics
5602.21	Felt other than needleloom, of wool or fine animal hair, not impregnated, coated, covered etc.
5602.29	Felt other than needleloom, of other textile materials, not impregnated, coated, covered etc.
5602.90	Felt of textile materials, nes
5603.00	Non-wovens, whether or not impregnated, coated, covered or laminated
5604.10	Rubber thread and cord, textile covered
5604.20	High tenacity yarn of polyester, nylon other polyamid, viscose rayon, coated etc.
5604.90	Textile yarn, strips & the like, impregnated coated/covered with rubber or plastics, nes

HS No.	Product Description
5605.00	Metallised yarn, beg textile yarn combind with/metal thread, strip/powder
5606.00	Gimped yarn nes; chenille yarn; loop wale-yarn
5607.10	Twine, cordage, ropes and cables, of jute or other textile bast fibres
5607.21	Binder or baler twine, of sisal or other textile fibres of the genus Agave
5607.29	Twine nes, cordage, ropes and cables, of sisal textile fibres
5607.30	Twine, cordage, ropes and cables, of abaca or other hard (leaf) fibres
5607.41	Binder or baler twine, of polyethylene or polypropylene
5607.49	Twine nes, cordage, ropes and cables, of polyethylene or polypropylene
5607.50	Twine, cordage, ropes and cables, of other synthetic fibres
5607.90	Twine, cordage, ropes and cables, of other materials
5608.11	Made up fishing nets, of man-made textile materials
5608.19	Knotted netting of twine/cordage/rope, and other made up nets of m-m textile materials
5608.90	Knotted netting of twine/cordage/rope, nes, and made up nets of other textile materials
5609.00	Articles of yarn, strip, twine, cordage, rope and cables, nes
Ch. 57	**Carpets and other textile floor coverings**
5701.10	Carpets of wool or fine animal hair, knotted
5701.90	Carpets of other textile materials, knotted
5702.10	Kelem, Schumacks, Karamanie and similar textile hand-woven rugs
5702.20	Floor coverings of coconut fibres (coir)
5702.31	Carpets of wool/fine animal hair, of woven pile construction, not made up nes
5702.32	Carpets of man-made textile materials, of woven pile construction, not made up, nes

HS No.	Product Description
5702.39	Carpets of other textile materials, of woven pile construction, not made up, nes
5702.41	Carpets of wool/fine animal hair, of woven pile construction, made up, nes
5702.42	Carpets of man-made textile materials, of woven pile construction, made up, nes
5702.49	Carpets of other textile materials, of woven pile construction, made up, nes
5702.51	Carpets of wool or fine animal hair, woven, not made up, nes
5702.52	Carpets of man-made textile materials, woven, not made up, nes
5702.59	Carpets of other textile materials, woven, not made up, nes
5702.91	Carpets of wool or fine animal hair, woven, made up, nes
5702.92	Carpets of man-made textile materials, woven, made up, nes
5702.99	Carpets of other textile materials, woven, made up, nes
5703.10	Carpets of wool or fine animal hair, tufted
5703.20	Carpets of nylon or other polyamides, tufted
5703.30	Carpets of other man-made textile materials, tufted
5703.90	Carpets of other textile materials, tufted
5704.10	Tiles of felt of textile materials, having a maximum surface area of 0.3 m2
5704.90	Carpets of felt of textile materials, nes
5705.00	Carpets and other textile floor coverings, nes
Ch. 58	**Special woven fabrics; tufted textile fabrics; lace; tapestries etc.**
5801.10	Woven pile fabrics of wool/fine animal hair, other than terry & narrow fabrics
5801.21	Woven uncut weft pile fabrics of cotton, other than terry and narrow fabrics
5801.22	Cut corduroy fabrics of cotton, other than narrow fabrics

HS No.	Product Description
5801.23	Woven weft pile fabrics of cotton, nes
5801.24	Woven warp pile fabrics of cotton, pingl (uncut),other than terry & narrow fabrics
5801.25	Woven warp pile fabrics of cotton, cut, other than terry and narrow fabrics
5801.26	Chenille fabrics of cotton, other than narrow fabrics
5801.31	Woven uncut weft pile fabrics of man-made fibres, other than terry & narrow fabrics.
5801.32	Cut corduroy fabrics of man-made fibres, other than narrow fabrics
5801.33	Woven weft pile fabrics of man-made fibres, nes
5801.34	Woven warp pile fabrics of man-made fibres, pingl (uncut), other than terry & narrow fabrics
5801.35	Woven warp pile fabrics of man-made fibres, cut, other than terry & narrow fabrics
5801.36	Chenille fabrics of man-made fibres, other than narrow fabrics
5801.90	Woven pile fabrics & chenille fabrics of other textile material, other than terry & narrow fabrics
5802.11	Terry towelling & similar woven terry fabries of cotton, other than narrow fabries, unbleached
5802.19	Terry towelling & similar woven terry fabrics of cotton, other than unbleached & other than narrow fabries
5802.20	Terry towellg & similar woven terry fabrics of other textile material, other than narrow fabrics
5802.30	Tufted textile fabrics, other than products of heading No. 57.03
5803.10	Gauze of cotton, other than narrow fabrics
5803.90	Gauze of other textile material, other than narrow fabrics
5804.10	Tulles & other net fabrics, not including woven, knitted or crocheted fabrics
5804.21	Mechanically made lace of man-made fibres, in the piece, in strips/motifs

HS No.	Product Description
5804.29	Mechanically made lace of other textile material, in the piece, in strips/in motifs
5804.30	Hand-made lace, in the piece, in strips or in motifs
5805.00	Hand-woven tapestries & needle-worked tapestries, whether or not made up
5806.10	Narrow woven pile fabrics and narrow chenille fabrics
5808.90	Ornamental trimmings in the piece, other than knitted; tassels, pompons & similar articles
5809.00	Woven fabrics of metal thread/of metallised yarn, for apparel, etc., nes
5810.10	Embroidery without visible ground, in the piece, in strips or in motifs
5810.91	Embroidery of cotton, in the piece, in strips or in motifs, nes
5810.92	Embroidery of man-made fibres, in the piece, in strips or in motifs, nes
5810.99	Embroidery of other textile materials, in the piece, in strips/motifs, nes
5811.00	Quilted textile products in the piece
Ch. 59	**Impregnated, coated, cover/laminated textile fabric etc.**
5901.10	Textile fabrics coatd with gum, of a kind used for outer covers of books
5901.90	Tracing cloth; prepared painting canvas; stiffened textile fabrics; for hats etc
5902.10	Tire cord fabric made of nylon or other polyamides high tenacity yarns
5902.20	Tire cord fabric made of polyester high tenacity yarns
5902.90	Tire cord fabric made of viscose rayon high tenacity yarns
5903.10	Textile fabrics impregnatd, coated, covered, or laminated with polyvinyl chloride, nes
5903.20	Textile fabrics impregnated, coated, covered, or laminated with polyurethane, nes
5903.90	Textile fabrics impregnated, coated, covered, or laminated with plastics, nes

HS No.	Product Description
5904.10	Lineoleum, whether or not cut to shape
5904.91	Floor coverings, other than linoleum, with a base of needleloom felt/non-wovens
5904.92	Floor coverings, other than linoleum, with other textile base
5905.00	Textile wall coverings
5906.10	Rubberised textile adhesive tape of a width not exceeding 20 cm
5906.91	Rubberised textile knitted or crocheted fabrics, nes
5906.99	Rubberised textile fabrics, nes
5907.00	Textile fabrics impregnated, coated, covered, nes; painted canvas (e.g., threatrical scenery)
5908.00	Textile wicks for lamps, stoves, etc., gas mantles & knitted gas mantle fabric
5909.00	Textile hosepiping p 6 and similar textile tubing
5910.00	Transmission or conveyor belts or belting of textile material
5911.10	Textile fabrics used for card clothing, and sim fabric for technical uses
5911.20	Textile bolting cloth, whether or not made up
5911.31	Textile fabrics used in paper-making or similar machines, <650 g/m2
5911.32	Textile fabrics used in paper-making or similar machines, weighing >/=650 g/m2
5911.40	Textile straining cloth used in oil presses or the like, inclusive of human hair
5911.90	Textile products and articles for technical uses, nes
Ch. 60	**Knitted or crocheted fabrics**
6001.10	Long pile knitted or crocheted textile fabrics
6001.21	Looped pile knitted or crocheted fabrics, of cotton
6001.22	Looped pile knitted or crocheted fabrics, of man-made fibres
6001.29	Looped pile knitted or crocheted fabrics, of other textile materials
6001.91	Pile knitted or crocheted fabrics, of cotton, nes

HS No.	Product Description
6001.92	Pile knitted or crocheted fabrics, of man-made fibres, nes
6001.99	Pile knitted or crocheted fabrics, of other textile materials, nes
6002.10	Knitted or crochetd textile fabrics, width</=30 cm,>/=5% of elastomeric/rubber, nes
6002.20	Knitted or crocheted textile fabrics, of a width not exceedg 30 cm, nes
6002.30	Knittd/crochetd textile fabrics, width > 30 cm,>/=5% of elastomeric/rubber, nes
6002.41	Warp knitted fabrics, of wool or fine animal hair, nes
6002.42	Warp knitted fabrics, of cotton, nes
6002.43	Warp knitted fabrics, of man-made fibres, nes
6002.49	Warp knitted fabrics, of other materials, nes
6002.91	Knitted or crocheted fabrics, of wool or of fine animal hair, nes
6002.92	Knitted or crocheted fabrics, of cotton, nes
6002.93	Knitted or crocheted fabrics, of man-made fibres, nes
6002.99	Knitted or crocheted fabrics, of other materials, nes
Ch. 61	**Art of apparel & clothing access, knitted or crocheted**
6101.10	Men/boys overcoats, anoraks etc., of wool or fine animal hair, knitted
6101.20	Men/boys overcoats, anoraks etc., of cotton, knitted
6101.30	Men/boys overcoats, anoraks etc., of man-made fibres, knitted
6101.90	Men/boys overcoats, anoraks etc., of other textile materials, knitted
6102.10	Women/girls overcoats, anoraks etc., of wool or fine animal hair, knitted
6102.20	Women/girls overcoats, anoraks etc., of cotton, knitted
6102.30	Women/girls overcoats, anoraks etc., of man-made fibres, knitted
6102.90	Women/girls overcoats, anoraks etc., of other textile materials, knitted

HS No.	Product Description
6103.11	Men/boys suits, of wool or fine animal hair, knitted
6103.12	Men/boys suits, of synthetic fibres, knitted
6103.19	Men/boys suits, of other textile materials, knitted
6103.21	Men/boys ensembles, of wool or fine animal hair, knitted
6103.22	Men/boys ensembles, of cotton, knitted
6103.23	Men/boys ensembles, of synthetic fibres, knitted
6103.29	Men/boys ensembles, of other textile materials, knitted
6103.31	Men/boys jackets and blazers, of wool or fine animal hair, knitted
6103.32	Men/boys jackets and blazers, of cotton, knitted
6103.33	Men/boys jackets and blazers, of synthetic fibres, knitted
6103.39	Men/boys jackets and blazers, of other textile materials, knitted
6103.41	Men/boys trousers and shorts, of wool or fine animal hair, knitted
6103.42	Men/boys trousers and shorts, of cotton, knitted
6103.43	Men/boys trousers and shorts, of synthetic fibres, knitted
6103.49	Men/boys trousers and shorts, of other textile materials, knitted
6104.11	Women/girls suits, of wool or fine animal hair, knitted
6104.12	Women/girls suits, of cotton, knitted
6104.13	Women/girls suits, of synthetic fibres, knitted
6104.19	Women/girls suits, of other textile materials, knitted
6104.21	Women/girls ensembles, of wool or fine animal hair, knitted
6104.22	Women/girls ensembles, of cotton, knitted
6104.23	Women/girls ensembles, of synthetic fibres, knitted
6104.29	Women/girls ensembles, of other textile materials, knitted
6104.31	Women/girls jackets, of wool or fine animal hair, knitted
6104.32	Women/girls jackets, of cotton, knitted
6104.33	Women/girls jackets, of synthetic fibres, knitted
6104.39	Women/girls jackets, of other textile materials, knitted
6104.41	Women/girls dresses, of wool or fine animal hair, knitted

HS No.	Product Description
6104.42	Women/girls dresses, of cotton, knitted
6104.43	Women/girls dresses, of synthetic fibres, knitted
6104.44	Women/girls dresses, of artificial fibres, knitted
6104.49	Women/girls dresses, of other textile materials, knitted
6104.51	Women/girls skirts, of wool or fine animal hair, knitted
6104.52	Women/girls skirts, of cotton, knitted
6104.53	Women/girls skirts, of synthetic fibres, knitted
6104.59	Women/girls skirts, of other textile materials, knitted
6104.61	Women/girls trousers and shorts, of wool or fine animal hair, knitted
6104.62	Women/girls trousers and shorts, of cotton, knitted
6104.63	Women/girls trousers and shorts, of synthetic fibres, knitted
6104.69	Women/girls trousers and shorts, of other textile materials, knitted
6105.10	Men/boys shirts, of cotton, knitted
6105.20	Men/boys shirts, of man-made fibres, knitted
6105.90	Men/boys shirts, of other textile materials, knitted
6106.10	Women/girls blouses and shirts, of cotton, knitted
6106.20	Women/girls blouses and shirts, of man-made fibres, knitted
6106.90	Women/girls blouses and shirts, of other materials, knitted
6107.11	Men/boys underpants and briefs, of cotton, knitted
6107.12	Men/boys underpants and briefs, of man-made fibres, knitted
6107.19	Men/boys underpants and briefs, of other textile materials, knitted
6107.21	Men/boys night-shirts and pyjamas, of cotton, knitted
6107.22	Men/boys night-shirts and pyjamas, of man-made fibres, knitted
6107.29	Men/boys night-shirts and pyjamas, of other textile materials, knitted
6107.91	Men/boys bathrobes, dressing gowns etc., of cotton, knitted

HS No.	Product Description
6107.92	Men/boys bathrobes, dressing gowns, etc., of man-made fibres, knitted
6107.99	Mens/boys bathrobes, dressg gowns, etc., of other textile materials, knitted
6108.11	Women/girls slips and petticoats, of man-made fibres, knitted
6108.19	Women/girls slips and petticoats, of other textile materials, knitted
6108.21	Women/girls briefs and panties, of cotton, knitted
6108.22	Women/girls briefs and panties, of man-made fibres, knitted
6108.29	Women/girls briefs and panties, of other textile materials, knitted
6108.31	Women/girls night-dresses and pyjamas, of cotton, knitted
6108.32	Women/girls night-dresses and pyjamas, of man-made fibres, knitted
6108.39	Women/girls night-dresses & pyjamas, of other textile materials, knitted
6108.91	Women/girls bathrobes, dressing gowns, etc., of cotton, knitted
6108.92	Women/girls bathrobes, dressing gowns, etc., of man-made fibres, knitted
6108.99	Women/girls bathrobes, dressing gowns, etc., of other textile materials, knitted
6109.10	T-shirts, singlets and other vests, of cotton, knitted
6109.90	T-shirts, singlets and other vests, of other textile materials, knitted
6110.10	Pullovers, cardigans & similar article of wool or fine animal hair, knitted
6110.20	Pullovers, cardigans and similar articles of cotton, knitted
6110.30	Pullovers, cardigans and similar articles of man-made fibres, knitted
6110.90	Pullovers, cardigans & similar articles of other textile materials, knitted

HS No.	Product Description
6111.10	Babies garments & clothing accessories of wool or fine animal hair, knitted
6111.20	Babies garments and clothing accessories of cotton, knitted
6111.30	Babies garments and clothing accessories of synthetic fibres, knitted
6111.90	Babies garments & clothing accessories of other textile materials, knitted
6112.11	Track suits, of cotton, knitted
6112.12	Track suits, of synthetic fibres, knitted
6112.19	Track suits, of other textile materials, knitted
6112.20	Ski suits, of textile materials, knitted
6112.31	Men/boys swimwear, of synthetic fibres, knitted
6112.39	Men/boys swimwear, of other textile materials, knitted
6112.41	Women/girls swimwear, of synthetic fibres, knitted
6112.49	Women/girls swimwear, of other textile materials, knitted
6113.00	Garments made up of impregnated, coated, covered or laminated textile knitted fabrics
6114.10	Garments nes, of wool or fine animal hair, knitted
6114.20	Garments nes, of cotton, knitted
6114.30	Garments nes, of man-made fibres, knitted
6114.90	Garments nes, of other textile materials, knitted
6115.11	Panty hose & tights, of synthetic fibres yarns <67 dtex/ single yarn knitted
6115.12	Panty hose & tights, of synthetic fibres yarns >/=67 dtex/ single yarn knitted
6115.19	Panty hose and tights, of other textile materials, knitted
6115.20	Women full-l/knee-l hosiery, of textile yarn<67 dtex/single yarn knitted
6115.91	Hosiery nes, of wool or fine animal hair, knitted
6115.92	Hosiery nes, of cotton, knitted
6115.93	Hosiery nes, of synthetic fibres, knitted
6115.99	Hosiery nes, of other textile materials, knitted

HS No.	Product Description
6116.10	Gloves impregnated, coated or covered with plastics or rubber, knitted
6116.91	Gloves, mittens and mitts, nes, of wool or fine animal hair, knitted
6116.92	Gloves, mittens and mitts, nes, of cotton, knitted
6116.93	Gloves, mittens and mitts, nes, of synthetic fibres, knitted
6116.99	Gloves, mittens and mitts, nes, of other textile materials, knitted
6117.10	Shawls, scarves, veils and the like, of textile materials, knitted
6117.20	Ties, bow ties and cravats, of textile materials, knitted
6117.80	Clothing accessories nes, of textile materials, knitted
6117.90	Parts of garments/of clothing accessories, of textile materials, knitted
Ch. 62	**Articles of apparel & clothing access, not knitted/ crocheted**
6201.11	Men/boys overcoats & similar articles of wool/fine animal hair, not knitted
6201.12	Men/boys overcoats and similar articles of cotton, not knitted
6201.13	Men/boys overcoats & similar articles of man-made fibres, not knitted
6201.19	Men/boys overcoats & similar articles of other textile materials, not knitted
6201.91	Men/boys anoraks & similar articles, of wool/fine animal hair, not knitted
6201.92	Men/boys anoraks and similar articles, of cotton, not knitted
6201.93	Men/boys anoraks and similar articles, of man-made fibres, not knitted
6201.99	Men/boys anoraks & similar articles, of other textile materials, not knitted
6202.11	Women/girls overcoats & similar articles of wool/fine animal hair not knitted
6202.12	Women/girls overcoats and similar articles of cotton, not knitted

HS No.	Product Description
6202.13	Women/girls overcoats & similar articles of man-made fibres, not knitted
6202.19	Women/girls overcoats & similar articles of other textile materials, not knitted
6202.91	Women/girls anoraks & similar article of wool/fine animal hair, not knitted
6202.92	Women/girls anoraks and similar article of cotton, not knitted
6202.93	Women/girls anoraks & similar article of man-made fibres, not knitted
6202.99	Womens/girls anoraks & similar article of other textile materials, not knitted
6203.11	Men/boys suits, of wool or fine animal hair, not knitted
6203.12	Men/boys suits, of synthetic fibres, not knitted
6203.19	Men/boys suits, of other textile materials, not knitted
6203.21	Men/boys ensembles, of wool or fine animal hair, not knitted
6203.22	Men/boys ensembles, of cotton, not knitted
6203.23	Men/boys ensembles, of synthetic fibres, not knitted
6203.29	Men/boys ensembles, of other textile materials, not knitted
6203.31	Men/boys jackets and blazers, of wool or fine animal hair, not knitted
6203.32	Men/boys jackets and blazers, of cotton, not knitted
6203.33	Men/boys jackets and blazers, of synthetic fibres, not knitted
6203.39	Men/boys jackets and blazers, of other textile materials, not knitted
6203.41	Men/boys trousers and shorts, of wool or fine animal hair, not knitted
6203.42	Men/boys trousers and shorts, of cotton, not knitted
6203.43	Men/boys trousers and shorts, of synthetic fibres, not knitted
6203.49	Men/boys trousers and shorts, of other textile materials, not knitted

HS No.	Product Description
6204.11	Women/girls suits, of wool or fine animal hair, not knitted
6204.12	Women/girls suits, of cotton, not knitted
6204.13	Women/girls suits, of synthetic fibres, not knitted
6204.19	Women/girls suits, of other textile materials, not knitted
6204.21	Women/girls ensembles, of wool or fine animal hair, not knitted
6204.22	Women/girls ensembles, of cotton, not knitted
6204.23	Women/girls ensembles, of synthetic fibres, not knitted
6204.29	Women/girls ensembles, of other textile materials, not knitted
6204.31	Women/girls jackets, of wool or fine animal hair, not knitted
6204.32	Women/girls jackets, of cotton, not knitted
6204.33	Women/girls jackets, of synthetic fibres, not knitted
6204.39	Women/girls jackets, of other textile materials, not knitted
6204.41	Women/girls dresses, of wool or fine animal hair, not knitted
6204.42	Women/girls dresses, of cotton, not knitted
6204.43	Women/girls dresses, of synthetic fibres, not knitted
6204.44	Women/girls dresses, of artificial fibres, not knitted
6204.49	Women/girls dresses, of other textile materials, not knitted
6204.51	Women/girls skirts, of wool or fine animal hair, not knitted
6204.52	Women/girls skirts, of cotton, not knitted
6204.53	Women/girls skirts, of synthetic fibres, not knitted
6204.59	Women/girls skirts, of other textile materials, not knitted
6204.61	Women/girls trousers & shorts, of wool or fine animal hair, not knitted
6204.62	Women/girls trousers and shorts, of cotton, not knitted
6204.63	Women/girls trousers and shorts, of synthetic fibres, not knitted
6204.69	Women/girls trousers & shorts, of other textile materials, not knitted

HS No.	Product Description
6205.10	Men/boys shirts, of wool or fine animal hair, not knitted
6205.20	Men/boys shirts, of cotton, not knitted
6205.30	Men/boys shirts, of man-made fibres, not knitted
6205.90	Men/boys shirts, of other textile materials, not knitted
6206.10	Women/girls blouses and shirts, of silk or silk waste, not knitted
6206.20	Women/girls blouses & shirts, of wool or fine animal hair, not knitted
6206.30	Women/girls blouses and shirts, of cotton, not knitted
6206.40	Women/girls blouses and shirts, of man-made fibres, not knitted
6206.90	Women/girls blouses and shirts, of other textile materials, not knitted
6207.11	Men/boys underpants and briefs, of cotton, not knitted
6207.19	Men/boys underpants and briefs, of other textile materials, not knitted
6207.21	Men/boys night-shirts and pyjamas, of cotton, not knitted
6207.22	Men/boys night-shirts and pyjamas, of man-made fibres, not knitted
6207.29	Men/boys night-shirts & pyjamas, of other textile materials, not knitted
6207.91	Men/boys bathrobes, dressing gowns, etc., of cotton, not knitted
6207.92	Men/boys bathrobes, dressing gowns, etc., of man-made fibres, not knitted
6207.99	Men/boys bathrobes, dressing gowns, etc., of other textile materials, not knitted
6208.11	Women/girls slips and petticoats, of man-made fibres, not knitted
6208.19	Women/girls slips & petticoats, of other textile materials, not knitted
6208.21	Women/girls night-dresses and pyjamas, of cotton, not knitted

HS No.	Product Description
6208.22	Women/girls nightdresses and pyjamas, of man-made fibres, not knitted
6208.29	Women/girls nightdresses & pyjamas, of other textile materials, not knitted
6208.91	Women/girls panties, bathrobes, etc., of cotton, not knitted
6208.92	Women/girls panties, bathrobes, etc., of man-made fibres, not knitted
6208.99	Women/girls panties, bathrobes, etc., of other textile materials, not knitted
6209.10	Babies garments & clothing accessories of wool or fine animal hair, not knitted
6209.20	Babies garments and clothing accessories of cotton, not knitted
6209.30	Babies garments & clothing accessories of synthetic fibres, not knitted
6209.90	Babies garments & clothing accessories of other textile materials, not knitted
6210.10	Garments made up of textile felts and of non-woven textile fabrics
6210.20	Men/boys overcoats & similar articles of impregnated, coated, covered etc., textile woven fabrics
6210.30	Women/girls overcoats & similar articles, of impregnated, coated, etc., textile woven fabrics
6210.40	Men/boys garments nes, made up of impregnated, coated, covered etc., textile woven fabrics
6210.50	Women/girls garments nes, of impregnatd, coated, covered, etc., textile woven fabrics
6211.11	Men/boys swimwear, of textile materials not knitted
6211.12	Women/girls swimwear, of textile materials, not knitted
6211.20	Ski suits, of textile materials, not knitted
6211.31	Men/boys garments nes, of wool or fine animal hair, not knitted
6211.32	Men/boys garments nes, of cotton, not knitted

HS No.	Product Description
6211.33	Men/boys garments nes, of man-made fibres, not knitted
6211.39	Men/boys garments nes, of other textile materials, not knitted
6211.41	Women/girls garments nes, of wool or fine animal hair, not knitted
6211.42	Women/girls garments nes, of cotton, not knitted
6211.43	Women/girls garments nes, of man-made fibres, not knitted
6211.49	Women/girls garments nes, of other textile materials, not knitted
6212.10	Brassieres and parts thereof, of textile materials
6212.20	Girdles, panty girdles and parts thereof, of textile materials
6212.30	Corselettes and parts thereof, of textile materials
6212.90	Corsets, braces & similar articles & parts thereof, of textile materials
6213.10	Handkerchiefs, of silk or silk waste, not knitted
6213.20	Handkerchiefs, of cotton, not knitted
6213.90	Handkerchiefs, of other textile materials, not knitted
6214.10	Shawls, scarves, veils and the like, of silk or silk waste, not knitted
6214.20	Shawls, scarves, veils & the like, of wool or fine animal hair, not knitted
6214.30	Shawls, scarves, veils and the like, of synthetic fibres, not knitted
6214.40	Shawls, scarves, veils and the like, of artificial fibres, not knitted
6214.90	Shawls, scarves, veils & the like, of other textile materials, not knitted
6215.10	Ties, bow ties and cravats, of silk or silk waste, not knitted
6215.20	Ties, bow ties and cravats, of man-made fibres, not knitted

HS No.	Product Description
6215.90	Ties, bow ties and cravats, of other textile materials, not knitted
6216.00	Gloves, mittens and mitts, of textile materials, not knitted
6217.10	Clothing accessories nes, of textile materials, not knitted
6217.90	Parts of garments or of clothing accessories nes, of textile materials, not knitted.
Ch. 63	**Other made up textile articles; sets; worn clothing etc.**
6301.10	Electric blankets, of textile materials
6301.20	Blankets (other than electric) & travelling rugs, of wool or fine animal hair
6301.30	Blankets (other than electric) and travelling rugs, of cotton
6301.40	Blankets (other than electric) and travelling rugs, of synthetic fibres
6301.90	Blankets (other than electric) and travelling rugs, of other textile materials
6302.10	Bed linen, of textile knitted or crocheted materials
6302.21	Bed linen, of cotton, printed, not knitted
6302.22	Bed linen, of man-made fibres, printed, not knitted
6302.29	Bed linen, of other textile materials, printed, not knitted
6302.31	Bed linen, of cotton, nes
6302.32	Bed linen, of man-made fibres, nes
6302.39	Bed linen, of other textile materials, nes
6302.40	Table linen, of textile knitted or crocheted materials
6302.51	Table linen, of cotton, not knitted
6302.52	Table linen, of flax, not knitted
6302.53	Table linen, of man-made fibres, not knitted
6302.59	Table linen, of other textile materials, not knitted
6302.60	Toilet & kitchen linen, of terry towellg or similar terry fabrics, of cotton
6302.91	Toilet and kitchen linen, of cotton, nes
6302.92	Toilet and kitchen linen, of flax

HS No.	Product Description
6302.93	Toilet and kitchen linen, of man-made fibres
6302.99	Toilet and kitchen linen, of other textile materials
6303.11	Curtains, drapes, interior blinds & curtain or bed valances, of cotton, knitted
6303.12	Curtains, drapes, interior blinds & curtain/bed valances, of synthetic fibres, knitted
6303.19	Curtains, drapes, interior blinds & curtain/bed valances, other textile matirials, knitted
6303.91	Curtains/drapes/interior blinds & curtain/bed valances, of cotton, not knitted
6303.92	Curtains/drapes/interior blinds curtain/bed valances, of synthetic fibres, not knitted
6303.99	Curtain/drape/interior blind curtain/bed valance, of other textile materials, not knitted
6304.11	Bedspreads of textile materials, nes, knitted or crocheted
6304.19	Bedspreads of textile materials, nes, not knitted or crocheted
6304.91	Furnishing articles nes, of textile materials, knitted or crocheted
6304.92	Furnishing articles nes, of cotton, not knitted or crocheted
6304.93	Furnishing articles nes, of synthetic fibres, not knitted or crocheted
6304.99	Furnishg articles nes, of other textile materials, not knitted or crochetd
6305.10	Sacks & bags, for packing of goods, of jute or of other textile bast fibres
6305.20	Sacks and bags, for packing of goods, of cotton
6305.31	Sacks & bags, for packing of goods, of polyethylene or polypropylene strips
6305.39	Sacks & bags, for packing of goods, of other man-made textile materials
6305.90	Sacks and bags, for packing of goods, of other textile materials

HS No.	Product Description
6306.11	Tarpaulins, awnings and sunblinds, of cotton
6306.12	Tarpaulins, awnings and sunblinds, of synthetic fibres
6306.19	Tarpaulins, awnings and sunblinds, of other textile materials
6306.21	Tents, of cotton
6306.22	Tents, of synthetic fibres
6306.29	Tents, of other textile materials
6306.31	Sails, of synthetic fibres
6306.39	Sails, of other textile materials
6306.41	Pneumatic mattresses, of cotton
6306.49	Pneumatic mattresses, of other textile materials
6306.91	Camping goods nes, of cotton
6306.99	Camping goods nes, of other textile materials
6307.10	Floor-cloths, dish-cloths, dusters & similar cleaning cloths, of textile materials
6307.20	Life jackets and life belts, of textile materials
6307.90	Made up articles, of textile materials, nes, including dress patterns
6308.00	Sets consisting of woven fabrics & yarn, for makg up into rugs, tapestries etc.
6309.00	Worn clothing and other worn articles

Textile and clothing products in Chapters 30-49, 64-96

3005.90	Wadding, gauze, bandages and the like
ex 3921.12} ex 3921.13} ex 3921.90}	Woven, knitted or non-woven fabrics coated, covered or laminated with plastics
ex 4202.12} ex 4202.22} ex 4202.32} ex 4202.92}	Luggage, handbags and flatgoods with an outer surface predominantly of textile materials

HS No.	Product Description
ex 6405.20	Footwear with soles and uppers of wool felt
ex 6406.10	Footwear uppers of which 50% or more of the external surface area is textile material
ex 6406.99	Leg warmers and gaiters of textile material
6501.00	Hat-forms, hat bodies and hoods of felt; plateaux and manchons of felt
6502.00	Hat-shapes, plaited or made by assembling strips of any material
6503.00	Felt hats and other felt headgear
6504.00	Hats & other headgear, plaited or made by assembling strips of any material
6505.90	Hats & other headgear, knitted or made up from lace, or other textile material
6601.10	Umbrellas and sun umbrellas, garden type
6601.91	Other umbrella types, telescopic shaft
6601.99	Other umbrellas
ex 7019.10	Yarns of fibre glass
ex 7019.20	Woven fabrics of fibre glass
8708.21	Safety seat belts for motor vehicles
8804.00	Parachutes; their parts and accessories
9113.90	Watch straps, bands and bracelets of textile materials
ex 9404.90	Pillow and cushions of cotton; quilts; eiderdowns; comforters and similar articles of textile materials
9502.91	Garments for dolls
ex 9612.10	Woven ribbons, of man-made fibres, other than those measuring less than 30 mm in width and permanently put up in cartridges

AGREEMENT ON TECHNICAL BARRIERS TO TRADE

Members,

Having regard to the Uruguay Round of Multilateral Trade Negotiations;

Desiring to further the objectives of GATT 1994;

Recognizing the important contribution that international standards and conformity assessment systems can make in this regard by improving efficiency of production and facilitating the conduct of international trade;

Desiring therefore to encourage the development of such international standards and conformity assessment systems;

Desiring however to ensure that technical regulations and standards, including packaging, marking and labelling requirements, and procedures for assessment of conformity with technical regulations and standards do not create unnecessary obstacles to international trade;

Recognizing that no country should be prevented from taking measures necessary to ensure the quality of its exports, or for the protection of human, animal or plant life or health, of the environment, or for the prevention of deceptive practices, at the levels it considers appropriate, subject to the requirement that they are not applied in a manner which would constitute a means of arbitrary or unjustifiable discrimination between countries where the same conditions prevail or a disguised restriction on international trade, and are otherwise in accordance with the provisions of this Agreement;

Recognizing that no country should be prevented from taking measures necessary for the protection of its essential security interest;

Recognizing the contribution which international standardization can make to the transfer of technology from developed to developing countries;

Recognizing that developing countries may encounter special difficulties in the formulation and application of technical regulations and standards and procedures for assessment of conformity with technical regulations and standards, and desiring to assist them in their endeavours in this regard;

Hereby *agree* as follows:

ARTICLE 1

General Provisions

1.1 General terms for standardization and procedures for assessment of conformity shall normally have the meaning given to them by definitions adopted within the United Nations system and by international standardizing bodies taking into account their context and in the light of the object and purpose of this Agreement.

1.2 However, for the purposes of this Agreement the meaning of the terms given in Annex 1 applies.

1.3 All products, including industrial and agricultural products, shall be subject to the provisions of this Agreement.

1.4 Purchasing specifications prepared by governmental bodies for production or consumption requirements of governmental bodies are not subject to the provisions of this Agreement but are addressed in the Agreement on Government Procurement, according to its coverage.

1.5 The provisions of this Agreement do not apply to sanitary and phytosanitary measures as defined in Annex A of the Agreement on the Application of Sanitary and Phytosanitary Measures.

1.6 All references in this Agreement to technical regulations, standards and conformity assessment procedures shall be construed to include any amendments thereto and any additions to the rules or the product coverage thereof, except amendments and additions of an insignificant nature.

TECHNICAL REGULATIONS AND STANDARDS

ARTICLE 2

Preparation, Adoption and Application of Technical Regulations by Central Government Bodies

With respect to their central government bodies:

2.1 Members shall ensure that in respect of technical regulations, products imported from the territory of any Member shall be accorded treatment no less favourable than that accorded to like products of national origin and to like products originating in any other country.

2.2 Members shall ensure that technical regulations are not prepared, adopted or applied with a view to or with the effect of creating unnecessary obstacles to international trade. For this purpose, technical regulations shall not be more trade-restrictive than necessary to fulfil a legitimate objective, taking account of the risks non-fulfilment would create. Such legitimate objectives are, *inter alia:* national security requirements; the prevention of deceptive practices; protection of human health or safety, animal or plant life or health, or the environment. In assessing such risks, relevant elements of consideration are, *inter alia:* available scientific and technical information, related processing technology or intended end-uses of products.

2.3 Technical regulations shall not be maintained if the circumstances or objectives giving rise to their adoption no longer exist or if the changed circumstances or objectives can be addressed in a less trade-restrictive manner.

2.4 Where technical regulations are required and relevant international standards exist or their completion is imminent, Members shall use them, or the relevant parts of them, as a basis for their technical regulations except when such international standards or relevant parts would be an ineffective or inappropriate means for the fulfilment of the legitimate objectives pursued, for instance because of fundamental climatic or geographical factors or fundamental technological problems.

2.5 A Member preparing, adopting or applying a technical regulation which may have a significant effect on trade of other Members shall, upon the request of another Member, explain the justification for that technical regulation in terms of the provisions of paragraphs 2 to 4. Whenever a technical regulation is prepared, adopted or applied for one of the legitimate objectives explicitly mentioned in paragraph 2, and is in accordance with relevant international standards, it shall be rebuttably presumed not to create an unnecessary obstacle to international trade.

2.6 With a view to harmonizing technical regulations on as wide a basis as possible, Members shall play a full part, within the limits of their resources, in the preparation by appropriate international standardizing bodies of international standards for products for which they either have adopted, or expect to adopt, technical regulations.

2.7 Members shall give positive consideration to accepting as equivalent technical regulations of other Members, even if these regulations differ from their own, provided they are satisfied that these regulations adequately fulfil the objectives of their own regulations.

2.8 Wherever appropriate, Members shall specify technical regulations based on product requirements in terms of performance rather than design or descriptive characteristics.

2.9 Whenever a relevant international standard does not exist or the technical content of a proposed technical regulation is not in accordance with the technical content of relevant international standards, and if the technical regulation may have a significant effect on trade of other Members, Members shall:

2.9.1 publish a notice in a publication at an early appropriate stage, in such a manner as to enable interested parties in other Members to become acquainted with it, that they propose to introduce a particular technical regulation;

2.9.2 notify other Members through the Secretariat of the products to be covered by the proposed technical regulation, together with a brief indication of its objective and rationale. Such notifications shall take place at an early appropriate stage, when amendments can still be introduced and comments taken into account;

2.9.3 upon request, provide to other Members particulars or copies of the proposed technical regulation and, whenever possible, identify the parts which in substance deviate from relevant international standards;

2.9.4 without discrimination, allow reasonable time for other Members to make comments in writing, discuss these comments upon request, and take these written comments and the results of these discussions into account.

2.10 Subject to the provisions in the lead-in to paragraph 9, where urgent problems of safety, health, environmental protection or national security arise or threaten to arise for a Member, that Member may omit such of the steps enumerated in paragraph 9 as it finds necessary, provided that the Member, upon adoption of a technical regulation, shall:

2.10.1 notify immediately other Members through the Secretariat of the particular technical regulation and the products covered, with a brief indication of the objective and the rationale of the technical regulation, including the nature of the urgent problems;

2.10.2 upon request, provide other Members with copies of the technical regulation;

2.10.3 without discrimination, allow other Members to present their comments in writing, discuss these comments upon request, and take these written comments and the results of these discussions into account.

2.11 Members shall ensure that all technical regulations which have been adopted are published promptly or otherwise made available in such a manner as to enable interested parties in other Members to become acquainted with them.

2.12 Except in those urgent circumstances referred to in paragraph 10, Members shall allow a reasonable interval between the publication of technical regulations and their entry into force in order to allow time for producers in exporting Members, and particularly in developing country Members, to adapt their products or methods of production to the requirements of the importing Member.

ARTICLE 3

Preparation, Adoption and Application of Technical Regulations by Local Government Bodies and Non-Governmental Bodies

With respect to their local government and non-governmental bodies within their territories:

3.1 Members shall take such reasonable measures as may be available to them to ensure compliance by such bodies with the provisions of Article 2, with the exception of the obligation to notify as referred to in paragraphs 9.2 and 10.1 of Article 2.

3.2 Members shall ensure that the technical regulations of local governments on the level directly below that of the central government in Members are notified in accordance with the provisions of paragraphs 9.2 and 10.1 of Article 2, noting that notification shall not be required for technical regulations the technical content of which is substantially the same as that of previously notified technical regulations of central government bodies of the Member concerned.

3.3 Members may require contact with other Members, including the notifications, provision of information, comments and discussions referred to in paragraphs 9 and 10 of Article 2, to take place through the central government.

3.4 Members shall not take measures which require or encourage local government bodies or non-governmental bodies within their territories to act in a manner inconsistent with the provisions of Article 2.

3.5 Members are fully responsible under this Agreement for the observance of all provisions of Article 2. Members shall formulate and implement positive measures and mechanisms in support of the observance of the provisions of Article 2 by other than central government bodies.

ARTICLE 4

Preparation, Adoption and Application of Standards

4.1 Members shall ensure that their central government standardizing bodies accept and comply with the Code of Good Practice for the Preparation, Adoption and Application of Standards in Annex 3 to this Agreement (referred to in this Agreement as the "Code of Good Practice"). They shall take such reasonable measures as may be available to them to ensure that local government and non-governmental standardizing bodies within their territories, as well as regional standardizing bodies of which they or one or more bodies within their territories are members, accept and comply with this Code of Good Practice. In addition, Members shall not take measures which have the effect of, directly or indirectly, requiring or encouraging such standardizing bodies to act in a manner inconsistent with the Code of Good Practice. The obligations of Members with respect to compliance of standardizing bodies with the provisions of the Code of Good Practice shall apply irrespective of whether or not a standardizing body has accepted the Code of Good Practice.

4.2 Standardizing bodies that have accepted and are complying with the Code of Good Practice shall be acknowledged by the Members as complying with the principles of this Agreement.

CONFORMITY WITH TECHNICAL REGULATIONS AND STANDARDS

ARTICLE 5

Procedures for Assessment of Conformity by Central Government Bodies

5.1 Members shall ensure that, in cases where a positive assurance of conformity with technical regulations or standards is required, their central government bodies apply the following provisions to products originating in the territories of other Members:

5.1.1 conformity assessment procedures are prepared, adopted and applied so as to grant access for suppliers of like products originating in the territories of other Members under conditions no less favourable than those accorded to suppliers of like products of national origin or originating in any other country, in a comparable situation; access entails suppliers' right to an assessment of conformity under the rules of the procedure, including, when foreseen by this procedure, the possibility to have conformity assessment activities undertaken at the site of facilities and to receive the mark of the system;

5.1.2 conformity assessment procedures are not prepared, adopted or applied with a view to or with the effect of creating unnecessary obstacles to international trade. This means, *inter alia*, that conformity assessment procedures shall not be more strict or be applied more strictly than is necessary to give the importing Member adequate confidence that products conform with the applicable technical regulations or standards, taking account of the risks non-conformity would create.

5.2 When implementing the provisions of paragraph 1, Members shall ensure that:

5.2.1 conformity assessment procedures are undertaken and completed as expeditiously as possible and in a no less favourable order for products originating in the territories of other Members than for like domestic products;

5.2.2 the standard processing period of each conformity assessment procedure is published or that the anticipated processing period is communicated to the applicant upon request; when receiving an application, the competent body promptly examines the completeness of the documentation and informs the applicant in a precise and complete manner of all deficiencies; the competent body transmits as soon as possible the results of the assessment in a precise and complete manner to the applicant so that corrective action may be taken if necessary; even when the application has deficiencies, the competent body proceeds as far as practicable with the conformity assessment if the applicant so requests; and that, upon request, the applicant is informed of the stage of the procedure, with any delay being explained;

5.2.3 information requirements are limited to what is necessary to assess conformity and determine fees;

5.2.4 the confidentiality of information about products originating in the territories of other Members arising from or supplied in connection with such conformity assessment procedures is respected in the same way as for domestic products and in such a manner that legitimate commercial interests are protected;

5.2.5 any fees imposed for assessing the conformity of products originating in the territories of other Members are equitable in relation to any fees chargeable for assessing the conformity of like products of national origin or originating in any other country, taking into account communication, transportation and other costs arising from differences between location of facilities of the applicant and the conformity assessment body;

5.2.6 the siting of facilities used in conformity assessment procedures and the selection of samples are not such as to cause unnecessary inconvenience to applicants or their agents;

5.2.7 whenever specifications of a product are changed subsequent to the determination of its conformity to the applicable technical regulations or standards, the conformity assessment procedure for the modified product is limited to what is necessary to determine whether adequate confidence exists that the product still meets the technical regulations or standards concerned;

5.2.8 a procedure exists to review complaints concerning the operation of a conformity assessment procedure and to take corrective action when a complaint is justified.

5.3 Nothing in paragraphs 1 and 2 shall prevent Members from carrying out reasonable spot checks within their territories.

5.4 In cases where a positive assurance is required that products conform with technical regulations or standards, and relevant guides or recommendations issued by international standardizing bodies exist or their completion is imminent, Members shall ensure that central government bodies use them, or the relevant parts of them, as a basis for their conformity assessment procedures, except where, as duly explained upon request, such guides or recommendations or relevant parts are inappropriate for the Members concerned, for, *inter alia*, such reasons as: national security requirements; the prevention of deceptive practices; protection of human health or safety, animal or plant life or health, or the environment; fundamental climatic or other geographical factors; fundamental technological or infrastructural problems.

5.5 With a view to harmonizing conformity assessment procedures on as wide a basis as possible, Members shall play a full part, within the limits of their resources, in the preparation by appropriate international standardizing bodies of guides and recommendations for conformity assessment procedures.

5.6 Whenever a relevant guide or recommendation issued by an international standardizing body does not exist or the technical content of a proposed conformity assessment procedure is not in accordance with relevant guides and recommendations issued by international standardizing bodies, and if the conformity assessment procedure may have a significant effect on trade of other Members, Members shall:

5.6.1 publish a notice in a publication at an early appropriate stage, in such a manner as to enable interested parties in other Members to become acquainted with it, that they propose to introduce a particular conformity assessment procedure;

5.6.2 notify other Members through the Secretariat of the products to be covered by the proposed conformity assessment procedure, together with a brief indication of its objective and rationale. Such notifications shall take place at an early appropriate stage, when amendments can still be introduced and comments taken into account;

5.6.3 upon request, provide to other Members particulars or copies of the proposed procedure and, whenever possible, identify the parts which in substance deviate from relevant guides or recommendations issued by international standardizing bodies;

5.6.4 without discrimination, allow reasonable time for other Members to make comments in writing, discuss these comments upon request, and take these written comments and the results of these discussions into account.

5.7 Subject to the provisions in the lead-in to paragraph 6, where urgent problems of safety, health, environmental protection or national security arise or threaten to arise for a Member, that Member may omit such of the steps enumerated in paragraph 6 as it finds necessary, provided that the Member, upon adoption of the procedure, shall:

5.7.1 notify immediately other Members through the Secretariat of the particular procedure and the products covered, with a brief indication of the objective and the rationale of the procedure, including the nature of the urgent problems;

5.7.2 upon request, provide other Members with copies of the rules of the procedure;

5.7.3 without discrimination, allow other Members to present their comments in writing, discuss these comments upon request, and take these written comments and the results of these discussions into account.

5.8 Members shall ensure that all conformity assessment procedures which have been adopted are published promptly or otherwise made available in such a manner as to enable interested parties in other Members to become acquainted with them.

5.9 Except in those urgent circumstances referred to in paragraph 7, Members shall allow a reasonable interval between the publication of requirements concerning conformity assessment procedures and their entry into force in order to allow time for producers in exporting Members, and particularly in developing country Members, to adapt their products or methods of production to the requirements of the importing Member.

ARTICLE 6

Recognition of Conformity Assessment by Central Government Bodies

With respect to their central government bodies:

6.1 Without prejudice to the provisions of paragraphs 3 and 4, Members shall ensure, whenever possible, that results of conformity assessment procedures in other Members are accepted, even when those procedures differ from their own, provided they are satisfied that those procedures offer an assurance of conformity with applicable technical regulations or standards equivalent to their own procedures.

It is recognized that prior consultations may be necessary in order to arrive at a mutually satisfactory understanding regarding, in particular:

6.1.1 adequate and enduring technical competence of the relevant conformity assessment bodies in the exporting Member, so that confidence in the continued reliability of their conformity assessment results can exist; in this regard, verified compliance, for instance through accreditation, with relevant guides or recommendations issued by international standardizing bodies shall be taken into account as an indication of adequate technical competence;

6.1.2 limitation of the acceptance of conformity assessment results to those produced by designated bodies in the exporting Member.

6.2 Members shall ensure that their conformity assessment procedures permit, as far as practicable, the implementation of the provisions in paragraph 1.

6.3 Members are encouraged, at the request of other Members, to be willing to enter into negotiations for the conclusion of agreements for the mutual recognition of results of each other's conformity assessment procedures. Members may require that such agreements fulfil the criteria of paragraph 1 and give mutual satisfaction regarding their potential for facilitating trade in the products concerned.

6.4 Members are encouraged to permit participation of conformity assessment bodies located in the territories of other Members in their conformity assessment procedures under conditions no less favourable than those accorded to bodies located within their territory or the territory of any other country.

ARTICLE 7

Procedures for Assessment of Conformity by Local Government Bodies

With respect to their local government bodies within their territories:

7.1 Members shall take such reasonable measures as may be available to them to ensure compliance by such bodies with the provisions of Articles 5 and 6, with the exception of the obligation to notify as referred to in paragraphs 6.2 and 7.1 of Article 5.

7.2 Members shall ensure that the conformity assessment procedures of local governments on the level directly below that of the central government in Members are notified in accordance with the provisions of paragraphs 6.2 and 7.1 of Article 5, noting that notifications shall not be required for conformity assessment procedures the technical content of which is substantially the same as that of previously notified conformity assessment procedures of central government bodies of the Members concerned.

7.3 Members may require contact with other Members, including the notifications, provision of information, comments and discussions referred to in paragraphs 6 and 7 of Article 5, to take place through the central government.

7.4 Members shall not take measures which require or encourage local government bodies within their territories to act in a manner inconsistent with the provisions of Articles 5 and 6.

7.5 Members are fully responsible under this Agreement for the observance of all provisions of Articles 5 and 6. Members shall formulate and implement positive measures and mechanisms in support of the observance of the provisions of Articles 5 and 6 by other than central government bodies.

ARTICLE 8

Procedures for Assessment of Conformity by Non-Governmental Bodies

8.1 Members shall take such reasonable measures as may be available to them to ensure that non-governmental bodies within their territories which operate conformity assessment procedures comply with the provisions of Articles 5 and 6, with the exception of the obligation to notify proposed conformity assessment procedures. In addition, Members shall not take measures which have the effect of, directly or indirectly, requiring or encouraging such bodies to act in a manner inconsistent with the provisions of Articles 5 and 6.

8.2 Members shall ensure that their central government bodies rely on conformity assessment procedures operated by non-governmental bodies only if these latter bodies comply with the provisions of Articles 5 and 6, with the exception of the obligation to notify proposed conformity assessment procedures.

ARTICLE 9

International and Regional Systems

9.1 Where a positive assurance of conformity with a technical regulation or standard is required, Members shall, wherever practicable, formulate and adopt international systems for conformity assessment and become members thereof or participate therein.

9.2 Members shall take such reasonable measures as may be available to them to ensure that international and regional systems for conformity assessment in which relevant bodies within their territories are members or participants comply with the provisions of Articles 5 and 6. In addition, Members shall not take any measures which have the effect of, directly or indirectly, requiring or encouraging such systems to act in a manner inconsistent with any of the provisions of Articles 5 and 6.

9.3 Members shall ensure that their central government bodies rely on international or regional conformity assessment systems only to the extent that these systems comply with the provisions of Articles 5 and 6, as applicable.

INFORMATION AND ASSISTANCE

ARTICLE 10

Information About Technical Regulations, Standards and Conformity Assessment Procedures

10.1 Each Member shall ensure that an enquiry point exists which is able to answer all reasonable enquiries from other Members and interested parties in other Members as well as to provide the relevant documents regarding:

10.1.1 any technical regulations adopted or proposed within its territory by central or local government bodies, by non-governmental bodies which have legal power to enforce a technical regulation, or by regional standardizing bodies of which such bodies are members or participants;

10.1.2 any standards adopted or proposed within its territory by central or local government bodies, or by regional standardizing bodies of which such bodies are members or participants;

10.1.3 any conformity assessment procedures, or proposed conformity assessment procedures, which are operated within its territory by central or local government bodies, or by non-governmental bodies which have legal power to enforce a technical regulation, or by regional bodies of which such bodies are members or participants;

10.1.4 the membership and participation of the Member, or of relevant central or local government bodies within its territory, in international and regional standardizing bodies and conformity assessment systems, as well as in bilateral and multilateral arrangements within the scope of this Agreement; it shall also be able to provide reasonable information on the provisions of such systems and arrangements;

10.1.5 the location of notices published pursuant to this Agreement, or the provision of information as to where such information can be obtained; and

10.1.6 the location of the enquiry points mentioned in paragraph 3.

10.2 If, however, for legal or administrative reasons more than one enquiry point is established by a Member, that Member shall provide to the other Members complete and unambiguous information on the scope of responsibility of each of these enquiry points. In addition, that Member shall ensure that any enquiries addressed to an incorrect enquiry point shall promptly be conveyed to the correct enquiry point.

10.3 Each Member shall take such reasonable measures as may be available to it to ensure that one or more enquiry points exist which are able to answer all reasonable enquiries from other Members and interested parties in other Members as well as to provide the relevant documents or information as to where they can be obtained regarding:

10.3.1 any standards adopted or proposed within its territory by non-governmental standardizing bodies, or by regional standardizing bodies of which such bodies are members or participants; and

10.3.2 any conformity assessment procedures, or proposed conformity assessment procedures, which are operated within its territory by non-governmental bodies, or by regional bodies of which such bodies are members or participants;

10.3.3 the membership and participation of relevant non-governmental bodies within its territory in international and regional standardizing bodies and conformity assessment systems, as well as in bilateral and multilateral arrangements within the scope of this Agreement; they shall also be able to provide reasonable information on the provisions of such systems and arrangements.

10.4 Members shall take such reasonable measures as may be available to them to ensure that where copies of documents are requested by other Members or by interested parties in other Members, in accordance with the provisions of this Agreement, they are supplied at an equitable price (if any) which shall, apart from the real cost of delivery, be the same for the nationals[1] of the Member concerned or of any other Member.

10.5 Developed country Members shall, if requested by other Members, provide, in English, French or Spanish, translations of the documents covered by a specific notification or, in case of voluminous documents, of summaries of such documents.

10.6 The Secretariat shall, when it receives notifications in accordance with the provisions of this Agreement, circulate copies of the notifications to all Members and interested international standardizing and conformity assessment bodies, and draw the attention of developing country Members to any notifications relating to products of particular interest to them.

10.7 Whenever a Member has reached an agreement with any other country or countries on issues related to technical regulations, standards or conformity assessment procedures which may have a significant effect on trade, at least one Member party to the agreement shall notify other Members through the Secretariat of the products to be covered by the agreement and include a brief description of the agreement. Members concerned are encouraged to enter, upon request, into consultations with other Members for the purposes of

1. "Nationals" here shall be deemed, in the case of a separate customs territory Member of the WTO, to mean persons, natural or legal, who are domiciled or who have a real and effective industrial or commercial establishment in that customs territory.

concluding similar agreements or of arranging for their participation in such agreements.

10.8 Nothing in this Agreement shall be construed as requiring:

10.8.1 the publication of texts other than in the language of the Member;

10.8.2 the provision of particulars or copies of drafts other than in the language of the Member except as stated in paragraph 5; or

10.8.3 Members to furnish any information, the disclosure of which they consider contrary to their essential security interests.

10.9 Notifications to the Secretariat shall be in English, French or Spanish.

10.10 Members shall designate a single central government authority that is responsible for the implementation on the national level of the provisions concerning notification procedures under this Agreement except those included in Annex 3.

10.11 If, however, for legal or administrative reasons the responsibility for notification procedures is divided among two or more central government authorities, the Member concerned shall provide to the other Members complete and unambiguous information on the scope of responsibility of each of these authorities.

ARTICLE 11

Technical Assistance to Other Members

11.1 Members shall, if requested, advise other Members, especially the developing country Members, on the preparation of technical regulations.

11.2 Members shall, if requested, advise other Members, especially the developing country Members, and shall grant them technical assistance on mutually agreed terms and conditions regarding the establishment of national standardizing bodies, and participation in the international standardizing bodies, and shall encourage their national standardizing bodies to do likewise.

11.3 Members shall, if requested, take such reasonable measures as may be available to them to arrange for the regulatory bodies within their territories to advise other Members, especially the developing country Members, and shall grant them technical assistance on mutually agreed terms and conditions regarding:

11.3.1 the establishment of regulatory bodies, or bodies for the assessment of conformity with technical regulations; and

11.3.2 the methods by which their technical regulations can best be met.

11.4 Members shall, if requested, take such reasonable measures as may be available to them to arrange for advice to be given to other Members, especially the developing country Members, and shall grant them technical assistance on mutually agreed terms and conditions regarding the establishment of bodies for the assessment of conformity with standards adopted within the territory of the requesting Member.

11.5 Members shall, if requested, advise other Members, especially the developing country Members, and shall grant them technical assistance on mutually agreed terms and conditions regarding the steps that should be taken by their producers if they wish to have access to systems for conformity assessment operated by governmental or non-governmental bodies within the territory of the Member receiving the request.

11.6 Members which are members or participants of international or regional systems for conformity assessment shall, if requested, advise other Members, especially the developing country Members, and shall grant them technical assistance on mutually agreed terms and conditions regarding the establishment of the institutions and legal framework which would enable them to fulfil the obligations of membership or participation in such systems.

11.7 Members shall, if so requested, encourage bodies within their territories which are members or participants of international or regional systems for conformity assessment to advise other Members, especially the developing country Members, and should consider requests for technical assistance from them regarding the establishment of the institutions which would enable the relevant bodies within their territories to fulfil the obligations of membership or participation.

11.8 In providing advice and technical assistance to other Members in terms of paragraphs 1 to 7, Members shall give priority to the needs of the least-developed country Members.

ARTICLE 12

Special and Differential Treatment of Developing Country Members

12.1 Members shall provide differential and more favourable treatment to developing country Members to this Agreement, through the following provisions as well as through the relevant provisions of other Articles of this Agreement.

12.2 Members shall give particular attention to the provisions of this Agreement concerning developing country Members' rights and obligations and shall take into account the special development, financial and trade needs of developing country Members in the implementation of this Agreement, both nationally and in the operation of this Agreement's institutional arrangements.

12.3 Members shall, in the preparation and application of technical regulations, standards and conformity assessment procedures, take account of the special development, financial and trade needs of developing country Members, with a view to ensuring that such technical regulations, standards and conformity assessment procedures do not create unnecessary obstacles to exports from developing country Members.

12.4 Members recognize that, although international standards, guides or recommendations may exist, in their particular technological and socio-economic conditions, developing country Members adopt certain technical regulations, standards or conformity assessment procedures aimed at preserving indigenous technology and production methods and processes compatible with their development needs. Members therefore recognize that developing country Members should not be expected to use international standards as a basis for their technical regulations or standards, including test methods, which are not appropriate to their development, financial and trade needs.

12.5 Members shall take such reasonable measures as may be available to them to ensure that international standardizing bodies and international systems for conformity assessment are organized and operated in a way which facilitates active and representative participation of relevant bodies in all Members, taking into account the special problems of developing country Members.

12.6 Members shall take such reasonable measures as may be available to them to ensure that international standardizing bodies, upon request of developing country Members, examine the possibility of, and, if practicable, prepare international standards concerning products of special interest to developing country Members.

12.7 Members shall, in accordance with the provisions of Article 11, provide technical assistance to developing country Members to ensure that the preparation and application of technical regulations, standards and conformity assessment procedures do not create unnecessary obstacles to the expansion and diversification of exports from developing country Members. In determining the terms and conditions of the technical assistance, account shall be taken of the stage of development of the requesting Members and in particular of the least-developed country Members.

12.8 It is recognized that developing country Members may face special problems, including institutional and infrastructural problems, in the field of preparation and application of technical regulations, standards and conformity assessment procedures. It is further recognized that the special development and trade needs of developing country Members, as well as their stage of technological development, may hinder their ability to discharge fully their obligations under this Agreement. Members, therefore, shall take this fact fully into account. Accordingly, with a view to ensuring that developing country Members are able to comply with this Agreement, the Committee on Technical Barriers to Trade provided for in Article 13 (referred to in this Agreement as the "Committee") is enabled to grant, upon request, specified, time-limited exceptions in whole or in part from obligations under this Agreement. When considering such requests the Committee shall take into account the special problems, in the field of preparation and application of technical regulations, standards and conformity assessment procedures, and the special development and trade needs of the developing country Member, as well as its stage of technological development, which may hinder its ability to discharge fully its obligations under this Agreement. The Committee shall, in particular, take into account the special problems of the least-developed country Members.

12.9 During consultations, developed country Members shall bear in mind the special difficulties experienced by developing country Members in formulating and implementing standards and technical regulations and conformity assessment procedures, and in their desire to assist developing country Members with their efforts in this direction, developed country Members shall take account of the special needs of the former in regard to financing, trade and development.

12.10 The Committee shall examine periodically the special and differential treatment, as laid down in this Agreement, granted to developing country Members on national and international levels.

INSTITUTIONS, CONSULTATION AND DISPUTE SETTLEMENT

ARTICLE 13

The Committee on Technical Barriers to Trade

13.1 A Committee on Technical Barriers to Trade is hereby established, and shall be composed of representatives from each of the Members. The Committee shall elect its own Chairman and shall meet as necessary, but no less than once a year, for the purpose of affording Members the opportunity of consulting on any matters relating to the operation of this Agreement or the furtherance of its objectives, and shall carry out such responsibilities as assigned to it under this Agreement or by the Members.

13.2 The Committee shall establish working parties or other bodies as may be appropriate, which shall carry out such responsibilities as may be assigned to them by the Committee in accordance with the relevant provisions of this Agreement.

13.3 It is understood that unnecessary duplication should be avoided between the work under this Agreement and that of governments in other technical bodies. The Committee shall examine this problem with a view to minimizing such duplication.

ARTICLE 14

Consultation and Dispute Settlement

14.1 Consultations and the settlement of disputes with respect to any matter affecting the operation of this Agreement shall take place under the auspices of the Dispute Settlement Body and shall follow, *mutatis mutandis*, the provisions of Articles XXII and XXIII of GATT 1994, as elaborated and applied by the Dispute Settlement Understanding.

14.2 At the request of a party to a dispute, or at its own initiative, a panel may establish a technical expert group to assist in questions of a technical nature, requiring detailed consideration by experts.

14.3 Technical expert groups shall be governed by the procedures of Annex 2.

14.4 The dispute settlement provisions set out above can be invoked in cases where a Member considers that another Member has not achieved satisfactory results under Articles 3, 4, 7, 8 and 9 and its trade interests are significantly affected. In this respect, such results shall be equivalent to those as if the body in question were a Member.

FINAL PROVISIONS

ARTICLE 15

Final Provisions

Reservations

15.1 Reservations may not be entered in respect of any of the provisions of this Agreement without the consent of the other Members.

Review

15.2 Each Member shall, promptly after the date on which the WTO Agreement enters into force for it, inform the Committee of measures in existence or taken to ensure the implementation and administration of this Agreement. Any changes of such measures thereafter shall also be notified to the Committee.

15.3 The Committee shall review annually the implementation and operation of this Agreement taking into account the objectives thereof.

15.4 Not later than the end of the third year from the date of entry into force of the WTO Agreement and at the end of each three-year period thereafter, the Committee shall review the operation and implementation of this Agreement, including the provisions relating to transparency, with a view to recommending an adjustment of the rights and obligations of this Agreement where necessary to ensure mutual economic advantage and balance of rights and obligations, without prejudice to the provisions of Article 12. Having regard, *inter alia,* to the experience gained in the implementation of the Agreement, the Committee shall, where appropriate, submit proposals for amendments to the text of this Agreement to the Council for Trade in Goods.

Annexes

15.5 The annexes to this Agreement constitute an integral part thereof.

ANNEX 1

TERMS AND THEIR DEFINITIONS FOR THE PURPOSE OF THIS AGREEMENT

The terms presented in the sixth edition of the ISO/IEC Guide 2: 1991, General Terms and Their Definitions Concerning Standardization and Related Activities, shall, when used in this Agreement, have the same meaning as given in the definitions in the said Guide taking into account that services are excluded from the coverage of this Agreement.

For the purpose of this Agreement, however, the following definitions shall apply:

1. *Technical regulation*

Document which lays down product characteristics or their related processes and production methods, including the applicable administrative provisions, with which compliance is mandatory. It may also include or deal exclusively with terminology, symbols, packaging, marking or labelling requirements as they apply to a product, process or production method.

Explanatory note

The definition in ISO/IEC Guide 2 is not self-contained, but based on the so-called "building block" system.

2. *Standard*

Document approved by a recognized body, that provides, for common and repeated use, rules, guidelines or characteristics for products or related processes and production methods, with which compliance is not mandatory. It may also include or deal exclusively with terminology, symbols, packaging, marking or labelling requirements as they apply to a product, process or production method.

Explanatory note

The terms as defined in ISO/IEC Guide 2 cover products, processes and services. This Agreement deals only with technical regulations, standards and conformity assessment procedures related to products or processes and production methods. Standards as defined by ISO/IEC Guide 2 may be mandatory or voluntary. For the purpose of this Agreement standards are defined as voluntary and technical regulations as mandatory documents. Standards prepared by the international standardization community are based on consensus. This Agreement covers also documents that are not based on consensus.

3. *Conformity assessment procedures*

Any procedure used, directly or indirectly, to determine that relevant requirements in technical regulations or standards are fulfilled.

Explanatory note

Conformity assessment procedures include, *inter alia*, procedures for sampling, testing and inspection; evaluation, verification and assurance of conformity; registration, accreditation and approval as well as their combinations.

4. *International body or system*

Body or system whose membership is open to the relevant bodies of at least all Members.

5. *Regional body or system*

Body or system whose membership is open to the relevant bodies of only some of the Members.

6. *Central government body*

Central government, its ministries and departments or any body subject to the control of the central government in respect of the activity in question.

Explanatory note:

In the case of the European Communities the provisions governing central government bodies apply. However, regional bodies or conformity assessment systems may be established within the European Communities, and in such cases would be subject to the provisions of this Agreement on regional bodies or conformity assessment systems.

7. *Local government body*

Government other than a central government (e.g. states, provinces, Länder, cantons, municipalities, etc.), its ministries or departments or any body subject to the control of such a government in respect of the activity in question.

8. *Non-governmental body*

Body other than a central government body or a local government body, including a non-governmental body which has legal power to enforce a technical regulation.

ANNEX 2

TECHNICAL EXPERT GROUPS

The following procedures shall apply to technical expert groups established in accordance with the provisions of Article 14.

1. Technical expert groups are under the panel's authority. Their terms of reference and detailed working procedures shall be decided by the panel, and they shall report to the panel.

2. Participation in technical expert groups shall be restricted to persons of professional standing and experience in the field in question.

3. Citizens of parties to the dispute shall not serve on a technical expert group without the joint agreement of the parties to the dispute, except in exceptional circumstances when the panel considers that the need for specialized scientific expertise cannot be fulfilled otherwise. Government officials of parties to the dispute shall not serve on a technical expert group. Members of technical expert groups shall serve in their individual capacities and not as government representatives, nor as representatives of any organization. Governments or organizations shall therefore not give them instructions with regard to matters before a technical expert group.

4. Technical expert groups may consult and seek information and technical advice from any source they deem appropriate. Before a technical expert group seeks such information or advice from a source within the jurisdiction of a Member, it shall inform the government of that Member. Any Member shall respond promptly and fully to any request by a technical expert group for such information as the technical expert group considers necessary and appropriate.

5. The parties to a dispute shall have access to all relevant information provided to a technical expert group, unless it is of a confidential nature. Confidential information provided to the technical expert group shall not be released without formal authorization from the government, organization or person providing the information. Where such information is requested from the technical expert group

but release of such information by the technical expert group is not authorized, a non-confidential summary of the information will be provided by the government, organization or person supplying the information.

6. The technical expert group shall submit a draft report to the Members concerned with a view to obtaining their comments, and taking them into account, as appropriate, in the final report, which shall also be circulated to the Members concerned when it is submitted to the panel.

ANNEX 3

CODE OF GOOD PRACTICE FOR THE PREPARATION, ADOPTION AND APPLICATION OF STANDARDS

General Provisions

A. For the purposes of this Code the definitions in Annex 1 of this Agreement shall apply.

B. This Code is open to acceptance by any standardizing body within the territory of a Member of the WTO, whether a central government body, a local government body, or a non-governmental body; to any governmental regional standardizing body one or more members of which are Members of the WTO; and to any non-governmental regional standardizing body one or more members of which are situated within the territory of a Member of the WTO (referred to in this Code collectively as "standardizing bodies" and individually as "the standardizing body").

C. Standardizing bodies that have accepted or withdrawn from this Code shall notify this fact to the ISO/IEC Information Centre in Geneva. The notification shall include the name and address of the body concerned and the scope of its current and expected standardization activities. The notification may be sent either directly to the ISO/IEC Information Centre, or through the national member body of ISO/IEC or, preferably, through the relevant national member or international affiliate of ISONET, as appropriate.

SUBSTANTIVE PROVISIONS

D. In respect of standards, the standardizing body shall accord treatment to products originating in the territory of any other Member of the WTO no less favourable than that accorded to like products of national origin and to like products originating in any other country.

E. The standardizing body shall ensure that standards are not prepared, adopted or applied with a view to, or with the effect of, creating unnecessary obstacles to international trade.

F. Where international standards exist or their completion is imminent, the standardizing body shall use them, or the relevant parts of them, as a basis for the standards it develops, except where such international standards or relevant parts would be ineffective or inappropriate, for instance, because of an insufficient level of protection or fundamental climatic or geographical factors or fundamental technological problems.

G. With a view to harmonizing standards on as wide a basis as possible, the standardizing body shall, in an appropriate way, play a full part, within the limits of its resources, in the preparation by relevant international standardizing bodies of international standards regarding subject matter for which it either has adopted, or expects to adopt, standards. For standardizing bodies within the territory of a Member, participation in a particular international standardization activity shall, whenever possible, take place through one delegation representing all standardizing bodies in the territory that have adopted, or expect to adopt, standards for the subject matter to which the international standardization activity relates.

H. The standardizing body within the territory of a Member shall make every effort to avoid duplication of, or overlap with, the work of other standardizing bodies in the national territory or with the work of relevant international or regional standardizing bodies. They shall also make every effort to achieve a national consensus on the standards they develop. Likewise the regional standardizing body shall make every effort to avoid duplication of, or overlap with, the work of relevant international standardizing bodies.

I. Wherever appropriate, the standardizing body shall specify standards based on product requirements in terms of performance rather than design or descriptive characteristics.

J. At least once every six months, the standardizing body shall publish a work programme containing its name and address, the standards it is currently preparing and the standards which it has adopted in the preceding period. A standard is under preparation from the moment a decision has been taken to develop a standard until that standard has been adopted. The titles of specific draft standards shall, upon request, be provided in English, French or Spanish. A notice of the existence of the work programme shall be published in a national or, as the case may be, regional publication of standardization activities.

The work programme shall for each standard indicate, in accordance with any ISONET rules, the classification relevant to the subject matter, the stage attained in the standard's development, and the references of any international standards taken as a basis. No later than at the time of publication of its work programme, the standardizing body shall notify the existence thereof to the ISO/IEC Information Centre in Geneva.

The notification shall contain the name and address of the standardizing body, the name and issue of the publication in which the work programme is published, the period to which the work programme applies, its price (if any), and how and where it can be obtained. The notification may be sent directly to the ISO/IEC Information Centre, or, preferably, through the relevant national member or international affiliate of ISONET, as appropriate.

K. The national member of ISO/IEC shall make every effort to become a member of ISONET or to appoint another body to become a member as well as to acquire the most advanced membership type possible for the ISONET member. Other standardizing bodies shall make every effort to associate themselves with the ISONET member.

L. Before adopting a standard, the standardizing body shall allow a period of at least 60 days for the submission of comments on the draft standard by interested parties within the territory of a Member of the WTO. This period may, however, be shortened in cases where urgent problems of safety, health or environment arise or threaten to arise. No later than at the start of the comment period, the standardizing body shall publish a notice announcing the period for commenting in the publication referred to in paragraph J. Such notification shall include, as far as practicable, whether the draft standard deviates from relevant international standards.

M. On the request of any interested party within the territory of a Member of the WTO, the standardizing body shall promptly provide, or arrange to provide, a copy of a draft standard which it has submitted for comments. Any fees charged for this service shall, apart from the real cost of delivery, be the same for foreign and domestic parties.

N. The standardizing body shall take into account, in the further processing of the standard, the comments received during the period for commenting. Comments received through standardizing bodies that have accepted this Code of Good Practice shall, if so requested, be replied to as promptly as possible. The reply shall include an explanation why a deviation from relevant international standards is necessary.

O. Once the standard has been adopted, it shall be promptly published.

P. On the request of any interested party within the territory of a Member of the WTO, the standardizing body shall promptly provide, or arrange to provide, a copy of its most recent work programme or of a standard which it produced. Any fees charged for this service shall, apart from the real cost of delivery, be the same for foreign and domestic parties.

Q. The standardizing body shall afford sympathetic consideration to, and adequate opportunity for, consultation regarding representations with respect to the operation of this Code presented by standardizing bodies that have accepted this Code of Good Practice. It shall make an objective effort to solve any complaints.

AGREEMENT ON TRADE-RELATED INVESTMENT MEASURES

Members,

Considering that Ministers agreed in the Punta del Este Declaration that "Following an examination of the operation of GATT Articles related to the trade restrictive and distorting effects of investment measures, negotiations should elaborate, as appropriate, further provisions that may be necessary to avoid such adverse effects on trade";

Desiring to promote the expansion and progressive liberalisation of world trade and to facilitate investment across international frontiers so as to increase the economic growth of all trading partners, particularly developing country Members, while ensuring free competition;

Taking into account the particular trade, development and financial needs of developing country Members, particularly those of the least-developed country Members;

Recognizing that certain investment measures can cause trade-restrictive and distorting effects;

Hereby *agree* as follows:

ARTICLE 1

Coverage

This Agreement applies to investment measures related to trade in goods only (referred to in this Agreement as "TRIMs").

ARTICLE 2

National Treatment and Quantitative Restrictions

1. Without prejudice to other rights and obligations under GATT 1994, no Member shall apply any TRIM that is inconsistent with the provisions of Article III or Article XI of GATT 1994.

2. An illustrative list of TRIMs that are inconsistent with the obligation of national treatment provided for in paragraph 4 of Article III of GATT 1994 and the obligation of general elimination of quantitative restrictions provided for in paragraph 1 of Article XI of GATT 1994 is contained in the Annex to this Agreement.

ARTICLE 3

Exceptions

All exceptions under GATT 1994 shall apply, as appropriate, to the provisions of this Agreement.

ARTICLE 4

Developing Country Members

A developing country Member shall be free to deviate temporarily from the provisions of Article 2 to the extent and in such a manner as Article XVIII of GATT 1994, the Understanding on the Balance-of-Payments Provisions of GATT 1994, and the Declaration on Trade Measures Taken for Balance-of-Payments Purposes adopted on 28 November 1979 (BISD 26S/205-209) permit the Member to deviate from the provisions of Articles III and XI of GATT 1994.

ARTICLE 5

Notification and Transitional Arrangements

1. Members, within 90 days of the date of entry into force of the WTO Agreement, shall notify the Council for Trade in Goods of all TRIMs they are applying that are not in conformity with the

provisions of this Agreement. Such TRIMs of general or specific application shall be notified, along with their principal features.[1]

2. Each Member shall eliminate all TRIMs which are notified under paragraph 1 within two years of the date of entry into force of the WTO Agreement in the case of a developed country Member, within five years in the case of a developing country Member, and within seven years in the case of a least-developed country Member.

3. On request, the Council for Trade in Goods may extend the transition period for the elimination of TRIMs notified under paragraph 1 for a developing country Member, including a least-developed country Member, which demonstrates particular difficulties in implementing the provisions of this Agreement. In considering such a request, the Council for Trade in Goods shall take into account the individual development, financial and trade needs of the Member in question.

4. During the transition period, a Member shall not modify the terms of any TRIM which it notifies under paragraph 1 from those prevailing at the date of entry into force of the WTO Agreement so as to increase the degree of inconsistency with the provisions of Article 2. TRIMs introduced less than 180 days before the date of entry into force of the WTO Agreement shall not benefit from the transitional arrangements provided in paragraph 2.

5. Notwithstanding the provisions of Article 2, a Member, in order not to disadvantage established enterprises which are subject to a TRIM notified under paragraph 1, may apply during the transition period the same TRIM to a new investment (*i*) where the products of such investment are like products to those of the established enterprises, and (*ii*) where necessary to avoid distorting the conditions of competition between the new investment and the established enterprises. Any TRIM so applied to a new investment shall be notified to the Council for Trade in Goods. The terms of such a TRIM shall be equivalent in their competitive effect to those applicable to the established enterprises, and it shall be terminated at the same time.

---

1. In the case of TRIMs applied under discretionary authority, each specific application shall be notified. Information that would prejudice the legitimate commercial interests of particular enterprises need not be disclosed.

ARTICLE 6

Transparency

1. Members reaffirm, with respect to TRIMs, their commitment to obligations on transparency and notification in Article X of GATT 1994, in the undertaking on "Notification" contained in the Understanding Regarding Notification, Consultation, Dispute Settlement and Surveillance adopted on 28 November 1979 and in the Ministerial Decision on Notification Procedures adopted on 15 April 1994.

2. Each Member shall notify the Secretariat of the publications in which TRIMs may be found, including those applied by regional and local governments and authorities within their territories.

3. Each Member shall accord sympathetic consideration to requests for information, and afford adequate opportunity for consultation, on any matter arising from this Agreement raised by another Member. In conformity with Article X of GATT 1994 no Member is required to disclose information the disclosure of which would impede law enforcement or otherwise be contrary to the public interest or would prejudice the legitimate commercial interests of particular enterprises, public or private.

ARTICLE 7

Committee on Trade-Related Investment Measures

1. A Committee on Trade-Related Investment Measures (referred to in this Agreement as the "Committee") is hereby established, and shall be open to all Members. The Committee shall elect its own Chairman and Vice-Chairman, and shall meet not less than once a year and otherwise at the request of any Member.

2. The Committee shall carry out responsibilities assigned to it by the Council for Trade in Goods and shall afford Members the opportunity to consult on any matters relating to the operation and implementation of this Agreement.

3. The Committee shall monitor the operation and implementation of this Agreement and shall report thereon annually to the Council for Trade in Goods.

ARTICLE 8

Consultation and Dispute Settlement

The provisions of Articles XXII and XXIII of GATT 1994, as

elaborated and applied by the Dispute Settlement Understanding, shall apply to consultations and the settlement of disputes under this Agreement.

ARTICLE 9

Review by the Council for Trade in Goods

Not later than five years after the date of entry into force of the WTO Agreement, the Council for Trade in Goods shall review the operation of this Agreement and, as appropriate, propose to the Ministerial Conference amendments to its text. In the course of this review, the Council for Trade in Goods shall consider whether the Agreement should be complemented with provisions on investment policy and competition policy.

ANNEX

Illustrative List

1. TRIMs that are inconsistent with the obligation of national treatment provided for in paragraph 4 of Article III of GATT 1994 include those which are mandatory or enforceable under domestic law or under administrative rulings, or compliance with which is necessary to obtain an advantage, and which require:

(a) the purchase or use by an enterprise of products of domestic origin or from any domestic source, whether specified in terms of particular products, in terms of volume or value of products, or in terms of a proportion of volume or value of its local production; or

(b) that an enterprise's purchases or use of imported products be limited to an amount related to the volume or value of local products that it exports.

2. TRIMs that are inconsistent with the obligation of general elimination of quantitative restrictions provided for in paragraph 1 of Article XI of GATT 1994 include those which are mandatory or enforceable under domestic law or under administrative rulings, or compliance with which is necessary to obtain an advantage, and which restrict:

(a) the importation by an enterprise of products used in or related to its local production, generally or to an amount related to the volume or value of local production that it exports;

(b) the importation by an enterprise of products used in or related to its local production by restricting its access to foreign exchange to an amount related to the foreign exchange inflows attributable to the enterprise; or

(c) the exportation or sale for export by an enterprise of products, whether specified in terms of particular products, in terms of volume or value of products, or in terms of a proportion of volume or value of its local production.

AGREEMENT ON IMPLEMENTATION OF ARTICLE VI OF THE GENERAL AGREEMENT ON TARIFFS AND TRADE 1994

Members hereby *agree* as follows:

PART I

ARTICLE 1

Principles

An anti-dumping measure shall be applied only under the circumstances provided for in Article VI of GATT 1994 and pursuant to investigations initiated[1] and conducted in accordance with the provisions of this Agreement. The following provisions govern the application of Article VI of GATT 1994 in so far as action is taken under anti-dumping legislation or regulations.

ARTICLE 2

Determination of Dumping

2.1 For the purpose of this Agreement, a product is to be considered as being dumped, i.e. introduced into the commerce of another country at less than its normal value, if the export price of the product exported from one country to another is less than the comparable price, in the ordinary course of trade, for the like product when destined for consumption in the exporting country.

2.2 When there are no sales of the like product in the ordinary course of trade in the domestic market of the exporting country or when, because of the particular market situation or the low volume

1. The term "initiated" as used in this Agreement means the procedural action by which a Member formally commences an investigation as provided in Article 5.

of the sales in the domestic market of the exporting country[2], such sales do not permit a proper comparison, the margin of dumping shall be determined by comparison with a comparable price of the like product when exported to an appropriate third country, provided that this price is representative, or with the cost of production in the country of origin plus a reasonable amount for administrative, selling and general costs and for profits.

2.2.1 Sales of the like product in the domestic market of the exporting country or sales to a third country at prices below per unit (fixed and variable) costs of production plus administrative, selling and general costs may be treated as not being in the ordinary course of trade by reason of price and may be disregarded in determining normal value only if the authorities[3] determine that such sales are made within an extended period of time[4] in substantial quantities[5] and are at prices which do not provide for the recovery of all costs within a reasonable period of time. If prices which are below per unit costs at the time of sale are above weighted average per unit costs for the period of investigation, such prices shall be considered to provide for recovery of costs within a reasonable period of time.

2.2.1.1 For the purpose of paragraph 2, costs shall normally be calculated on the basis of records kept by the exporter or producer under investigation, provided that

2. Sales of the like product destined for consumption in the domestic market of the exporting country shall normally be considered a sufficient quantity for the determination of the normal value if such sales constitute 5 per cent or more of the sales of the product under consideration to the importing Member, provided that a lower ratio should be acceptable where the evidence demonstrates that domestic sales at such lower ratio are nonetheless of sufficient magnitude to provide for a proper comparison.

3. When in this Agreement the term "authorities" is used, it shall be interpreted as meaning authorities at an appropriate senior level.

4. The extended period of time should normally be one year but shall in no case be less than six months.

5. Sales below per unit costs are made in substantial quantities when the authorities establish that the weighted average selling price of the transactions under consideration for the determination of the normal value is below the weighted average per unit costs, or that the volume of sales below per unit costs represents not less than 20 per cent of the volume sold in transactions under consideration for the determination of the normal value.

such records are in accordance with the generally accepted accounting principles of the exporting country and reasonably reflect the costs associated with the production and sale of the product under consideration. Authorities shall consider all available evidence on the proper allocation of costs, including that which is made available by the exporter or producer in the course of the investigation provided that such allocations have been historically utilized by the exporter or producer, in particular in relation to establishing appropriate amortization and depreciation periods and allowances for capital expenditures and other development costs. Unless already reflected in the cost allocations under this sub-paragraph, costs shall be adjusted appropriately for those non-recurring items of cost which benefit future and/or current production, or for circumstances in which costs during the period of investigation are affected by start-up operations.[6]

2.2.2 For the purpose of paragraph 2, the amounts for administrative, selling and general costs and for profits shall be based on actual data pertaining to production and sales in the ordinary course of trade of the like product by the exporter or producer under investigation. When such amounts cannot be determined on this basis, the amounts may be determined on the basis of:

(i) the actual amounts incurred and realized by the exporter or producer in question in respect of production and sales in the domestic market of the country of origin of the same general category of products;

(ii) the weighted average of the actual amounts incurred and realized by other exporters or producers subject to investigation in respect of production and sales of the like product in the domestic market of the country of origin;

6. The adjustment made for start-up operations shall reflect the costs at the end of the start-up period or, if that period extends beyond the period of investigation, the most recent costs which can reasonably be taken into account by the authorities during the investigation.

(iii) any other reasonable method, provided that the amount for profit so established shall not exceed the profit normally realized by other exporters or producers on sales of products of the same general category in the domestic market of the country of origin.

2.3 In cases where there is no export price or where it appears to the authorities concerned that the export price is unreliable because of association or a compensatory arrangement between the exporter and the importer or a third party, the export price may be constructed on the basis of the price at which the imported products are first resold to an independent buyer, or if the products are not resold to an independent buyer, or not resold in the condition as imported, on such reasonable basis as the authorities may determine.

2.4 A fair comparison shall be made between the export price and the normal value. This comparison shall be made at the same level of trade, normally at the ex-factory level, and in respect of sales made at as nearly as possible the same time. Due allowance shall be made in each case, on its merits, for differences which affect price comparability, including differences in conditions and terms of sale, taxation, levels of trade, quantities, physical characteristics, and any other differences which are also demonstrated to affect price comparability.[7] In the cases referred to in paragraph 3, allowances for costs, including duties and taxes, incurred between importation and resale, and for profits accruing, should also be made. If in these cases price comparability has been affected, the authorities shall establish the normal value at a level of trade equivalent to the level of trade of the constructed export price, or shall make due allowance as warranted under this paragraph. The authorities shall indicate to the parties in question what information is necessary to ensure a fair comparison and shall not impose an unreasonable burden of proof on those parties.

2.4.1 When the comparison under paragraph 4 requires a conversion of currencies, such conversion should be

7. It is understood that some of the above factors may overlap, and authorities shall ensure that they do not duplicate adjustments that have been already made under this provision.

made using the rate of exchange on the date of sale[8], provided that when a sale of foreign currency on forward markets is directly linked to the export sale involved, the rate of exchange in the forward sale shall be used. Fluctuations in exchange rates shall be ignored and in an investigation the authorities shall allow exporters at least 60 days to have adjusted their export prices to reflect sustained movements in exchange rates during the period of investigation.

2.4.2 Subject to the provisions governing fair comparison in paragraph 4, the existence of margins of dumping during the investigation phase shall normally be established on the basis of a comparison of a weighted average normal value with a weighted average of prices of all comparable export transactions or by a comparison of normal value and export prices on a transaction-to-transaction basis. A normal value established on a weighted average basis may be compared to prices of individual export transactions if the authorities find a pattern of export prices which differ significantly among different purchasers, regions or time periods, and if an explanation is provided as to why such differences cannot be taken into account appropriately by the use of a weighted average-to-weighted average or transaction-to-transaction comparison.

2.5 In the case where products are not imported directly from the country of origin but are exported to the importing Member from an intermediate country, the price at which the products are sold from the country of export to the importing Member shall normally be compared with the comparable price in the country of export. However, comparison may be made with the price in the country of origin, if, for example, the products are merely transshipped through the country of export, or such products are not produced in the country of export, or there is no comparable price for them in the country of export.

2.6 Throughout this Agreement the term "like product" ("produit

8. Normally, the date of sale would be the date of contract, purchase order, order confirmation, or invoice, whichever establishes the material terms of sale.

similaire") shall be interpreted to mean a product which is identical, i.e. alike in all respects to the product under consideration, or in the absence of such a product, another product which, although not alike in all respects, has characteristics closely resembling those of the product under consideration.

2.7 This Article is without prejudice to the second Supplementary Provision to paragraph 1 of Article VI in Annex I to GATT 1994.

ARTICLE 3

Determination of Injury[9]

3.1 A determination of injury for purposes of Article VI of GATT 1994 shall be based on positive evidence and involve an objective examination of both *(a)* the volume of the dumped imports and the effect of the dumped imports on prices in the domestic market for like products, and *(b)* the consequent impact of these imports on domestic producers of such products.

3.2 With regard to the volume of the dumped imports, the investigating authorities shall consider whether there has been a significant increase in dumped imports, either in absolute terms or relative to production or consumption in the importing Member. With regard to the effect of the dumped imports on prices, the investigating authorities shall consider whether there has been a significant price undercutting by the dumped imports as compared with the price of a like product of the importing Member, or whether the effect of such imports is otherwise to depress prices to a significant degree or prevent price increases, which otherwise would have occurred, to a significant degree. No one or several of these factors can necessarily give decisive guidance.

3.3 Where imports of a product from more than one country are simultaneously subject to anti-dumping investigations, the investigating authorities may cumulatively assess the effects of such imports only if they determine that *(a)* the margin of dumping established in relation to the imports from each country is more than *de minimis* as defined in paragraph 8 of Article 5 and the volume of imports from each country is not negligible and *(b)* a cumulative

---

9. Under this Agreement the term "injury" shall, unless otherwise specified, be taken to mean material injury to a domestic industry, threat of material injury to a domestic industry or material retardation of the establishment of such an industry and shall be interpreted in accordance with the provisions of this Article.

assessment of the effects of the imports is appropriate in light of the conditions of competition between the imported products and the conditions of competition between the imported products and the like domestic product.

3.4 The examination of the impact of the dumped imports on the domestic industry concerned shall include an evaluation of all relevant economic factors and indices having a bearing on the state of the industry, including actual and potential decline in sales, profits, output, market share, productivity, return on investments, or utilization of capacity; factors affecting domestic prices; the magnitude of the margin of dumping; actual and potential negative effects on cash flow, inventories, employment, wages, growth, ability to raise capital or investments. This list is not exhaustive, nor can one or several of these factors necessarily give decisive guidance.

3.5 It must be demonstrated that the dumped imports are, through the effects of dumping, as set forth in paragraphs 2 and 4, causing injury within the meaning of this Agreement. The demonstration of a causal relationship between the dumped imports and the injury to the domestic industry shall be based on an examination of all relevant evidence before the authorities. The authorities shall also examine any known factors other than the dumped imports which at the same time are injuring the domestic industry, and the injuries caused by these other factors must not be attributed to the dumped imports. Factors which may be relevant in this respe l ct include, *inter alia*, the volume and prices of imports not sold at dumping prices, contraction in demand or changes in the patterns of consumption, trade restrictive practices of and competition between the foreign and domestic producers, developments in technology and the export performance and productivity of the domestic industry.

3.6 The effect of the dumped imports shall be assessed in relation to the domestic production of the like product when available data permit the separate identification of that production on the basis of such criteria as the production process, producers' sales and profits. If such separate identification of that production is not possible, the effects of the dumped imports shall be assessed by the examination of the production of the narrowest group or range of products, which i cludes the like product, for which the necessary information can be provided.

3.7 A determination of a threat of material injury shall be based on facts and not merely on allegation, conjecture or remote possibility. The change in circumstances which would create a situation in which the dumping would cause injury must be clearly foreseen and imminent.[10] In making a determination regarding the existence of a threat of material injury, the authorities should consider, *inter alia*, such factors as:

(i) a significant rate of increase of dumped imports into the domestic market indicating the likelihood of substantially increased importation;

(ii) sufficient freely disposable, or an imminent, substantial increase in, capacity of the exporter indicating the likelihood of substantially increased dumped exports to the importing Member's market, taking into account the availability of other export markets to absorb any additional exports;

(iii) whether imports are entering at prices that will have a significant depressing or suppressing effect on domestic prices, and would likely increase demand for further imports; and

(iv) inventories of the product being investigated.

No one of these factors by itself can necessarily give decisive guidance but the totality of the factors considered must lead to the conclusion that further dumped exports are imminent and that, unless protective action is taken, material injury would occur.

3.8 With respect to cases where injury is threatened by dumped imports, the application of anti-dumping measures shall be considered and decided with special care.

ARTICLE 4

Definition of Domestic Industry

4.1 For the purposes of this Agreement, the term "domestic industry" shall be interpreted as referring to the domestic producers as a whole of the like products or to those of them whose collective

10. One example, though not an exclusive one, is that there is convincing reason to believe that there will be, in the near future, substantially increased importation of the product at dumped prices.

output of the products constitutes a major proportion of the total domestic production of those products, except that:

(i) when producers are related[11] to the exporters or importers or are themselves importers of the allegedly dumped product, the term "domestic industry" may be interpreted as referring to the rest of the producers;

(ii) in exceptional circumstances the territory of a Member may, for the production in question, be divided into two or more competitive markets and the producers within each market may be regarded as a separate industry if *(a)* the producers within such market sell all or almost all of their production of the product in question in that market, and *(b)* the demand in that market is not to any substantial degree supplied by producers of the product in question located elsewhere in the territory. In such circumstances, injury may be found to exist even where a major portion of the total domestic industry is not injured, provided there is a concentration of dumped imports into such an isolated market and provided further that the dumped imports are causing injury to the producers of all or almost all of the production within such market.

4.2 When the domestic industry has been interpreted as referring to the producers in a certain area, i.e. a market as defined in paragraph 1(ii), anti-dumping duties shall be levied[12] only on the products in question consigned for final consumption to that area. When the constitutional law of the importing Member does not permit the levying of anti-dumping duties on such a basis, the importing Member may levy the anti-dumping duties without limitation only if

11. For the purpose of this paragraph, producers shall be deemed to be related to exporters or importers only if *(a)* one of them directly or indirectly controls the other; or *(b)* both of them are directly or indirectly controlled by a third person; or *(c)* together they directly or indirectly control a third person, provided that there are grounds for believing or suspecting that the effect of the relationship is such as to cause the producer concerned to behave differently from non-related producers. For the purpose of this paragraph, one shall be deemed to control another when the former is legally or operationally in a position to exercise restraint or direction over the latter.

12. As used in this Agreement "levy" shall mean the definitive or final legal assessment or collection of a duty or tax.

(a) the exporters shall have been given an opportunity to cease exporting at dumped prices to the area concerned or otherwise give assurances pursuant to Article 8 and adequate assurances in this regard have not been promptly given, and *(b)* such duties cannot be levied only on products of specific producers which supply the area in question.

4.3 Where two or more countries have reached under the provisions of paragraph 8(a) of Article XXIV of GATT 1994 such a level of integration that they have the characteristics of a single, unified market, the industry in the entire area of integration shall be taken to be the domestic industry referred to in paragraph 1.

4.4 The provisions of paragraph 6 of Article 3 shall be applicable to this Article.

ARTICLE 5

Initiation and Subsequent Investigation

5.1 Except as provided for in paragraph 6, an investigation to determine the existence, degree and effect of any alleged dumping shall be initiated upon a written application by or on behalf of the domestic industry.

5.2 An application under paragraph 1 shall include evidence of *(a)* dumping, *(b)* injury within the meaning of Article VI of GATT 1994 as interpreted by this Agreement and *(c)* a causal link between the dumped imports and the alleged injury. Simple assertion, unsubstantiated by relevant evidence, cannot be considered sufficient to meet the requirements of this paragraph. The application shall contain such information as is reasonably available to the applicant on the following:

(i) the identity of the applicant and a description of the volume and value of the domestic production of the like product by the applicant. Where a written application is made on behalf of the domestic industry, the application shall identify the industry on behalf of which the application is made by a list of all known domestic producers of the like product (or associations of domestic producers of the like product) and, to the extent possible, a description of the volume and value of domestic production of the like product accounted for by such producers;

(ii) a complete description of the allegedly dumped product, the names of the country or countries of origin or export in question, the identity of each known exporter or foreign producer and a list of known persons importing the product in question;

(iii) information on prices at which the product in question is sold when destined for consumption in the domestic markets of the country or countries of origin or export (or, where appropriate, information on the prices at which the product is sold from the country or countries of origin or export to a third country or countries, or on the constructed value of the product) and information on export prices or, where appropriate, on the prices at which the product is first resold to an independent buyer in the territory of the importing Member;

(iv) information on the evolution of the volume of the allegedly dumped imports, the effect of these imports on prices of the like product in the domestic market and the consequent impact of the imports on the domestic industry, as demonstrated by relevant factors and indices having a bearing on the state of the domestic industry, such as those listed in paragraphs 2 and 4 of Article 3.

5.3 The authorities shall examine the accuracy and adequacy of the evidence provided in the application to determine whether there is sufficient evidence to justify the initiation of an investigation.

5.4 An investigation shall not be initiated pursuant to paragraph 1 unless the authorities have determined, on the basis of an examination of the degree of support for, or opposition to, the application expressed[13] by domestic producers of the like product, that the application has been made by or on behalf of the domestic industry.[14] The application shall be considered to have been made "by or on

13. In the case of fragmented industries involving an exceptionally large number of producers, authorities may determine support and opposition by using statistically valid sampling techniques.

14. Members are aware that in the territory of certain Members employees of domestic producers of the like product or representatives of those employees may make or support an application for an investigation under paragraph 1.

behalf of the domestic industry" if it is supported by those domestic producers whose collective output constitutes more than 50 per cent of the total production of the like product produced by that portion of the domestic industry expressing either support for or opposition to the application. However, no investigation shall be initiated when domestic producers expressly supporting the application account for less than 25 per cent of total production of the like product produced by the domestic industry.

5.5 The authorities shall avoid, unless a decision has been made to initiate an investigation, any publicizing of the application for the initiation of an investigation. However, after receipt of a properly documented application and before proceeding to initiate an investigation, the authorities shall notify the government of the exporting Member concerned.

5.6 If, in special circumstances, the authorities concerned decide to initiate an investigation without having received a written application by or on behalf of a domestic industry for the initiation of such investigation, they shall proceed only if they have sufficient evidence of dumping, injury and a causal link, as described in paragraph 2, to justify the initiation of an investigation.

5.7 The evidence of both dumping and injury shall be considered simultaneously *(a)* in the decision whether or not to initiate an investigation, and *(b)* thereafter, during the course of the investigation, starting on a date not later than the earliest date on which in accordance with the provisions of this Agreement provisional measures may be applied.

5.8 An application under paragraph 1 shall be rejected and an investigation shall be terminated promptly as soon as the authorities concerned are satisfied that there is not sufficient evidence of either dumping or of injury to justify proceeding with the case. There shall be immediate termination in cases where the authorities determine that the margin of dumping is *de minimis*, or that the volume of dumped imports, actual or potential, or the injury, is negligible. The margin of dumping shall be considered to be *de minimis* if this margin is less than 2 per cent, expressed as a percentage of the export price. The volume of dumped imports shall normally be regarded as negligible if the volume of dumped imports from a particular country is found to account for less than 3 per cent of imports of the like product in the importing Member, unless countries which individually account for less than 3 per cent of the imports of the like product in the importing Member collectively account for more than 7 per cent of imports of the like product in the importing Member.

5.9 An anti-dumping proceeding shall not hinder the procedures of customs clearance.

5.10 Investigations shall, except in special circumstances, be concluded within one year, and in no case more than 18 months, after their initiation.

ARTICLE 6

Evidence

6.1 All interested parties in an anti-dumping investigation shall be given notice of the information which the authorities require and ample opportunity to present in writing all evidence which they consider relevant in respect of the investigation in question.

6.1.1 Exporters or foreign producers receiving questionnaires used in an anti-dumping investigation shall be given at least 30 days for reply.[15] Due consideration should be given to any request for an extension of the 30-day period and, upon cause shown, such an extension should be granted whenever practicable.

6.1.2 Subject to the requirement to protect confidential information, evidence presented in writing by one interested party shall be made available promptly to other interested parties participating in the investigation.

6.1.3 As soon as an investigation has been initiated, the authorities shall provide the full text of the written application received under paragraph 1 of Article 5 to the known exporters[16] and to the authorities of the

15. As a general rule, the time-limit for exporters shall be counted from the date of receipt of the questionnaire, which for this purpose shall be deemed to have been received one week from the date on which it was sent to the respondent or transmitted to the appropriate diplomatic representative of the exporting Member or, in the case of a separate customs territory Member of the WTO, an official representative of the exporting territory.

16. It being understood that, where the number of exporters involved is particularly high, the full text of the written application should instead be provided only to the authorities of the exporting Member or to the relevant trade association.

exporting Member and shall make it available, upon request, to other interested parties involved. Due regard shall be paid to the requirement for the protection of confidential information, as provided for in paragraph 5.

6.2 Throughout the anti-dumping investigation all interested parties shall have a full opportunity for the defence of their interests. To this end, the authorities shall, on request, provide opportunities for all interested parties to meet those parties with adverse interests, so that opposing views may be presented and rebuttal arguments offered. Provision of such opportunities must take account of the need to preserve confidentiality and of the convenience to the parties. There shall be no obligation on any party to attend a meeting, and failure to do so shall not be prejudicial to that party's case. Interested parties shall also have the right, on justification, to present other information orally.

6.3 Oral information provided under paragraph 2 shall be taken into account by the authorities only in so far as it is subsequently reproduced in writing and made available to other interested parties, as provided for in subparagraph 1.2.

6.4 The authorities shall whenever practicable provide timely opportunities for all interested parties to see all information that is relevant to the presentation of their cases, that is not confidential as defined in paragraph 5, and that is used by the authorities in an anti-dumping investigation, and to prepare presentations on the basis of this information.

6.5 Any information which is by nature confidential (for example, because its disclosure would be of significant competitive advantage to a competitor or because its disclosure would have a significantly adverse effect upon a person supplying the information or upon a person from whom that person acquired the information), or which is provided on a confidential basis by parties to an investigation shall, upon good cause shown, be treated as such by the authorities. Such information shall not be disclosed without specific permission of the party submitting it.[17]

6.5.1 The authorities shall require interested parties providing confidential information to furnish non-confidential

17. Members are aware that in the territory of certain Members disclosure pursuant to a narrowly-drawn protective order may be required.

summaries thereof. These summaries shall be in sufficient detail to permit a reasonable understanding of the substance of the information submitted in confidence. In exceptional circumstances, such parties may indicate that such information is not susceptible of summary. In such exceptional circumstances, a statement of the reasons why summarization is not possible must be provided.

6.5.2 If the authorities find that a request for confidentiality is not warranted and if the supplier of the information is either unwilling to make the information public or to authorize its disclosure in generalized or summary form, the authorities may disregard such information unless it can be demonstrated to their satisfaction from appropriate sources that the information is correct.[18]

6.6 Except in circumstances provided for in paragraph 8, the authorities shall during the course of an investigation satisfy themselves as to the accuracy of the information supplied by interested parties upon which their findings are based.

6.7 In order to verify information provided or to obtain further details, the authorities may carry out investigations in the territory of other Members as required, provided they obtain the agreement of the firms concerned and notify the representatives of the government of the Member in question, and unless that Member objects to the investigation. The procedures described in Annex I shall apply to investigations carried out in the territory of other Members. Subject to the requirement to protect confidential information, the authorities shall make the results of any such investigations available, or shall provide disclosure thereof pursuant to paragraph 9, to the firms to which they pertain and may make such results available to the applicants.

6.8 In cases in which any interested party refuses access to, or otherwise does not provide, necessary information within a reasonable period or significantly impedes the investigation, preliminary and final determinations, affirmative or negative, may be made on the basis of the facts available. The provisions of Annex II shall be observed in the application of this paragraph.

---

18. Members agree that requests for confidentiality should not be arbitrarily rejected.

6.9 The authorities shall, before a final determination is made, inform all interested parties of the essential facts under consideration which form the basis for the decision whether to apply definitive measures. Such disclosure should take place in sufficient time for the parties to defend their interests.

6.10 The authorities shall, as a rule, determine an individual margin of dumping for each known exporter or producer concerned of the product under investigation. In cases where the number of exporters, producers, importers or types of products involved is so large as to make such a determination impracticable, the authorities may limit their examination either to a reasonable number of interested parties or products by using samples which are statistically valid on the basis of information available to the authorities at the time of the selection, or to the largest percentage of the volume of the exports from the country in question which can reasonably be investigated.

6.10.1 Any selection of exporters, producers, importers or types of products made under this paragraph shall preferably be chosen in consultation with and with the consent of the exporters, producers or importers concerned.

6.10.2 In cases where the authorities have limited their examination, as provided for in this paragraph, they shall nevertheless determine an individual margin of dumping for any exporter or producer not initially selected who submits the necessary information in time for that information to be considered during the course of the investigation, except where the number of exporters or producers is so large that individual examinations would be unduly burdensome to the authorities and prevent the timely completion of the investigation. Voluntary responses shall not be discouraged.

6.11 For the purposes of this Agreement, "interested parties" shall include:

(i) an exporter or foreign producer or the importer of a product subject to investigation, or a trade or business association a majority of the members of which are producers, exporters or importers of such product;

(ii) the government of the exporting Member; and

(iii) a producer of the like product in the importing Member or a trade and business association a majority of the members of which produce the like product in the territory of the importing Member.

This list shall not preclude Members from allowing domestic or foreign parties other than those mentioned above to be included as interested parties.

6.12 The authorities shall provide opportunities for industrial users of the product under investigation, and for representative consumer organizations in cases where the product is commonly sold at the retail level, to provide information which is relevant to the investigation regarding dumping, injury and causality.

6.13 The authorities shall take due account of any difficulties experienced by interested parties, in particular small companies, in supplying information requested, and shall provide any assistance practicable.

6.14 The procedures set out above are not intended to prevent the authorities of a Member from proceeding expeditiously with regard to initiating an investigation, reaching preliminary or final determinations, whether affirmative or negative, or from applying provisional or final measures, in accordance with relevant provisions of this Agreement.

ARTICLE 7

Provisional Measures

7.1 Provisional measures may be applied only if:

(i) an investigation has been initiated in accordance with the provisions of Article 5, a public notice has been given to that effect and interested parties have been given adequate opportunities to submit information and make comments;

(ii) a preliminary affirmative determination has been made of dumping and consequent injury to a domestic industry; and

(iii) the authorities concerned judge such measures necessary to prevent injury being caused during the investigation.

7.2 Provisional measures may take the form of a provisional duty or, preferably, a security - by cash deposit or bond - equal to the amount of the anti-dumping duty provisionally estimated, being not greater than the provisionally estimated margin of dumping. Withholding of appraisement is an appropriate provisional measure, provided that the normal duty and the estimated amount of the anti-dumping duty be indicated and as long as the withholding of appraisement is subject to the same conditions as other provisional measures.

7.3 Provisional measures shall not be applied sooner than 60 days from the date of initiation of the investigation.

7.4 The application of provisional measures shall be limited to as short a period as possible, not exceeding four months or, on decision of the authorities concerned, upon request by exporters representing a significant percentage of the trade involved, to a period not exceeding six months. When authorities, in the course of an investigation, examine whether a duty lower than the margin of dumping would be sufficient to remove injury, these periods may be six and nine months, respectively.

7.5 The relevant provisions of Article 9 shall be followed in the application of provisional measures.

ARTICLE 8

Price Undertakings

8.1 Proceedings may[19] be suspended or terminated without the imposition of provisional measures or anti-dumping duties upon receipt of satisfactory voluntary undertakings from any exporter to revise its prices or to cease exports to the area in question at dumped prices so that the authorities are satisfied that the injurious effect of the dumping is eliminated. Price increases under such undertakings shall not be higher than necessary to eliminate the margin of dumping. It is desirable that the price increases be less than the margin of dumping if such increases would be adequate to remove the injury to the domestic industry.

8.2 Price undertakings shall not be sought or accepted from exporters unless the authorities of the importing Member have made a preliminary affirmative determination of dumping and injury caused by such dumping.

19. The word "may" shall not be interpreted to allow the simultaneous continuation of proceedings with the implementation of price undertakings except as provided in paragraph 4.

8.3 Undertakings offered need not be accepted if the authorities consider their acceptance impractical, for example, if the number of actual or potential exporters is too great, or for other reasons, including reasons of general policy. Should the case arise and where practicable, the authorities shall provide to the exporter the reasons which have led them to consider acceptance of an undertaking as inappropriate, and shall, to the extent possible, give the exporter an opportunity to make comments thereon.

8.4 If an undertaking is accepted, the investigation of dumping and injury shall nevertheless be completed if the exporter so desires or the authorities so decide. In such a case, if a negative determination of dumping or injury is made, the undertaking shall automatically lapse, except in cases where such a determination is due in large part to the existence of a price undertaking. In such cases, the authorities may require that an undertaking be maintained for a reasonable period consistent with the provisions of this Agreement. In the event that an affirmative determination of dumping and injury is made, the undertaking shall continue consistent with its terms and the provisions of this Agreement.

8.5 Price undertakings may be suggested by the authorities of the importing Member, but no exporter shall be forced to enter into such undertakings. The fact that exporters do not offer such undertakings, or do not accept an invitation to do so, shall in no way prejudice the consideration of the case. However, the authorities are free to determine that a threat of injury is more likely to be realized if the dumped imports continue.

8.6 Authorities of an importing Member may require any exporter from whom an undertaking has been accepted to provide periodically information relevant to the fulfilment of such an undertaking and to permit verification of pertinent data. In case of violation of an undertaking, the authorities of the importing Member may take, under this Agreement in conformity with its provisions, expeditious actions which may constitute immediate application of provisional measures using the best information available. In such cases, definitive duties may be levied in accordance with this Agreement on products entered for consumption not more than 90 days before the application of such provisional measures, except that any such retroactive assessment shall not apply to imports entered before the violation of the undertaking.

ARTICLE 9

Imposition and Collection of Anti-Dumping Duties

9.1 The decision whether or not to impose an anti-dumping duty in cases where all requirements for the imposition have been fulfilled, and the decision whether the amount of the anti-dumping duty to be imposed shall be the full margin of dumping or less, are decisions to be made by the authorities of the importing Member. It is desirable that the imposition be permissive in the territory of all Members, and that the duty be less than the margin if such lesser duty would be adequate to remove the injury to the domestic industry.

9.2 When an anti-dumping duty is imposed in respect of any product, such anti-dumping duty shall be collected in the appropriate amounts in each case, on a non-discriminatory basis on imports of such product from all sources found to be dumped and causing injury, except as to imports from those sources from which price undertakings under the terms of this Agreement have been accepted. The authorities shall name the supplier or suppliers of the product concerned. If, however, several suppliers from the same country are involved, and it is impracticable to name all these suppliers, the authorities may name the supplying country concerned. If several suppliers from more than one country are involved, the authorities may name either all the suppliers involved, or, if this is impracticable, all the supplying countries involved.

9.3 The amount of the anti-dumping duty shall not exceed the margin of dumping as established under Article 2.

9.3.1 When the amount of the anti-dumping duty is assessed on a retrospective basis, the determination of the final liability for payment of anti-dumping duties shall take place as soon as possible, normally within 12 months, and in no case more than 18 months, after the date on which a request for a final assessment of the amount of the anti-dumping duty has been made.[20] Any refund shall be made promptly and normally in not more than 90 days following the determination of final liability made pursuant to this sub-paragraph. In any case, where a

20. It is understood that the observance of the time-limits mentioned in this subparagraph and in subparagraph 3.2 may not be possible where the product in question is subject to judicial review proceedings.

refund is not made within 90 days, the authorities shall provide an explanation if so requested.

9.3.2 When the amount of the anti-dumping duty is assessed on a prospective basis, provision shall be made for a prompt refund, upon request, of any duty paid in excess of the margin of dumping. A refund of any such duty paid in excess of the actual margin of dumping shall normally take place within 12 months, and in no case more than 18 months, after the date on which a request for a refund, duly supported by evidence, has been made by an importer of the product subject to the anti-dumping duty. The refund authorized should normally be made within 90 days of the above-noted decision.

9.3.3 In determining whether and to what extent a reimbursement should be made when the export price is constructed in accordance with paragraph 3 of Article 2, authorities should take account of any change in normal value, any change in costs incurred between importation and resale, and any movement in the resale price which is duly reflected in subsequent selling prices, and should calculate the export price with no deduction for the amount of anti-dumping duties paid when conclusive evidence of the above is provided.

9.4 When the authorities have limited their examination in accordance with the second sentence of paragraph 10 of Article 6, any anti-dumping duty applied to imports from exporters or producers not included in the examination shall not exceed:

(i) the weighted average margin of dumping established with respect to the selected exporters or producers or,

(ii) where the liability for payment of anti-dumping duties is calculated on the basis of a prospective normal value, the difference between the weighted average normal value of the selected exporters or producers and the export prices of exporters or producers not individually examined,

provided that the authorities shall disregard for the purpose of this paragraph any zero and *de minimis* margins and margins established under the circumstances referred to in paragraph 8 of Article 6. The authorities shall apply individual duties or normal values to imports from any exporter or producer not included in the examination who has provided the necessary information during the course of the investigation, as provided for in subparagraph 10.2 of Article 6.

9.5 If a product is subject to anti-dumping duties in an importing Member, the authorities shall promptly carry out a review for the purpose of determining individual margins of dumping for any exporters or producers in the exporting country in question who have not exported the product to the importing Member during the period of investigation, provided that these exporters or producers can show that they are not related to any of the exporters or producers in the exporting country who are subject to the anti-dumping duties on the product. Such a review shall be initiated and carried out on an accelerated basis, compared to normal duty assessment and review proceedings in the importing Member. No anti-dumping duties shall be levied on imports from such exporters or producers while the review is being carried out. The authorities may, however, withhold appraisement and/or request guarantees to ensure that, should such a review result in a determination of dumping in respect of such producers or exporters, anti-dumping duties can be levied retroactively to the date of the initiation of the review.

ARTICLE 10
Retroactivity

10.1 Provisional measures and anti-dumping duties shall only be applied to products which enter for consumption after the time when the decision taken under paragraph 1 of Article 7 and paragraph 1 of Article 9, respectively, enters into force, subject to the exceptions set out in this Article.

10.2 Where a final determination of injury (but not of a threat thereof or of a material retardation of the establishment of an industry) is made or, in the case of a final determination of a threat of injury, where the effect of the dumped imports would, in the absence of the provisional measures, have led to a determination of injury, anti-dumping duties may be levied retroactively for the period for which provisional measures, if any, have been applied.

10.3 If the definitive anti-dumping duty is higher than the provisional duty paid or payable, or the amount estimated for the purpose of the security, the difference shall not be collected. If the definitive duty is lower than the provisional duty paid or payable, or the amount estimated for the purpose of the security, the difference shall be reimbursed or the duty recalculated, as the case may be.

10.4 Except as provided in paragraph 2, where a determination of threat of injury or material retardation is made (but no injury has yet occurred) a definitive anti-dumping duty may be imposed only from the date of the determination of threat of injury or material retardation, and any cash deposit made during the period of the application of provisional measures shall be refunded and any bonds released in an expeditious manner.

10.5 Where a final determination is negative, any cash deposit made during the period of the application of provisional measures shall be refunded and any bonds released in an expeditious manner.

10.6 A definitive anti-dumping duty may be levied on products which were entered for consumption not more than 90 days prior to the date of application of provisional measures, when the authorities determine for the dumped product in question that:

(i) there is a history of dumping which caused injury or that the importer was, or should have been, aware that the exporter practises dumping and that such dumping would cause injury, and

(ii) the injury is caused by massive dumped imports of a product in a relatively short time which in light of the timing and the volume of the dumped imports and other circumstances (such as a rapid build-up of inventories of the imported product) is likely to seriously undermine the remedial effect of the definitive anti-dumping duty to be applied, provided that the importers concerned have been given an opportunity to comment.

10.7 The authorities may, after initiating an investigation, take such measures as the withholding of appraisement or assessment as may be necessary to collect anti-dumping duties retroactively, as provided for in paragraph 6, once they have sufficient evidence that the conditions set forth in that paragraph are satisfied.

10.8 No duties shall be levied retroactively pursuant to paragraph 6 on products entered for consumption prior to the date of initiation of the investigation.

ARTICLE 11

Duration and Review of Anti-Dumping Duties and Price Undertakings

11.1 An anti-dumping duty shall remain in force only as long as and to the extent necessary to counteract dumping which is causing injury.

11.2 The authorities shall review the need for the continued imposition of the duty, where warranted, on their own initiative or, provided that a reasonable period of time has elapsed since the imposition of the definitive anti-dumping duty, upon request by any interested party which submits positive information substantiating the need for a review.[21] Interested parties shall have the right to request the authorities to examine whether the continued imposition of the duty is necessary to offset dumping, whether the injury would be likely to continue or recur if the duty were removed or varied, or both. If, as a result of the review under this paragraph, the authorities determine that the anti-dumping duty is no longer warranted, it shall be terminated immediately.

11.3 Notwithstanding the provisions of paragraphs 1 and 2, any definitive anti-dumping duty shall be terminated on a date not later than five years from its imposition (or from the date of the most recent review under paragraph 2 if that review has covered both dumping and injury, or under this paragraph), unless the authorities determine, in a review initiated before that date on their own initiative or upon a duly substantiated request made by or on behalf of the domestic industry within a reasonable period of time prior to that date, that the expiry of the duty would be likely to lead to continuation or recurrence of dumping and injury.[22] The duty may remain in force pending the outcome of such a review.

11.4 The provisions of Article 6 regarding evidence and procedure shall apply to any review carried out under this Article. Any such

---

21. A determination of final liability for payment of anti-dumping duties, as provided for in paragraph 3 of Article 9, does not by itself constitute a review within the meaning of this Article.

22. When the amount of the anti-dumping duty is assessed on a retrospective basis, a finding in the most recent assessment proceeding under subparagraph 3.1 of Article 9 that no duty is to be levied shall not by itself require the authorities to terminate the definitive duty.

review shall be carried out expeditiously and shall normally be concluded within 12 months of the date of initiation of the review.

11.5 The provisions of this Article shall apply *mutatis mutandis* to price undertakings accepted under Article 8.

ARTICLE 12

Public Notice and Explanation of Determinations

12.1 When the authorities are satisfied that there is sufficient evidence to justify the initiation of an anti-dumping investigation pursuant to Article 5, the Member or Members the products of which are subject to such investigation and other interested parties known to the investigating authorities to have an interest therein shall be notified and a public notice shall be given.

12.1.1 A public notice of the initiation of an investigation shall contain, or otherwise make available through a separate report[23], adequate information on the following:

(i) the name of the exporting country or countries and the product involved;

(ii) the date of initiation of the investigation;

(iii) the basis on which dumping is alleged in the application;

(iv) a summary of the factors on which the allegation of injury is based;

(v) the address to which representations by interested parties should be directed;

(vi) the time-limits allowed to interested parties for making their views known.

12.2 Public notice shall be given of any preliminary or final determination, whether affirmative or negative, of any decision to accept an undertaking pursuant to Article 8, of the termination of such an undertaking, and of the termination of a definitive anti-dumping duty. Each such notice shall set forth, or otherwise make available through a separate report, in sufficient detail the findings and conclusions reached on all issues of fact and law considered material by the investigating authorities. All such notices and reports

23. Where authorities provide information and explanations under the provisions of this Article in a separate report, they shall ensure that such report is readily available to the public.

shall be forwarded to the Member or Members the products of which are subject to such determination or undertaking and to other interested parties known to have an interest therein.

12.2.1 A public notice of the imposition of provisional measures shall set forth, or otherwise make available through a separate report, sufficiently detailed explanations for the preliminary determinations on dumping and injury and shall refer to the matters of fact and law which have led to arguments being accepted or rejected. Such a notice or report shall, due regard being paid to the requirement for the protection of confidential information, contain in particular:

(i) the names of the suppliers, or when this is impracticable, the supplying countries involved;

(ii) a description of the product which is sufficient for customs purposes;

(iii) the margins of dumping established and a full explanation of the reasons for the methodology used in the establishment and comparison of the export price and the normal value under Article 2;

(iv) considerations relevant to the injury determination as set out in Article 3;

(v) the main reasons leading to the determination.

12.2.2 A public notice of conclusion or suspension of an investigation in the case of an affirmative determination providing for the imposition of a definitive duty or the acceptance of a price undertaking shall contain, or otherwise make available through a separate report, all relevant information on the matters of fact and law and reasons which have led to the imposition of final measures or the acceptance of a price undertaking, due regard being paid to the requirement for the protection of confidential information. In particular, the notice or report shall contain the information described in subparagraph 2.1, as well as the reasons for the acceptance or rejection of relevant arguments or claims made by the exporters and importers, and the basis for any decision made under subparagraph 10.2 of Article 6.

12.2.3 A public notice of the termination or suspension of an investigation following the acceptance of an undertaking pursuant to Article 8 shall include, or otherwise make available through a separate report, the non-confidential part of this undertaking.

12.3 The provisions of this Article shall apply *mutatis mutandis* to the initiation and completion of reviews pursuant to Article 11 and to decisions under Article 10 to apply duties retroactively.

ARTICLE 13

Judicial Review

Each Member whose national legislation contains provisions on anti-dumping measures shall maintain judicial, arbitral or administrative tribunals or procedures for the purpose, *inter alia*, of the prompt review of administrative actions relating to final determinations and reviews of determinations within the meaning of Article 11. Such tribunals or procedures shall be independent of the authorities responsible for the determination or review in question.

ARTICLE 14

Anti-Dumping Action on Behalf of a Third Country

14.1 An application for anti-dumping action on behalf of a third country shall be made by the authorities of the third country requesting action.

14.2 Such an application shall be supported by price information to show that the imports are being dumped and by detailed information to show that the alleged dumping is causing injury to the domestic industry concerned in the third country. The government of the third country shall afford all assistance to the authorities of the importing country to obtain any further information which the latter may require.

14.3 In considering such an application, the authorities of the importing country shall consider the effects of the alleged dumping on the industry concerned as a whole in the third country; that is to say, the injury shall not be assessed in relation only to the effect of the alleged dumping on the industry's exports to the importing country or even on the industry's total exports.

14.4 The decision whether or not to proceed with a case shall rest with the importing country. If the importing country decides that it is prepared to take action, the initiation of the approach to the Council for Trade in Goods seeking its approval for such action shall rest with the importing country.

ARTICLE 15

Developing Country Members

It is recognized that special regard must be given by developed country Members to the special situation of developing country Members when considering the application of anti-dumping measures under this Agreement. Possibilities of constructive remedies provided for by this Agreement shall be explored before applying anti-dumping duties where they would affect the essential interests of developing country Members.

PART II

ARTICLE 16

Committee on Anti-Dumping Practices

16.1 There is hereby established a Committee on Anti-Dumping Practices (referred to in this Agreement as the "Committee") composed of representatives from each of the Members. The Committee shall elect its own Chairman and shall meet not less than twice a year and otherwise as envisaged by relevant provisions of this Agreement at the request of any Member. The Committee shall carry out responsibilities as assigned to it under this Agreement or by the Members and it shall afford Members the opportunity of consulting on any matters relating to the operation of the Agreement or the furtherance of its objectives. The WTO Secretariat shall act as the secretariat to the Committee.

16.2 The Committee may set up subsidiary bodies as appropriate.

16.3 In carrying out their functions, the Committee and any subsidiary bodies may consult with and seek information from any source they deem appropriate. However, before the Committee or a subsidiary body seeks such information from a source within the jurisdiction of a Member, it shall inform the Member involved. It shall obtain the consent of the Member and any firm to be consulted.

16.4 Members shall report without delay to the Committee all preliminary or final anti-dumping actions taken. Such reports shall be available in the Secretariat for inspection by other Members. Members shall also submit, on a semi-annual basis, reports of any anti-dumping actions taken within the preceding six months. The semi-annual reports shall be submitted on an agreed standard form.

16.5 Each Member shall notify the Committee *(a)* which of its authorities are competent to initiate and conduct investigations referred to in Article 5 and *(b)* its domestic procedures governing the initiation and conduct of such investigations.

ARTICLE 17

Consultation and Dispute Settlement

17.1 Except as otherwise provided herein, the Dispute Settlement Understanding is applicable to consultations and the settlement of disputes under this Agreement.

17.2 Each Member shall afford sympathetic consideration to, and shall afford adequate opportunity for consultation regarding, representations made by another Member with respect to any matter affecting the operation of this Agreement.

17.3 If any Member considers that any benefit accruing to it, directly or indirectly, under this Agreement is being nullified or impaired, or that the achievement of any objective is being impeded, by another Member or Members, it may, with a view to reaching a mutually satisfactory resolution of the matter, request in writing consultations with the Member or Members in question. Each Member shall afford sympathetic consideration to any request from another Member for consultation.

17.4 If the Member that requested consultations considers that the consultations pursuant to paragraph 3 have failed to achieve a mutually agreed solution, and if final action has been taken by the administering authorities of the importing Member to levy definitive anti-dumping duties or to accept price undertakings, it may refer the matter to the Dispute Settlement Body ("DSB"). When a provisional measure has a significant impact and the Member that requested consultations considers that the measure was taken contrary to the provisions of paragraph 1 of Article 7, that Member may also refer such matter to the DSB.

17.5 The DSB shall, at the request of the complaining party, establish a panel to examine the matter based upon:

(i) a written statement of the Member making the request indicating how a benefit accruing to it, directly or indirectly, under this Agreement has been nullified or impaired, or that the achieving of the objectives of the Agreement is being impeded, and

(ii) the facts made available in conformity with appropriate domestic procedures to the authorities of the importing Member.

17.6 In examining the matter referred to in paragraph 5:

(i) in its assessment of the facts of the matter, the panel shall determine whether the authorities' establishment of the facts was proper and whether their evaluation of those facts was unbiased and objective. If the establishment of the facts was proper and the evaluation was unbiased and objective, even though the panel might have reached a different conclusion, the evaluation shall not be overturned;

(ii) the panel shall interpret the relevant provisions of the Agreement in accordance with customary rules of interpretation of public international law. Where the panel finds that a relevant provision of the Agreement admits of more than one permissible interpretation, the panel shall find the authorities' measure to be in conformity with the Agreement if it rests upon one of those permissible interpretations.

17.7 Confidential information provided to the panel shall not be disclosed without formal authorization from the person, body or authority providing such information. Where such information is requested from the panel but release of such information by the panel is not authorized, a non-confidential summary of the information, authorized by the person, body or authority providing the information, shall be provided.

PART III

ARTICLE 1

Final Provisions

18.1 No specific action against dumping of exports from another

Member can be taken except in accordance with the provisions of GATT 1994, as interpreted by this Agreement.[24]

18.2 Reservations may not be entered in respect of any of the provisions of this Agreement without the consent of the other Members.

18.3 Subject to subparagraphs 3.1 and 3.2, the provisions of this Agreement shall apply to investigations, and reviews of existing measures, initiated pursuant to applications which have been made on or after the date of entry into force for a Member of the WTO Agreement.

18.3.1 With respect to the calculation of margins of dumping in refund procedures under paragraph 3 of Article 9, the rules used in the most recent determination or review of dumping shall apply.

18.3.2 For the purposes of paragraph 3 of Article 11, existing anti-dumping measures shall be deemed to be imposed on a date not later than the date of entry into force for a Member of the WTO Agreement, except in cases in which the domestic legislation of a Member in force on that date already included a clause of the type provided for in that paragraph.

18.4 Each Member shall take all necessary steps, of a general or particular character, to ensure, not later than the date of entry into force of the WTO Agreement for it, the conformity of its laws, regulations and administrative procedures with the provisions of this Agreement as they may apply for the Member in question.

18.5 Each Member shall inform the Committee of any changes in its laws and regulations relevant to this Agreement and in the administration of such laws and regulations.

18.6 The Committee shall review annually the implementation and operation of this Agreement taking into account the objectives thereof. The Committee shall inform annually the Council for Trade in Goods of developments during the period covered by such reviews.

18.7 The Annexes to this Agreement constitute an integral part thereof.

---

24. This is not intended to preclude action under other relevant provisions of GATT 1994, as appropriate.

ANNEX I

PROCEDURES FOR ON-THE-SPOT INVESTIGATIONS PURSUAN TO PARAGRAPH 7 OF ARTICLE 6

1. Upon initiation of an investigation, the authorities of the exporting Member and the firms known to be concerned should be informed of the intention to carry out on-the-spot investigations.

2. If in exceptional circumstances it is intended to include non-governmental experts in the investigating team, the firms and the authorities of the exporting Member should be so informed. Such non-governmental experts should be subject to effective sanctions for breach of confidentiality requirements.

3. It should be standard practice to obtain explicit agreement of the firms concerned in the exporting Member before the visit is finally scheduled.

4. As soon as the agreement of the firms concerned has been obtained, the investigating authorities should notify the authorities of the exporting Member of the names and addresses of the firms to be visited and the dates agreed.

5. Sufficient advance notice should be given to the firms in question before the visit is made.

6. Visits to explain the questionnaire should only be made at the request of an exporting firm. Such a visit may only be made if *(a)* the authorities of the importing Member notify the representatives of the Member in question and *(b)* the latter do not object to the visit.

7. As the main purpose of the on-the-spot investigation is to verify information provided or to obtain further details, it should be carried out after the response to the questionnaire has been received unless the firm agrees to the contrary and the government of the exporting Member is informed by the investigating authorities of the anticipated visit and does not object to it; further, it should be standard practice prior to the visit to advise the firms concerned of the general nature of the information to be verified and of any further information which needs to be provided, though this should not preclude requests to be made on the spot for further details to be provided in the light of information obtained.

8. Enquiries or questions put by the authorities or firms of the exporting Members and essential to a successful on-the-spot

investigation should, whenever possible, be answered before the visit is made.

ANNEX II

BEST INFORMATION AVAILABLE IN TERMS OF PARAGRAPH 8 OF ARTICLE 6

1. As soon as possible after the initiation of the investigation, the investigating authorities should specify in detail the information required from any interested party, and the manner in which that information should be structured by the interested party in its response. The authorities should also ensure that the party is aware that if information is not supplied within a reasonable time, the authorities will be free to make determinations on the basis of the facts available, including those contained in the application for the initiation of the investigation by the domestic industry.

2. The authorities may also request that an interested party provide its response in a particular medium (e.g. computer tape) or computer language. Where such a request is made, the authorities should consider the reasonable ability of the interested party to respond in the preferred medium or computer language, and should not request the party to use for its response a computer system other than that used by the party. The authority should not maintain a request for a computerized response if the interested party does not maintain computerized accounts and if presenting the response as requested would result in an unreasonable extra burden on the interested party, e.g. it would entail unreasonable additional cost and trouble. The authorities should not maintain a request for a response in a particular medium or computer language if the interested party does not maintain its computerized accounts in such medium or computer language and if presenting the response as requested would result in an unreasonable extra burden on the interested party, e.g. it would entail unreasonable additional cost and trouble.

3. All information which is verifiable, which is appropriately submitted so that it can be used in the investigation without undue difficulties, which is supplied in a timely fashion, and, where applicable, which is supplied in a medium or computer language requested by the authorities, should be taken into account when determinations are made. If a party does not respond in the preferred medium or computer language but the authorities find that the circumstances set out in paragraph 2 have been satisfied, the failure

to respond in the preferred medium or computer language should not be considered to significantly impede the investigation.

4. Where the authorities do not have the ability to process information if provided in a particular medium (e.g. computer tape), the information should be supplied in the form of written material or any other form acceptable to the authorities.

5. Even though the information provided may not be ideal in all respects, this should not justify the authorities from disregarding it, provided the interested party has acted to the best of its ability.

6. If evidence or information is not accepted, the supplying party should be informed forthwith of the reasons therefor, and should have an opportunity to provide further explanations within a reasonable period, due account being taken of the time-limits of the investigation. If the explanations are considered by the authorities as not being satisfactory, the reasons for the rejection of such evidence or information should be given in any published determinations.

7. If the authorities have to base their findings, including those with respect to normal value, on information from a secondary source, including the information supplied in the application for the initiation of the investigation, they should do so with special circumspection. In such cases, the authorities should, where practicable, check the information from other independent sources at their disposal, such as published price lists, official import statistics and customs returns, and from the information obtained from other interested parties during the investigation. It is clear, however, that if an interested party does not cooperate and thus relevant information is being withheld from the authorities, this situation could lead to a result which is less favourable to the party than if the party did cooperate.

AGREEMENT ON IMPLEMENTATION OF ARTICLE VII OF THE GENERAL AGREEMENT ON TARIFFS AND TRADE 1994

GENERAL INTRODUCTORY COMMENTARY

1. The primary basis for customs value under this Agreement is "transaction value" as defined in Article 1. Article 1 is to be read together with Article 8 which provides, *inter alia*, for adjustments to the price actually paid or payable in cases where certain specific

elements which are considered to form a part of the value for customs purposes are incurred by the buyer but are not included in the price actually paid or payable for the imported goods. Article 8 also provides for the inclusion in the transaction value of certain considerations which may pass from the buyer to the seller in the form of specified goods or services rather than in the form of money. Articles 2 through 7 provide methods of determining the customs value whenever it cannot be determined under the provisions of Article 1.

2. Where the customs value cannot be determined under the provisions of Article 1 there should normally be a process of consultation between the customs administration and importer with a view to arriving at a basis of value under the provisions of Article 2 or 3. It may occur, for example, that the importer has information about the customs value of identical or similar imported goods which is not immediately available to the customs administration in the port of importation. On the other hand, the customs administration may have information about the customs value of identical or similar imported goods which is not readily available to the importer. A process of consultation between the two parties will enable information to be exchanged, subject to the requirements of commercial confidentiality, with a view to determining a proper basis of value for customs purposes.

3. Articles 5 and 6 provide two bases for determining the customs value where it cannot be determined on the basis of the transaction value of the imported goods or of identical or similar imported goods. Under paragraph 1 of Article 5 the customs value is determined on the basis of the price at which the goods are sold in the condition as imported to an unrelated buyer in the country of importation. The importer also has the right to have goods which are further processed after importation valued under the provisions of Article 5 if the importer so requests. Under Article 6 the customs value is determined on the basis of the computed value. Both these methods present certain difficulties and because of this the importer is given the right, under the provisions of Article 4, to choose the order of application of the two methods.

4. Article 7 sets out how to determine the customs value in cases where it cannot be determined under the provisions of any of the preceding Articles.

Members,

Having regard to the Multilateral Trade Negotiations;

Desiring to further the objectives of GATT 1994 and to secure additional benefits for the international trade of developing countries;

Recognizing the importance of the provisions of Article VII of GATT 1994 and desiring to elaborate rules for their application in order to provide greater uniformity and certainty in their implementation;

Recognizing the need for a fair, uniform and neutral system for the valuation of goods for customs purposes that precludes the use of arbitrary or fictitious customs values;

Recognizing that the basis for valuation of goods for customs purposes should, to the greatest extent possible, be the transaction value of the goods being valued;

Recognizing that customs value should be based on simple and equitable criteria consistent with commercial practices and that valuation procedures should be of general application without distinction between sources of supply;

Recognizing that valuation procedures should not be used to combat dumping;

Hereby *agree* as follows:

PART I

RULES ON CUSTOMS VALUATION

ARTICLE 1

1. The customs value of imported goods shall be the transaction value, that is the price actually paid or payable for the goods when sold for export to the country of importation adjusted in accordance with the provisions of Article 8, provided:

(a) that there are no restrictions as to the disposition or use of the goods by the buyer other than restrictions which:

(i) are imposed or required by law or by the public authorities in the country of importation;

(ii) limit the geographical area in which the goods may be resold; or

(iii) do not substantially affect the value of the goods;

(b) that the sale or price is not subject to some condition or consideration for which a value cannot be determined with respect to the goods being valued;

(c) that no part of the proceeds of any subsequent resale, disposal or use of the goods by the buyer will accrue directly or indirectly to the seller, unless an appropriate adjustment can be made in accordance with the provisions of Article 8; and

(d) that the buyer and seller are not related, or where the buyer and seller are related, that the transaction value is acceptable for customs purposes under the provisions of paragraph 2.

2. (a) In determining whether the transaction value is acceptable for the purposes of paragraph 1, the fact that the buyer and the seller are related within the meaning of Article 15 shall not in itself be grounds for regarding the transaction value as unacceptable. In such case the circumstances surrounding the sale shall be examined and the transaction value shall be accepted provided that the relationship did not influence the price. If, in the light of information provided by the importer or otherwise, the customs administration has grounds for considering that the relationship influenced the price, it shall communicate its grounds to the importer and the importer shall be given a reasonable opportunity to respond. If the importer so requests, the communication of the grounds shall be in writing.

(b) In a sale between related persons, the transaction value shall be accepted and the goods valued in accordance with the provisions of paragraph 1 whenever the importer demonstrates that such value closely approximates to one of the following occurring at or about the same time:

(i) the transaction value in sales to unrelated buyers of identical or similar goods for export to the same country of importation;

(ii) the customs value of identical or similar goods as determined under the provisions of Article 5;

(iii) the customs value of identical or similar goods as determined under the provisions of Article 6;

In applying the foregoing tests, due account shall be taken of demonstrated differences in commercial levels, quantity levels, the elements enumerated in Article 8 and costs incurred by the seller in sales in which the seller and the buyer are not related that are not incurred by the seller in sales in which the seller and the buyer are related.

(c) The tests set forth in paragraph 2(b) are to be used at the initiative of the importer and only for comparison purposes. Substitute values may not be established under the provisions of paragraph 2(b).

ARTICLE 2

1. (a) If the customs value of the imported goods cannot be determined under the provisions of Article 1, the customs value shall be the transaction value of identical goods sold for export to the same country of importation and exported at or about the same time as the goods being valued.

(b) In applying this Article, the transaction value of identical goods in a sale at the same commercial level and in substantially the same quantity as the goods being valued shall be used to determine the customs value. Where no such sale is found, the transaction value of identical goods sold at a different commercial level and/or in different quantities, adjusted to take account of differences attributable to commercial level and/or to quantity, shall be used, provided that such adjustments can be made on the basis of demonstrated evidence which clearly establishes the reasonableness and accuracy of the adjustment, whether the adjustment leads to an increase or a decrease in the value.

2. Where the costs and charges referred to in paragraph 2 of Article 8 are included in the transaction value, an adjustment shall be made to take account of significant differences in such costs and charges between the imported goods and the identical goods in question arising from differences in distances and modes of transport.

3. If, in applying this Article, more than one transaction value of identical goods is found, the lowest such value shall be used to determine the customs value of the imported goods.

ARTICLE 3

1. (a) If the customs value of the imported goods cannot be determined under the provisions of Articles 1 and 2, the customs value shall be the transaction value of similar goods sold for export to the same country of importation and exported at or about the same time as the goods being valued.

   (b) In applying this Article, the transaction value of similar goods in a sale at the same commercial level and in substantially the same quantity as the goods being valued shall be used to determine the customs value. Where no such sale is found, the transaction value of similar goods sold at a different commercial level and/or in different quantities, adjusted to take account of differences attributable to commercial level and/or to quantity, shall be used, provided that such adjustments can be made on the basis of demonstrated evidence which clearly establishes the reasonableness and accuracy of the adjustment, whether the adjustment leads to an increase or a decrease in the value.

2. Where the costs and charges referred to in paragraph 2 of Article 8 are included in the transaction value, an adjustment shall be made to take account of significant differences in such costs and charges between the imported goods and the similar goods in question arising from differences in distances and modes of transport.

3. If, in applying this Article, more than one transaction value of similar goods is found, the lowest such value shall be used to determine the customs value of the imported goods.

ARTICLE 4

If the customs value of the imported goods cannot be determined under the provisions of Articles 1, 2 and 3, the customs value shall be determined under the provisions of Article 5 or, when the customs value cannot be determined under that Article, under the provisions of Article 6 except that, at the request of the importer, the order of application of Articles 5 and 6 shall be reversed.

ARTICLE 5

1. (a) If the imported goods or identical or similar imported goods are sold in the country of importation in the condition as imported, the customs value of the imported goods under the provisions of this Article shall be based on the unit price at which the imported goods or identical or similar imported goods are so sold in the greatest aggregate quantity, at or about the time of the importation of the goods being valued, to persons who are not related to the persons from whom they buy such goods, subject to deductions for the following:

(i) either the commissions usually paid or agreed to be paid or the additions usually made for profit and general expenses in connection with sales in such country of imported goods of the same class or kind;

(ii) the usual costs of transport and insurance and associated costs incurred within the country of importation;

(iii) where appropriate, the costs and charges referred to in paragraph 2 of Article 8; and

(iv) the customs duties and other national taxes payable in the country of importation by reason of the importation or sale of the goods.

(b) If neither the imported goods nor identical nor similar imported goods are sold at or about the time of importation of the goods being valued, the customs value shall, subject otherwise to the provisions of paragraph 1(a), be based on the unit price at which the imported goods or identical or similar imported goods are sold in the country of importation in the condition as imported at the earliest date after the importation of the goods being valued but before the expiration of 90 days after such importation.

2. If neither the imported goods nor identical nor similar imported goods are sold in the country of importation in the condition as imported, then, if the importer so requests, the customs value shall be based on the unit price at which the imported goods, after further

processing, are sold in the greatest aggregate quantity to persons in the country of importation who are not related to the persons from whom they buy such goods, due allowance being made for the value added by such processing and the deductions provided for in paragraph 1(a).

ARTICLE 6

1. The customs value of imported goods under the provisions of this Article shall be based on a computed value. Computed value shall consist of the sum of:

(a) the cost or value of materials and fabrication or other processing employed in producing the imported goods;

(b) an amount for profit and general expenses equal to that usually reflected in sales of goods of the same class or kind as the goods being valued which are made by producers in the country of exportation for export to the country of importation;

(c) the cost or value of all other expenses necessary to reflect the valuation option chosen by the Member under paragraph 2 of Article 8.

2. No Member may require or compel any person not resident in its own territory to produce for examination, or to allow access to, any account or other record for the purposes of determining a computed value. However, information supplied by the producer of the goods for the purposes of determining the customs value under the provisions of this Article may be verified in another country by the authorities of the country of importation with the agreement of the producer and provided they give sufficient advance notice to the government of the country in question and the latter does not object to the investigation.

ARTICLE 7

1. If the customs value of the imported goods cannot be determined under the provisions of Articles 1 through 6, inclusive, the customs value shall be determined using reasonable means consistent with the principles and general provisions of this Agreement and of Article VII of GATT 1994 and on the basis of data available in the country of importation.

2. No customs value shall be determined under the provisions of this Article on the basis of:

(a) the selling price in the country of importation of goods produced in such country;

(b) a system which provides for the acceptance for customs purposes of the higher of two alternative values;

(c) the price of goods on the domestic market of the country of exportation;

(d) the cost of production other than computed values which have been determined for identical or similar goods in accordance with the provisions of Article 6;

(e) the price of the goods for export to a country other than the country of importation;

(f) minimum customs values; or

(g) arbitrary or fictitious values.

3. If the importer so requests, the importer shall be informed in writing of the customs value determined under the provisions of this Article and the method used to determine such value.

ARTICLE 8

1. In determining the customs value under the provisions of Article 1, there shall be added to the price actually paid or payable for the imported goods:

(a) the following, to the extent that they are incurred by the buyer but are not included in the price actually paid or payable for the goods:

(i) commissions and brokerage, except buying commissions;

(ii) the cost of containers which are treated as being one for customs purposes with the goods in question;

(iii) the cost of packing whether for labour or materials;

(b) the value, apportioned as appropriate, of the following goods and services where supplied directly or indirectly by the buyer free of charge or at reduced cost for use in connection with the production and sale for export of the imported goods, to the extent that such value has not been included in the price actually paid or payable:

(i) materials, components, parts and similar items incorporated in the imported goods;

(ii) tools, dies, moulds and similar items used in the production of the imported goods;

(iii) materials consumed in the production of the imported goods;

(iv) engineering, development, artwork, design work, and plans and sketches undertaken elsewhere than in the country of importation and necessary for the production of the imported goods;

(c) royalties and licence fees related to the goods being valued that the buyer must pay, either directly or indirectly, as a condition of sale of the goods being valued, to the extent that such royalties and fees are not included in the price actually paid or payable;

(d) the value of any part of the proceeds of any subsequent resale, disposal or use of the imported goods that accrues directly or indirectly to the seller.

2. In framing its legislation, each Member shall provide for the inclusion in or the exclusion from the customs value, in whole or in part, of the following:

(a) the cost of transport of the imported goods to the port or place of importation;

(b) loading, unloading and handling charges associated with the transport of the imported goods to the port or place of importation; and

(c) the cost of insurance.

3. Additions to the price actually paid or payable shall be made under this Article only on the basis of objective and quantifiable data.

4. No additions shall be made to the price actually paid or payable in determining the customs value except as provided in this Article.

ARTICLE 9

1. Where the conversion of currency is necessary for the

determination of the customs value, the rate of exchange to be used shall be that duly published by the competent authorities of the country of importation concerned and shall reflect as effectively as possible, in respect of the period covered by each such document of publication, the current value of such currency in commercial transactions in terms of the currency of the country of importation.

2. The conversion rate to be used shall be that in effect at the time of exportation or the time of importation, as provided by each Member.

ARTICLE 10

All information which is by nature confidential or which is provided on a confidential basis for the purposes of customs valuation shall be treated as strictly confidential by the authorities concerned who shall not disclose it without the specific permission of the person or government providing such information, except to the extent that it may be required to be disclosed in the context of judicial proceedings.

ARTICLE 11

1. The legislation of each Member shall provide in regard to a determination of customs value for the right of appeal, without penalty, by the importer or any other person liable for the payment of the duty.

2. An initial right of appeal without penalty may be to an authority within the customs administration or to an independent body, but the legislation of each Member shall provide for the right of appeal without penalty to a judicial authority.

3. Notice of the decision on appeal shall be given to the appellant and the reasons for such decision shall be provided in writing. The appellant shall also be informed of any rights of further appeal.

ARTICLE 12

Laws, regulations, judicial decisions and administrative rulings of general application giving effect to this Agreement shall be published in conformity with Article X of GATT 1994 by the country of importation concerned.

ARTICLE 13

If, in the course of determining the customs value of imported goods, it becomes necessary to delay the final determination of such customs value, the importer of the goods shall nevertheless be able to withdraw them from customs if, where so required, the importer provides sufficient guarantee in the form of a surety, a deposit or some other appropriate instrument, covering the ultimate payment of customs duties for which the goods may be liable. The legislation of each Member shall make provisions for such circumstances.

ARTICLE 14

The notes at Annex I to this Agreement form an integral part of this Agreement and the Articles of this Agreement are to be read and applied in conjunction with their respective notes. Annexes II and III also form an integral part of this Agreement.

ARTICLE 15

1. In this Agreement:

   (a) "customs value of imported goods" means the value of goods for the purposes of levying ad valorem duties of customs on imported goods;

   (b) "country of importation" means country or customs territory of importation; and

   (c) "produced" includes grown, manufactured and mined.

2. In this Agreement:

   (a) "identical goods" means goods which are the same in all respects, including physical characteristics, quality and reputation. Minor differences in appearance would not preclude goods otherwise conforming to the definition from being regarded as identical;

   (b) "similar goods" means goods which, although not alike in all respects, have like characteristics and like component materials which enable them to perform the same functions and to be commercially interchangeable. The quality of the goods, their reputation and the existence of a trademark are among the factors to be considered in determining whether goods are similar;

   (c) the terms "identical goods" and "similar goods" do not include, as the case may be, goods which incorporate or reflect engineering, development, artwork, design work, and plans and sketches for which no adjustment has been made under paragraph 1(b)(iv) of Article 8 because such elements were undertaken in the country of importation;

(d) goods shall not be regarded as "identical goods" or "similar goods" unless they were produced in the same country as the goods being valued;

(e) goods produced by a different person shall be taken into account only when there are no identical goods or similar goods, as the case may be, produced by the same person as the goods being valued.

3. In this Agreement "goods of the same class or kind" means goods which fall within a group or range of goods produced by a particular industry or industry sector, and includes identical or similar goods.

4. For the purposes of this Agreement, persons shall be deemed to be related only if:

(a) they are officers or directors of one another's businesses;

(b) they are legally recognized partners in business;

(c) they are employer and employee;

(d) any person directly or indirectly owns, controls or holds 5 per cent or more of the outstanding voting stock or shares of both of them;

(e) one of them directly or indirectly controls the other;

(f) both of them are directly or indirectly controlled by a third person;

(g) together they directly or indirectly control a third person; or

(h) they are members of the same family.

5. Persons who are associated in business with one another in that one is the sole agent, sole distributor or sole concessionaire, however described, of the other shall be deemed to be related for the purposes of this Agreement if they fall within the criteria of paragraph 4.

ARTICLE 16

Upon written request, the importer shall have the right to an explanation in writing from the customs administration of the country of importation as to how the customs value of the importer's goods was determined.

ARTICLE 17

Nothing in this Agreement shall be construed as restricting or calling into question the rights of customs administrations to satisfy themselves as to the truth or accuracy of any statement, document or declaration presented for customs valuation purposes.

PART II

ADMINISTRATION, CONSULTATIONS AND DISPUTE SETTLEMENT

ARTICLE 18

Institutions

1. There is hereby established a Committee on Customs Valuation (referred to in this Agreement as "the Committee") composed of representatives from each of the Members. The Committee shall elect its own Chairman and shall normally meet once a year, or as is otherwise envisaged by the relevant provisions of this Agreement, for the purpose of affording Members the opportunity to consult on matters relating to the administration of the customs valuation system by any Member as it might affect the operation of this Agreement or the furtherance of its objectives and carrying out such other responsibilities as may be assigned to it by the Members. The WTO Secretariat shall act as the secretariat to the Committee.

2. There shall be established a Technical Committee on Customs Valuation (referred to in this Agreement as "the Technical Committee") under the auspices of the Customs Co-operation Council (referred to in this Agreement as "the CCC"), which shall carry out the responsibilities described in Annex II to this Agreement and shall operate in accordance with the rules of procedure contained therein.

ARTICLE 19

Consultations and Dispute Settlement

1. Except as otherwise provided herein, the Dispute Settlement Understanding is applicable to consultations and the settlement of disputes under this Agreement.

2. If any Member considers that any benefit accruing to it, directly or indirectly, under this Agreement is being nullified or impaired, or that the achievement of any objective of this Agreement is being impeded, as a result of the actions of another Member or of other Members, it may, with a view to reaching a mutually satisfactory solution of this matter, request consultations with the Member or Members in question. Each Member shall afford sympathetic consideration to any request from another Member for consultations.

3. The Technical Committee shall provide, upon request, advice and assistance to Members engaged in consultations.

4. At the request of a party to the dispute, or on its own initiative, a panel established to examine a dispute relating to the provisions of this Agreement may request the Technical Committee to carry out an examination of any questions requiring technical consideration. The panel shall determine the terms of reference of the Technical Committee for the particular dispute and set a time period for receipt of the report of the Technical Committee. The panel shall take into consideration the report of the Technical Committee. In the event that the Technical Committee is unable to reach consensus on a matter referred to it pursuant to this paragraph, the panel should afford the parties to the dispute an opportunity to present their views on the matter to the panel.

5. Confidential information provided to the panel shall not be disclosed without formal authorization from the person, body or authority providing such information. Where such information is requested from the panel but release of such information by the panel is not authorized, a non-confidential summary of this information, authorized by the person, body or authority providing the information, shall be provided.

PART III

SPECIAL AND DIFFERENTIAL TREATMENT

ARTICLE 20

1. Developing country Members not party to the Agreement on Implementation of Article VII of the General Agreement on Tariffs and Trade done on 12 April 1979 may delay application of the provisions of this Agreement for a period not exceeding five years

from the date of entry into force of the WTO Agreement for such Members. Developing country Members who choose to delay application of this Agreement shall notify the Director-General of the WTO accordingly.

2. In addition to paragraph 1, developing country Members not party to the Agreement on Implementation of Article VII of the General Agreement on Tariffs and Trade done on 12 April 1979 may delay application of paragraph 2(b)(iii) of Article 1 and Article 6 for a period not exceeding three years following their application of all other provisions of this Agreement. Developing country Members that choose to delay application of the provisions specified in this paragraph shall notify the Director-General of the WTO accordingly.

3. Developed country Members shall furnish, on mutually agreed terms, technical assistance to developing country Members that so request. On this basis developed country Members shall draw up programmes of technical assistance which may include, *inter alia,* training of personnel, assistance in preparing implementation measures, access to sources of information regarding customs valuation methodology, and advice on the application of the provisions of this Agreement.

PART IV

FINAL PROVISIONS

ARTICLE 21

Reservations

Reservations may not be entered in respect of any of the provisions of this Agreement without the consent of the other Members.

ARTICLE 22

National Legislation

1. Each Member shall ensure, not later than the date of application of the provisions of this Agreement for it, the conformity of its laws, regulations and administrative procedures with the provisions of this Agreement.

2. Each Member shall inform the Committee of any changes in its laws and regulations relevant to this Agreement and in the administration of such laws and regulations.